MARINA WARNER AND THE ETHICS OF TELLING SILENCED STORIES

MARINA WARNER AND THE ETHICS OF TELLING SILENCED STORIES

Lisa Propst

McGill-Queen's University Press
Montreal & Kingston • London • Chicago

ISBN 978-0-2280-0403-5 (cloth)
ISBN 978-0-2280-0404-2 (paper)
ISBN 978-0-2280-0506-3 (ePDF)
ISBN 978-0-2280-0507-0 (ePUB)

Legal deposit fourth quarter 2020
Bibliothèque nationale du Québec

Printed in Canada on acid-free paper that is 100% ancient forest free (100% post-consumer recycled), processed chlorine free

This book has been published with the help of a grant from the Canadian Federation for the Humanities and Social Sciences, through the Awards to Scholarly Publications Program, using funds provided by the Social Sciences and Humanities Research Council of Canada.

Funded by the Government of Canada | Financé par le gouvernement du Canada | Canada

Canada Council for the Arts | Conseil des arts du Canada

We acknowledge the support of the Canada Council for the Arts.

Nous remercions le Conseil des arts du Canada de son soutien.

Library and Archives Canada Cataloguing in Publication

Title: Marina Warner and the ethics of telling silenced stories / Lisa Propst.

Names: Propst, Lisa Gena, 1979- author.

Description: Includes bibliographical references and index.

Identifiers: Canadiana (print) 20200287893 | Canadiana (ebook) 20200288024 | ISBN 9780228004035 (hardcover) | ISBN 9780228004042 (softcover) | ISBN 9780228005063 (PDF) | ISBN 9780228005070 (ePUB)

Subjects: LCSH: Warner, Marina, 1946- – Criticism and interpretation. | LCSH: English literature – 20th century – History and criticism.

Classification: LCC PR6073.A7274 Z825 2020 | DDC 823/.914 – dc23

This book was designed and typeset by Peggy & Co. Design in 10.5/13 Sabon.

Contents

Acknowledgments

The number of people whose generosity and support have contributed to this manuscript leaves me humbled. My heartfelt gratitude goes to Christopher Robinson and Stephen Casper for their ongoing mentorship, for reading an entire draft (parts repeatedly), and for giving me the confidence to think of this project as a real book. The book was strengthened by the feedback of many people who generously read sections and offered their insights. I am grateful to Camille Frazier, Joanne Lipson Freed, Claudia Hoffmann, Sarah Kastner, Jennifer Knack, Anna Sheftel, and Annegret Staiger. Samantha Stinson, my academic "accountabilibuddy," helped me think about the book in terms of manageable writing goals. Michael Garcia answered questions and provided insights from his experiences with his first monograph. Laura Ettinger enriched my thinking through wide-ranging discussions about research and writing. And I am deeply thankful to my late colleague Joseph Duemer for the mentorship he provided and the time we spent talking about the ethical challenges of representing other people's suffering. I'm grateful to all of my colleagues from the Clarkson Humanities and Social Sciences Department for inspiring and supportive conversations about the research process. I'm grateful, too, to the Impossible Projects Working Group for ongoing discussions about the roles of literature and scholarship in responding to silencing and marginalization.

Early versions of some arguments in this book were presented at the Northeast Modern Language Association, the Modern Language Association, the American Comparative Literature Association, the Louisville Conference on Literature and Culture since 1900, and the Impossible Projects Working Group, among others. Each of these opportunities helped me hone my ideas and think through the issues more clearly, and I deeply appreciate the dialogues enabled by these forums. This book grew out of my Oxford University D.Phil. dissertation, though it is a very different text. I am very grateful to Hermione Lee for her support and advice throughout the D.Phil., and to the many colleagues and students that have helped to shape my thinking and writing since then. I'm also thankful to Clarkson University for material support for conference travel and other research costs and to the SSHRC Awards to Scholarly Publications Program.

I owe sincere thanks to Mark Abley at McGill-Queen's University Press for his enthusiasm when I first contacted him about this book and for his feedback on the manuscript. And I am especially grateful to Richard Ratzlaff at MQUP for the support and generosity he has shown in shepherding the book through the publication process. I owe thanks, as well, to Grace Rosalie Seybold for her careful copy-editing, to MQUP's marketing and production team, to Judy Dunlop for indexing, and to the anonymous reviewers, whose suggestions pushed my thinking further and made this a better book.

Much of chapter 3 is derived from the article "Unsettling Stories: Disruptive Narrative Strategies in Marina Warner's *Indigo* and *The Leto Bundle*," *Studies in the Novel* 41, no. 3 (Fall 2009): 330–47, © University of North Texas. I am grateful to Johns Hopkins University Press for permission to reprint material from that article here.

Marina Warner has inspired me since I first encountered her work as a master's student. I am infinitely grateful for her kindness and generosity, in particular her willingness to talk with me about her writing, first when I was a graduate student more than ten years ago and more recently in 2019 as I was finishing this book. I deeply hope I have done justice to her work.

Last, my deepest thanks go to my family: to my parents and Alanna for their confidence and support; to Jan, for being a reader, sounding board, and constant source of encouragement; and of course, to Kai.

Abbreviations

I have used in-text citations for books by Warner that I analyze at length. The abbreviations are below.

BB	*From the Beast to the Blonde: On Fairy Tales and Their Tellers*
DE	*The Dragon Empress: Life and Times of Tz'u-hsi 1835–1908: Empress Dowager of China*
FAH	*Fly Away Home: Stories*
I	*Indigo, or, Mapping the Waters*
IDW	*In a Dark Wood*
LB	*The Leto Bundle*
LF	*The Lost Father*
MIHK	*Murderers I Have Known, and Other Stories*
NGB	*No Go the Bogeyman: Scaring, Lulling, and Making Mock*
SM	*Stranger Magic: Charmed States and the Arabian Nights*
SP	*The Skating Party*

MARINA WARNER AND THE ETHICS OF TELLING SILENCED STORIES

Introduction

Stories of Silencing and the Dangers of Appropriation

Creating spaces for silenced voices is a crucial task in a world where those whose stories go unheard are vulnerable to poverty and discrimination. Groups that cannot gain political attention are denied institutional resources and often basic human rights. The effects of social silencing are visible daily in the detention of undocumented immigrants, the treatment of detainees in the "war on terror," and the disproportionate imprisonment of people of colour by the US and Canadian justice systems. As Marina Warner observes, every day we encounter images that present some people as less than human. Consequently, "the character of our representations matters most urgently."[1]

In view of the inextricable connection between representation and rights, in the second half of the twentieth century telling unheard stories became central to a broad range of fields, including women's studies, postcolonial studies, trauma studies, oral history, and anthropology. Yet claiming to give voice to people who have been silenced always risks appropriating those people's stories. To speak on behalf of another person can be a means of silencing that person once more. Projects that call attention to suffering often oversimplify complex lives by casting their subjects as passive victims in need of rescue. This dilemma is apparent in aid campaigns that expose atrocities but reduce the people in their frames to anonymous violated bodies. Efforts to retrieve unheard stories can also carry out exclusions in other ways. They can ignore the complexities of individual lives in the desire to convey collective experience. They can leave out voices that challenge the writer's interpretive frameworks. Even in the most well-intentioned acts of advocacy, the desire to raise awareness or change socio-political conditions sits uneasily beside the instrumentalization of another person's life, a problem compounded by cultural economies in which academics, artists, and journalists gain professional stature from the images they produce. The proliferation of social media has turned public representations of the self and others into a day-to-day activity carried out on a global scale, making the ethical dilemmas of representation ever more salient.

In *Marina Warner and the Ethics of Telling Silenced Stories*, I argue that the work of Marina Warner offers some of the most provocative contemporary interventions into these dilemmas. As a novelist, historian, and public intellectual, Warner is well known across and beyond the UK for writing about people subjected to silencing. What has received far less attention is that in varied and often subtle ways, both her fiction and her non-fiction grapple with the drawbacks of using narrative to combat silencing. Warner's work persistently negotiates two opposing pressures: the desire to tell stories that have been ignored and the dangers of appropriating other people's histories by laying claim to them in ways that perpetuate unequal power relations. I contend that through stylistic features that question her authority to tell the stories of other people, Warner explores the limits of narrative as a means to redress silencing. At the same time, the formal elements of her work that point toward those limits demonstrate the value of literature as a site for developing ethical relationships. In Warner's work, narrative strategies such as stylized voices and conspicuous silences offer reminders that the writer cannot simply "give voice" to other people. They complicate responses based on empathy or compassion and invite readers to question the ethical implications of their reactions to the figures they read about – and to the real-life people who inspired the texts. They encourage readers to ask how they themselves are bound up in the structural conditions that shape those figures' lives and to assert responsibility toward people who may be geographically or temporally distant from them.

Warner started her career by writing about women relegated to the margins of historical records, from female rulers to housewives and immigrants. From the 1990s onward, her writing turned to groups subjected to violence and oppression. Her best known novel, *Indigo, or, Mapping the Waters* (1992), envisions the colonization of St. Kitts in the Caribbean from the perspectives of the Indigenous Caribs and Arawaks as well as the British colonial officials. Her next novel, *The Leto Bundle* (2001), tells the story of a single mother and refugee who is reincarnated across centuries and countries until she becomes an asylum-seeker in present-day Britain. Warner's short stories from the new millennium, while widely varied in subject matter, keep returning to the struggles and survival strategies of families caught in the Iraq War and the Israeli-Palestinian conflict. Yet Warner is conscious that efforts to combat marginalization or violence through acts of imagination create "a bristling and jagged, intractable problem."[2] Sympathizing with a suffering individual can forestall deeper examination of the conditions that cause suffering. Both the storyteller and the reader, Warner points out, can co-opt stories of suffering as part of "an economy of virtue." In condemning wrongs, they may lay claim to a condition of innocence and even merit.[3] These problems are particularly salient when the storyteller holds a position of relative privilege and the act of telling stories reaffirms that privilege by granting her a platform denied to the people she writes about.

Warner's life history places her in a complicated position for a writer dedicated to marginalized stories. She is a white British woman who grew up in a wealthy family. Her paternal grandfather was a cricketing hero; her paternal grandmother was a port heiress. Her father descended from the first colonial administrators in the West Indies, and he was proud of that history, so Warner grew up surrounded by icons of the colonial past. She had an elite education. As a child she attended a convent school in Berkshire. Later, she studied French and Italian at the University of Oxford. For decades she remained an independent scholar, but by the early 2000s she was firmly part of the British academic establishment. In 2015 she was named Dame Commander of the Order of the British Empire, the female equivalent of a knighthood.

With her privileged background, Warner may be a surprising subject for a book focused on the ethics of representation. However, she persistently explores the ethical challenges of writing about people whose histories have not been granted due attention and whose experiences she does not share. Not long after publishing *Indigo*, she admitted that she worried about "interloping on territory from which accidents of history had morally barred [her]."[4] As a descendant of colonial officials, she felt that she had "the wrong voice" to tell that story.[5] Yet she argued that not to write about that history would do no good, and that "it is important … for anyone and everyone to challenge received ideas."[6] Warner's work is suffused with efforts to respond to histories of injustice while resisting claims to authority over those histories.

With emotionally evocative storylines and complex, likeable characters, Warner invites readers to develop affective relationships with the characters in her work. Yet she also unsettles those relationships. She shows that, as Joanne Lipson Freed insists, literature must not allow imagined connections "to be mistaken for reality, for to do so would deny concrete and consequential differences in power."[7] It is all too easy for readers to connect to fictional characters while ignoring the conditions that divide them from real-life people in positions of vulnerability. Warner's novels both evoke and undermine identification with the characters on the page. They hold out and complicate the illusion of understanding. They offer readers interpretations that seem to make sense of her characters, including the comments of other characters and seemingly omniscient narrators. At the same time, they provoke questions and uncertainties that cannot be resolved through those interpretive scripts. Thus the novels invite readers to wonder what the characters would have said about their own lives – and, since fictional characters do not have lives beyond the page, how real people in similar positions would have told their stories. In this way they offer reminders that Warner is not retrieving voices but inventing them.

These narrative strategies are important because past silencing cannot simply be undone by present-day retrieval. Efforts to retrieve lost voices, as Gayatri Spivak famously pointed out in her essay "Can the Subaltern Speak?" cannot erase the structural conditions that caused their silencing in the first place. Moreover, silencing does not always involve preventing a person from speaking. It often involves the refusal of the surrounding society to hear, or the failure to hear certain elements of a story, a phenomenon that Rosemary Jolly labels "deaf listening." Recuperative narratives – narratives that strive to tell marginalized stories – can themselves be forms of "deaf listening." They may "'hear' or capture certain subjects within the contemporary social, political and cultural moment," but ignore or exclude others.[8] Consequently, it is important not just to write about stories and bodies that have been overlooked, but to consider how existing representational frameworks construct those bodies and which bodies they exclude.

Warner's desire to recover marginalized stories and her recognition of the limits of recovery efforts are not always reconciled. They remain in tension in her fictions and histories as well as her essays. She often speaks of her drive to retrieve silenced voices.[9] In a 2013 interview with Sateesh Maharaj, she describes writers "as the mouthpiece to channel elements of the past; untold stories of human suffering and experience that should be known."[10] In this context, it is perhaps no surprise that literary critics overwhelmingly cast her as a writer who strives to give voice to the silenced.[11] However, far from extolling the capacity of literature to redress silencing, Warner asks how to tell silenced stories without colonizing them once more. In her interview with Maharaj, she acknowledges the space separating her from the histories she writes about. She speaks of finding "traces" of old stories and "coming at [them] from another angle," using imagination to call attention to devalued histories.[12] By admitting that she approaches those "traces" from her own angle, she shows that her texts are not "retrievals" but imagined entries into the lives of others.

In her 2002 Amnesty Lecture in Human Rights at the University of Oxford, Warner asked, "Writers, pen-pushers, ivory-tower dwellers, bookworms and clerics … what part can we play? Where does literature intersect with life – with lives – how can we contribute to an increment of justice in the world?"[13] From a humanist perspective, literature contributes to justice because it helps people empathize with one another.[14] Definitions of empathy abound, but I am following Suzanne Keen in defining empathy as feeling what another person feels or "might be expected to feel" in a given context.[15] Yet empirical research has questioned whether empathy for fictional characters genuinely leads to real-world empathy or pro-social behaviour.[16] Moreover, when people think they are empathizing with someone else, they can be wrong about what that person actually feels (a problem compounded in empathizing with fictional characters, who do not "feel" in the way that real people do). Empathy can lead people to ignore important aspects of someone else's situation and subsume that person's experiences to their own.[17] In this book, I suggest that Warner's work contributes to ethical relationships while complicating responses based on empathy. Enjoining readers to feel compassion, outrage, even empathy for her characters, and distancing readers at the same time, Warner's writing often elicits uncertainty about how to relate to characters and their situations. This uncertainty promotes critical inquiry. It invites readers to analyze the social, political, and economic structures that might link them to the characters and to ask what the stories on the page suggest about their own complicities in unequal power relations.

Consequently, Warner's work has important political implications. This is not to suggest that either her fiction or her non-fiction is didactic. Far from it; she is a storyteller first and foremost. In a 2017 lecture titled "The Truth in Stories" at University College Dublin, Warner insisted, "A story is above all a form of enquiry. It's not a solution or explanation … To borrow from the language of maths, stories are conjectures, not theorems."[18] One might say the same of Warner's non-fiction, which explores its subjects in a spirit of enquiry rather than argument. At the same time, her "Truth in Stories" lecture proclaimed the ethical and political importance of stories. She declared, "Stories are a form of action, the way we insert ourselves into the human world."[19] Elsewhere she has quoted Ursula LeGuin on the connections between literature and politics: "Resistance and change often begin in art. Very often in our art, the art of words."[20] To make a claim for the political importance of Warner's work is not to cast literature as a pragmatic interventionist tool. Rather, it is to insist that literature and art can "bring about shifts in public awareness and understanding, both intellectually and affectively, of political issues."[21] Warner's novels provoke readers to ask hard questions about their own responsibilities when faced with stories of silencing. Literature is a fertile ground for such inquiry because people construct and interpret selves and surroundings through narrative. Human beings "both inhabit and create stories by which we live our lives. To the extent to which we can train ourselves to … evaluate the stories we inhabit as if by default, stories that we assume are the conventions of the social and political context into which we are born, we *can* take responsibility for 'authoring' ourselves."[22] This is inevitably an ongoing process, one that can never be complete but that has significant ethical and political stakes.

This Introduction outlines the tension between Warner's commitment to silenced stories and her exploration of the dangers of appropriating the voices of others. It begins by offering readers a brief biography in the knowledge that Warner's life and works are not well known outside the UK, and that even readers within the UK may be familiar with only a handful of frequently cited details. The Introduction then identifies the quandaries that face any effort to respond to marginalization or injustice through narrative and the particular challenges associated with representing suffering through fiction. It concludes with an outline of the chapters to follow.

WRITER, ICONOCLAST, AND DAME COMMANDER OF THE ORDER OF THE BRITISH EMPIRE: A BRIEF BIOGRAPHY

Warner's personal history shaped her interest in exclusions and margins, though she recognizes that she writes about marginalization from a position of social and economic privilege. Warner spent her childhood as "a migrant between worlds."[23] Far from disenfranchising her, though, her migrations marked a cosmopolitan and glamorous lifestyle. In 1947, a year after her birth in London, her family moved to Cairo and became part of the city's colonial elite. During the Second World War, her father had been stationed in Egypt with the eighth army. He loved Cairo largely due to the racetrack and parties frequented by colonial officials.[24] When the war ended he convinced the owner of W.H. Smith, who had been in his regiment, to let him open a wholesaler in Cairo. "Of course we were expats and colonials," Warner mused decades later, "but from a child's point of view it was very glamorous," with a view of the pyramids from the family terrace.[25]

As a student Warner often felt alienated from her peers, though she continued to enjoy the comforts of the British upper classes. When she was young, nationalist riots forced the family out of Cairo, first to London and then to Brussels. She insisted on going to boarding school, though when her parents sent her to a convent school in Berkshire called St. Mary's, she was mocked because her English was "so peculiar," with its tinge of foreignness and lack of slang.[26] At seventeen, Warner left for Lady Margaret Hall, a college of the University of Oxford, to study French and Italian. Actress Diana Quick, a contemporary of Warner's at Oxford, describes her as "very stylish and confident," with "a ready-made social circle" and "a phenomenal capacity for hard work."[27] Not long after finishing her degree Warner published her first article, a feature in *Vogue Magazine* critiquing the university for its chauvinism, "backbiting and intrigue." She observed ruefully that female students remained "blue-stocking grotesques" to many of their male classmates.[28] She was hardly a marginalized figure; Quick recalls Warner appearing on television week after week in a quiz show called *Double Your Money* and winning enough to fly to Paris for the weekend.[29] Still, her experiences moving from one culture to another and her nonconformity as a student left her attuned to cultural margins and exclusions.

The early years of her career were highly exploratory. She started out as a journalist at London's *Daily Telegraph Magazine.* After a year she left to write her first novel, which was never published, then took up a position as Features Editor for *Vogue*. She modelled as well, and "was much photographed by famous photographers," as she recalled with some pride decades later.[30] Warner wrote her first published book, *The Dragon Empress: Life and Times of Tz'u-hsi 1835–1908: Empress Dowager of China* (1972), when Cecil Day-Lewis, poet laureate and editorial director for Chatto and Windus, encouraged her to try writing non-fiction. After that she travelled to Vietnam with William Shawcross, her first husband, who had been assigned to cover the Vietnam War for the *Sunday Times*. There, she wrote articles for the London papers about the effects of the war on Vietnamese civilians, her journalism moving swiftly from *Vogue*'s socialites to women ignored by political pundits. Her next book, *Alone of All Her Sex: The Myth and Cult of the Virgin Mary* (1976), inaugurated her reputation as a scholar of female images at the height of the women's liberation movement. Still, she was never part of the movement in any straightforward way. She was working for *Vogue* when activists such as Sheila Rowbotham organized the first women's liberation conference in 1970 at Ruskin College, Oxford. In Warner's words, she was "never … much of a joiner."[31] One of her strongest influences was fellow iconoclast Angela Carter, whom she met in the offices of *Vogue* in the 1960s and praised for the unconventionality of her feminism.[32]

Warner remained an independent scholar throughout the 1980s and 1990s as her reputation as a novelist and scholar grew. She did not take up a faculty position until 2004, when she joined the interdisciplinary Department of Literature, Film and Theatre Studies at the University of Essex. In 2014 she moved to the Department of Literature and Humanities at Birkbeck College. During the preceding decades, she often wished she could be "enfolded and enclosed" in the academic world.[33] Still, her independence derived largely from her own choices. In 2000 Roy Foster, then Carroll Professor of Irish History at Oxford, mused that an academic post "would be hers for the asking," but resisting a university affiliation maximized Warner's freedom to follow her interests.[34]

Warner is sensitive to the position of privilege from which she addresses social justice issues. In a 1995 interview with Gilles Menegaldo, she invokes Henrik Ibsen's belief that the mission of a writer is "to sit in judgment on himself." She explains that in her work she strives to reckon with the circumstances and social structures in which she is located. She muses, "a lot of the literature that I'm interested in attempts to do that, often from a position of lack of privilege. I'm interested in the literature of the colonized, in feminist literature that takes a kind of partisan approach to the problems of women. Although in my own case, I actually had a very privileged life. So I'm aware that I can't claim victim status."[35] Warner insists that reckoning with injustice is not solely the task of the oppressed; privilege confers both a duty and a platform to think critically about injustice and its effects.

Driven by this conviction, Warner has participated in social justice advocacy throughout her career. Until the early 1990s she was part of the UK Campaign for Nuclear Disarmament. She sat on the management committee for the National Council for One Parent Families and the council for Charter 88, a pressure group that fought for constitutional reform to guarantee civil liberties and human rights. She later became a trustee of openDemocracy, an independent online news platform that emphasizes human rights, social democracy, and gender equality. As Warner gained academic status, she sought ways to leverage that status in the service of social advocacy. In 2005 she became a fellow of the British Academy; twelve years later she received the British Academy Medal for services to academia. In 2015 she was selected to chair the judging panel for the Man Booker Prize, one of the most prestigious literary awards in the world. In 2017 she became the first female president of the Royal Society of Literature. She has used this recognition to promote public discussion about pressing social issues. She has contributed to books such as Victoria Brittain's *Shadow Lives: The Forgotten Women of the War on Terror* (2013) and the Gatwick Detainees Welfare Group's *Refugee Tales II* (2017), composed of stories told to writers by refugees in indefinite detention in the UK. Her lectures increasingly bridge literary and humanitarian concerns, with an emphasis on the work stories can do in the face of displacement.

In 2015, when the Norwegian government awarded Warner the Holberg Prize, one of the largest international prizes for scholarship in the arts, humanities, and social sciences, she used the money to start a project called "Stories in Transit." The project focuses on developing storytelling initiatives within refugee communities. Warner does not presume that without such projects, refugees would be unable to tell their own stories. In her words, "music, confabulation, art, and so on cannot be altogether stifled. Yet creating conditions for expressions and exchanges to happen remains vital, even when other resources are extremely stretched."[36] With "Stories in Transit," Warner explores how to support the circulation of migrants' stories across borders and languages. She asks how storytelling can help refugee communities and whether stories can "provide a form of shelter" or belonging.[37] Talking to me in 2019, she depicted the project as a way to build community across linguistic and cultural boundaries.[38] The concerns at the centre of "Stories in Transit" reflect issues that have shaped her work throughout her career. She has consistently sought not just to raise awareness about lives excluded from dominant discourses, but to create a more inclusive society through the circulation of stories.

Warner's reputation as a scholar-novelist is contradictory. As a public intellectual, Warner is a household name, at least in the UK. Yet she seldom appears in the "Best British Novelist" lists compiled by news outlets such as the *Times* and the BBC.[39] Her fiction has not received the same acclaim as novels by Angela Carter, A.S. Byatt, or Jeanette Winterson, contemporaries who share her use of myth and fairy tale tropes, subversion of gender norms, and concern about silenced figures and unheard stories. This may be at least partially due to her ornate prose and frequent literary and artistic allusions. These stylistic qualities can prevent readers from getting caught up in a story. So, too, can the tensions in her fiction between intimacy and distance, which sometimes work against the pleasures of losing oneself in a character's life. However, I argue that Warner's fiction does not just contain rich and often haunting storytelling; it offers important ethical and political provocations. Some of the stylistic attributes that complicate the pleasures of the literary text, such as elements that may distance readers from characters, give her fiction its greatest ethical import as they invite readers to consider the positions they occupy within the real-world social structures fictionalized on the page. These stylistic features, coupled with her broad commitment to exploring marginalization and silencing through narrative, tie her fiction to her work as a public intellectual and activist as examples of the roles the humanities can play in promoting global justice.

TRANSFORMING LIVES INTO STORIES

Warner insists that both fiction and non-fiction can bear witness to experiences that have gone unheard. She proclaims that "where documents no longer exist, imagination provides new witnesses,"[40] a tenet that underpins her novels *The Lost Father* (1988), *Indigo*, and *The Leto Bundle*. In this context, "witnessing" does not refer to eyewitness testimony or transparent access to facts. Instead, witnessing asserts the importance of lives and experiences left out of historical documents. Witnessing in this sense creates an ethical relationship between the writer or the reader and the people whose lives they imagine, even if those people are long gone. It involves declaring oneself responsible to those people and their legacies.[41]

This use of literature to depict lives ignored by dominant narratives seems like an act of translation in the most common use of the term: expressing something in new words or a new form. Yet as Warner reminds readers, "stories and words rediscovered and retrieved in this way never truly are restored: in the transition to text, they become an invented language."[42] The "life" on the page becomes something very different from the life it commemorates, a textual artifact rather than a literal recuperation. Thus, if Warner translates lives into fiction, it is through transmutation or transformation. The author, as Warner remarks, is "a magician of language, imposing a despotic subjective vision on his (or her) public."[43] Warner acknowledges that she cannot simply create space for the voices of others, but invariably transforms them into her own story. This transformation can be a productive act. It can form bridges between people.[44] But it cannot convey silenced voices or experiences in any transparent sense.

This means that while Warner is deeply invested in re-imagining silenced stories, her work confronts a tangle of quandaries endemic to appropriation. In its broadest sense, appropriation involves laying claim to something and making it one's own. In literature, "appropriation" generally describes any re-invention of a well-known text that transforms it "into a wholly new cultural product."[45] This is a value-neutral description, though literary appropriation is frequently driven by "a political or ethical commitment," providing a new lens onto a canonical text in order to centre a previously marginalized viewpoint.[46] Appropriation in the more commonly used sense reinforces unequal power relations. In Edward Said's *Orientalism* (1978), a touchstone for analyses of literary appropriation, appropriation marks the process whereby Europeans interpret and represent the "Orient" as a means of asserting European superiority. Theorizations of appropriation developed through several interwoven conversations in the 1980s and 1990s. By the early 1990s, "cultural appropriation" was a buzzword in scholarly dialogue and the popular press, often used interchangeably with "appropriation of voice." Definitions of cultural appropriation are varied and often contested, but in line with popular usage, it is perhaps best characterized by a dominant cultural group using the experiences or cultural products of a less privileged group in a way that perpetuates unjust hierarchies.[47] Some of the most influential 1990s debates on cultural appropriation addressed appropriations of Indigenous voices, a point emblematized by Anishinaabekwe poet Lenore Keeshig-Tobias's influential essay "Stop Stealing Native Stories" (1990). More than two decades later, debates about cultural appropriation remain "as relevant, and difficult, as ever," as indicated by Lionel Shriver's polarizing remarks at the 2016 Brisbane Writers Festival and Hal Niedzviecki's glib proposal for a Canadian "appropriation prize" in 2017.[48]

But harmful appropriations of voice do not come only from glib presumptions that one is free to write about any cultural group one chooses. They can also come from well-meaning efforts to combat silencing. Concurrent with the rise of debates about cultural appropriation, postcolonial theorists such as Gayatri Spivak and Rey Chow deconstructed recuperative narratives that sought to give voice to marginalized people.[49] Transnational feminists of colour critiqued Western feminist discourses that homogenized "third world women" even in the effort to address experiential differences between women with varying levels of privilege.[50] Experimental work in cultural anthropology and oral history questioned the authority of the scholar to speak for the informant or interviewee.[51] bell hooks put the issue plainly: too often acts of retrieval tacitly say, "No need to hear your voice when I can talk about you better than you can speak about yourself. No need to hear your voice. Only tell me about your pain. I want to know your story. And then I will tell it back to you in a new way."[52] This is the challenge Warner faces in striving to combat discursive silencing by telling marginalized stories.

On one hand, Warner embraces appropriation as a literary strategy for challenging dominant narratives. She reinvents canonical stories to combat patriarchal and imperialist exclusions. She re-imagines well-known myths, fairy tales, biblical scenes, and Shakespeare plays to showcase the experiences of groups on the margins of the stories. These rewritings align her with a corpus of writers for whom literary appropriation is a means of "voicing the silenced or absent characters of the canon."[53] Examples include feminist contemporaries such as Angela Carter, Adrienne Rich, Michèle Roberts, and Sara Maitland as well as postcolonial writers as varied as Jean Rhys, Aimé Césaire, and Derek Walcott, all figures Warner admires and cites as inspirations. In the spirit of what Rich labels "re-vision," Warner appropriates old stories in "the act of looking back, of seeing with fresh eyes, of entering an old text from a new critical direction … not to pass on a tradition but to break its hold over us."[54] Like many feminist and postcolonial appropriations, Warner's versions of Shakespeare plays and fairy tales invite readers "to look anew" at texts and histories "we might otherwise have felt we had 'understood' or interpreted to our own satisfaction."[55] Yet such rewritings inevitably risk appropriation in the harmful sense, representing the experiences of a person or group in ways that subordinate them. Publishing a piece of literature – whether fiction or history – inherently rests on a tacit claim to discursive authority.[56] The writer makes a bid to be heard, to be respected, and to influence readers. When the narrative involves the experiences of an individual or population already subjected to silencing, this claim to authority risks denying the authority of those people over their life stories and entrenching the power of the author at the expense of the people she represents.

The problems involved in the appropriation of voice are not confined to representations of trauma or persecution, although they are most acute in those areas. They can arise any time one person represents another with comparatively less power or privilege. Even representations of people with comparable power, such as political and social elites, can be appropriative when they contribute to cultural stereotypes or turn individual life stories into myths in ways unjust to the people in question. For instance, Warner's first book, her biography of the Chinese empress dowager Tz'u-hsi – the woman pictured on the cover of this monograph – depicts an individual who wielded great political power but whose life story was appropriated by British journalists and Sinologists who cast her as a monstrous and unnatural figure. In taking up Tz'u-hsi as an exemplar of the capacity of women to wield power, Warner faced the challenge of telling her story without furthering that appropriation, whether by replicating Orientalist tropes at the core of the existing myth or simply by flattening out the complexities of Tz'u-hsi's life in the service of her own argument.

In her search for ways to tell stories about people subjected to marginalization, Warner insists that, as many scholars have argued, this quandary is not merely a matter of who can speak for whom.[57] To "solve" the problem of representation by speaking only for one's own cultural group is to reify group boundaries, presuming an illusory homogeneity within the group, and to ignore the narrative construction involved in all representation.[58] In addition, the idea that one can only speak for oneself promotes political paralysis and navel-gazing. It invariably leads to focusing on the social positions of the privileged at the expense of addressing inequalities or injustices.[59] More productive is critical attention to the power relations that enable and are enabled by acts of representation. Warner's work provokes precisely this critical attention. From dramatizations of the harm done by characters' readings of one another to strategies that invite readers to question their understandings of the characters, her work invites consideration of the power relations created by well-meaning responses to other people's experiences. In this way her books resonate with a broad transition in feminist and postcolonial studies from the question of "who can speak"[60] to concerns about how people are heard and what forms of representation can promote new kinds of community, coalition, and accountability.[61]

Varied formal strategies in Warner's fiction – and even her non-fiction – question her authority as a writer. Her biography of the empress dowager invites readers to approach it from multiple angles while suggesting that there are still more stories to tell and that she can only offer a partial account of her subject's life. From this early biography to her novels *Indigo* and *The Leto Bundle*, Warner combines assiduous historical research with conspicuous gaps, as pieces of her protagonists' lives invoke curiosity but remain resolutely withheld. In much of her fiction, lyrical speech and formal diction remind readers that characters are literary constructs and not transparent "retrievals" of voice. In some of Warner's short stories from the twenty-first century, inspired by violence in the Middle East, the metamorphoses of the characters prevent readers from grasping them in full. They point toward the ways the conflicts in the Middle East and the people affected by them exceed the fiction on the page. Some of the formal elements I analyze in this book may stem from more deliberate narrative strategies than others. I realize that in some cases, the examples I offer might not mark conscious efforts on Warner's part to unsettle her narrative authority or distance readers from the text. However, I argue that they all reflect Warner's abiding concerns with the ethics of telling other people's stories. Both her fiction and her non-fiction show sensitivity to the limits of her access to the lives of others and the ways people can appropriate and distort others' stories. They juxtapose "the seductions of recovery and the occlusions such retrieval mandates."[62] Through their sensitivity to those occlusions, Warner's works push readers to take up the challenge articulated by bell hooks and Gayatri Spivak: to speak to and with silenced people rather than speaking for them. They encourage readers to consider what broader histories and political structures may be obscured by efforts to bear witness to individual suffering and resilience, and how they, themselves, may be implicated in those political structures.

By charging readers to ask how to respond to lives affected by injustice, Warner invites them to undertake an act similar to what Jacques Derrida labels "absolute hospitality." For Derrida, absolute hospitality forms the core of ethical relationships. It entails boundless responsibility toward people who cannot necessarily be named in advance, or even at all: people who may not have recognizable positions within existing social structures.[63] When Warner pushes readers to probe their responsibilities toward people – dead or alive – in conditions similar to the ones she depicts, she invites them to undertake a similarly boundless undertaking. There is no endpoint to the task of figuring out how to respond to the needs of another person, given that selves and needs are constantly changing. This task only multiplies when one declares oneself responsible to the needs – and memory – of a group of people too large to delimit.

In drawing on a deconstructionist vision of boundless hospitality toward people who exceed one's understanding, I am mindful of Richard Kearney's warning that ethical theories based on the ineffable otherness of other people can preclude meaningful connection and moral judgment. For Kearney, an ethics premised on "the unmediatable … nature of alterity" makes the "other" so foreign to the self that friendship or coalition becomes impossible. Moreover, in his view this approach makes it impossible to distinguish between a vulnerable "other" to be supported and a genocidal "other" to be opposed.[64] However, I argue that one can declare oneself responsible, without limit, in the face of the inherent vulnerability of all people, without giving up the ability to distinguish between cruelty and need. Furthermore, acknowledging that all people exceed our understanding does not have to alienate us from one another. While Warner's work hints at the limits of readers' ability to grasp the lives of other people, she invites readers to undertake ongoing efforts at understanding and imagination in a continuous commitment to those lives.

Warner insists on the power of stories as a "weapon of the weaponless" (*BB* 412).[65] Stories can change the ways we – all people – think about who we are and how we are connected to one another. They can lead us to assert solidarity with, and accountability toward, people who seem culturally and geographically distant. In this way narrative can "remake the world in the image of desire," a phrase Warner borrows from Gillian Beer (*BB* xii), by inspiring ethical and political change. At the same time, even the most well-meaning narratives can inadvertently re-inscribe injustice. Warner heeds the exhortation of Walter Benjamin to defend stories lost to the histories of victors; she makes it her task "to brush history against the grain."[66] Nevertheless, she acknowledges that the victors' histories are not the only ones with the capacity to appropriate their subjects. The desire to bring the dead back to life, the drive to expose suffering, and the commitment to scenes of agency amid oppression can all simplify and distort.

SUBVERTING SPECTACLES OF SUFFERING

Many of Warner's early works focus not on trauma or violence but on the lives of the elite, from her biography of the Chinese empress dowager Tz'u-hsi to her first two novels, which centre on wealthy British families. Yet from the 1990s onward, Warner's writing increasingly focuses on war, colonialism, and the treatment of migrants and refugees – concerns that shape some of her earliest journalism as well. Warner repeatedly grapples with the challenges of bearing witness to violence across distances of time and space, and she insists that temporal and geographical distance do not constitute ethical distance.

In using real-life suffering as an inspiration for fiction – and, indeed, in writing journalistic articles about the Vietnam War – Warner confronts a number of questions that have long histories in scholarship on trauma and representation. These questions include how to express the weight of suffering without numbing spectators on the one hand or inducing facile identification on the other.[67] They include how to bear witness to violence when witnesses are often "implicated in hegemonic practices of domination, exploitation, and violence."[68] They include whether trauma is in fact unrepresentable, a tenet at the core of Western trauma theory. Western literary scholarship's affirmation of the unrepresentability of trauma grew out of Holocaust studies in the late 1980s and early 1990s.[69] Yet this presumption of unrepresentability risks homogenizing diverse experiences of pain, and trauma writers employ more varied aesthetic and epistemological approaches than the fragmented, non-linear aesthetics associated with the breakdown of narrative.[70]

In this section of the Introduction, I explore Warner's comments on ways of representing suffering. I show that she is conscious of the messiness of the issue and the impossibility of one approach solving all of the problems involved. The formal strategies an author uses to represent suffering are always ethically fraught, and they can compound the violence the author seeks to condemn. Literature, art, and journalism can "show a suffering that is outrageous, unjust, and should be repaired," as Susan Sontag writes about photographs of violence.[71] But they can also create a "voyeuristic lure." They can evoke relief: "This is not happening to *me*." When they lead to feelings of powerlessness, they can engender boredom and apathy.[72] Still, Warner insists, literary responses to suffering are crucial tools in opposing injustice. In her words, literature can help people examine "what is unjust or what could be redressed or what could be rewritten" in the service of "a more livable, more congenial world."[73] It can help readers understand painful experiences – even if that understanding is only partial – and it can promote commitments to redressing violence.

Warner criticizes spectacles of violence that use suffering to entertain or enthrall. As she argues, "sensations of excitement and thrills, produced by live action death and violence, all too often make us collusive with the violence represented."[74] People too often take pleasure in images of violence, a response exacerbated by representations that de-emphasize its bodily consequences.[75] In a humanist vein, Warner proclaims that "when we *read* about pain and suffering and death, we empathise," whereas digitization aestheticizes pain.[76] When viewers watch Frodo plunge down a mountainside in *Lord of the Rings* and emerge with only a "charming cosmetic scratch" on his cheek, they are numbed to the materiality of violence.[77] Contemporary mass media has produced "a disregard for the reality of flesh, mortality, and pain" by normalizing physical trauma through film and celebrating state violence against political enemies in the news.[78] These comments may set up an unduly rigid binary between literature and visual media. Elsewhere Warner complicates that binary by examining how fiction, like popular media, can contribute to both distance and prurience. Her point, however, is that popular aesthetic conventions hinder the understanding of suffering: "the new kind of realism" common to mainstream films and video games "never admits what blows or blades really inflict or the consequences of violence."[79]

However, while Warner insists on the fleshly realities of violence, she does not simply express them through realist aesthetics, and she is skeptical about the "turmoil of passions" inspired by gore.[80] In a review of the London Globe Theatre's 2014 production of *Titus Andronicus*, she reminds readers that powerful feelings arising from spectacles of suffering may not spur people to respond, but instead may act "more like a drug, setting us all ablaze but ultimately inhibiting action."[81] The catharsis that renders tragic stories pleasurable can stop viewers from taking action or examining their complicity in oppression.[82] Warner recognizes that such spectacles can be divisive. As Sara Ahmed warns, they can produce "an appropriation that transforms and perhaps even neutralizes their pain into our sadness." While blurring the distinction between the pain of someone else and one's own emotional response, such catharsis can paradoxically reify the boundaries between "they" who suffer and "we" who watch from a distance.[83] If empathy underpins interpersonal connection and mutual care, it also risks exploiting someone else's pain "to feel oneself feeling."[84] In addition, empathy created by spectacles of suffering can oversimplify the affective consequences of oppression. Oppression and domination can cause "psychic colonization," in the words of Kelly Oliver. They can lead to unconscious responses such as shame, anger, and alienation, which affect the formation of a person's subjectivity (their sense of themselves as an individual with agency).[85] This is not just an individual phenomenon, but a social one. Because these affective responses are unconscious, they cannot be transparent to the person who experiences them, let alone to someone else. Any effort at understanding them requires "incessant interpretation" and not just empathy for more visible manifestations of suffering.[86]

Warner's essays and lectures reveal ambivalence about empathy. In 2006, giving a plenary lecture at the annual English Graduate Conference at the University of Oxford, she praised the power of images to provoke empathy. "Come to Hecuba," the paper that grew out of her lecture, argues that feeling *with* someone rather than simply witnessing a landscape of horrors can serve as a "motor of revelation and of action."[87] Feeling the carnage of the Trojan War with the devastated queen, Hecuba, gives more weight to the loss than any panorama of destruction. On the other hand, in informal conversation after her Oxford plenary lecture, Warner acknowledged that the value and dangers of empathy are always in tension.[88]

In a 2005 essay called "Angels and Engines: The Culture of Apocalypse," Warner insists, "Either we admit artifice, stage unreality honestly, and keep faith with the laws of time and the flesh, with the reality of pain and suffering, or we risk deepening the current disregard for the consequences of violence."[89] Her writing gains much of its force from aesthetic properties that call attention to the artifice of her texts – their status as literary constructions – at the same time as they evoke the corporeal realities of suffering. In this way her work demonstrates what Dominick LaCapra calls "empathic unsettlement." LaCapra explains the term in *Writing History, Writing Trauma* (2001), calling for affective responses to traumas that resist appropriating them. Empathic unsettlement is suspicious of empathy that places someone else's story in the service of the empathizer's needs, such as catharsis or reassurance. It is an effort at understanding that drives the individual to question what is at stake in their responses to violence. Yet as a representational practice it "cannot be reduced to formulas or rules of method." Its stylistic attributes must be reinvented anew in response to each narrative and historical situation.[90] Warner's writing often creates opportunities to empathize with suffering characters but simultaneously unsettles that empathy, inviting readers to examine whether they have colluded in injustice, benefited from it, or perhaps simply ignored it, and what they owe its victims. In an echo of Sontag's exhortation to people who bear witness to violence, Warner's writing provides space for "reflection on how our privileges are located on the same map as their [other people's] suffering, and may – in ways we might prefer not to imagine – be linked to their suffering."[91] Thus it gives weight to suffering in a very different way from spectacles of gore in mainstream media.

In her writing on violence, Warner carries out what Kearney calls "narrative as impossible story: storytelling which forever fails to *cure* trauma" – and recognizes its inability to do so – "but never fails to try to *heal* it."[92] Kearney applies this phrase to writers trying to heal their own traumas through writing, but it also applies well to Warner's efforts to respond to violence through narrative. Warner does not presume that writing about violence can undo the harms violence has caused. Instead her writing invites ongoing effort to determine how to bring about greater justice.

Storytelling that invites critical self-assessment from readers carries its own risks. Nothing forces readers to engage in this kind of self-questioning. Many people read fiction purely or predominantly for pleasure, and readers can easily consume Warner's novels without critiquing their affective responses. Alternatively, a reader uncomfortably alienated by her distancing strategies can close the book and turn away, responding with neither compassion nor critical inquiry. Yet these risks in themselves are highly valuable. In a public sphere filled with representations of violence and oppression, we need ongoing opportunities to assess the ways we depict and respond to such experiences.

Warner's concerns about appropriating the lives of others are important not just for literature and art, but for journalists, policy-makers, and human rights activists. The tension between raising awareness about atrocities and potentially contributing to the degradation of victims confronts everyone who seeks to represent people outside centres of power. In mainstream news, this challenge is vividly apparent in debates over whether to share graphic images of suffering, from the notorious photographs of torture at Abu Ghraib prison to the images of three-year-old Syrian refugee Alan Kurdi, who drowned in 2015 trying to reach asylum in Europe. News outlets constantly navigate between conveying the human cost of war and contributing to that cost through tableaus of gore that distract from the humanity of their subjects. Facebook, Twitter, and YouTube multiply opportunities to publicize oppression and foster political awareness, but just as easily enable voyeurism. As emerging media make it ever easier to generate public discussion about injustice – and, conversely, to turn violence into spectacle – Warner's work becomes increasingly crucial to the ways we think about silence and voice.

OVERVIEW

This book takes a combined chronological and genre-based approach. In chapter 1, I read Warner's first book, *The Dragon Empress* (1972), and her Vietnam War journalism as early examples of the ways she negotiates the challenges of writing across cultural differences. I argue that in each case her writing reveals valuable narrative strategies for confronting the risks of appropriating other people's voices. The power relations involved in these two projects contrast starkly. In the first case, she writes about an extremely powerful figure, albeit one caricatured and vilified by a century of British writers. In the second, she writes about people subjected to the violence and economic precarity caused by war. However, I contend that both the biography and the journalism question the ability of Warner and her readers to grasp the lives she depicts. First, by offering readers multiple interpretive lenses, Warner suggests that no stories she tells could encompass the lives of her subjects in full. Second, by disrupting the sense of intimacy her texts seem to create, she calls attention to the layers of mediation that separate readers from her subjects. I contend that these narrative strategies have important ethical implications. Inflated presumptions of cultural understanding have often been used to justify perceptions of superiority or dominance.[93] By contrast, disrupting presumptions of understanding can undermine feelings of superiority and promote openness to experiences that lie outside one's grasp.

Chapter 2 extends my analysis of ways of interpreting people's lives across social differences: differences that create social or political hierarchies, such as nationality, race, or socio-economic class.[94] Turning from biography and journalism to Warner's early novels, I analyze how Warner depicts female characters interpreting the lives of women in cultures and situations different from their own. I probe these depictions for the ways they invite readers to respond to the lives of others – both fictional characters and real people. Here I focus on the consequences of identifying with other people's experiences of marginalization. I argue that Warner's early novels portray the dangers of acts of identification that overlook differences of experience and structural inequalities. Yet they hint that identifying with someone else can be a way of building solidarity when it leads to ongoing efforts to imagine that person's life. Like the texts I discuss in chapter 1, Warner's early novels suggest that openness to multiple stories and rejection of cognitive mastery can promote ethical relationships. This portrayal of ways of reading has important implications for Warner's practice as a writer, as she shows in *The Lost Father*, the last novel I analyze in the chapter. Warner implies that her role is not simply to evoke identification or empathy for silenced characters, but to provoke ongoing efforts to imagine the lives of silenced people outside the confines of the text.

Chapter 3 builds on my argument about the ways Warner complicates reader responses based on identification and empathy. Here, I turn to the power and limits of recuperative narratives: narratives that set out to tell stories relegated to the margins of historical and political discourses. Warner's novels *Indigo* and *The Leto Bundle* are generally read as texts that "give voice" to the stories of colonized people, single mothers, and refugees. Yet I argue that, like *The Lost Father* and the works I discuss in chapter 1, these novels call attention to the distance between the vision of the writer and the experiences of the people who inspired her narratives. Even as the novels provide vivid depictions that evoke investment in the lives of the characters, they unsettle the illusion of presence. They promote and disrupt empathetic responses in ways that invite both critical inquiry and ongoing efforts to imagine the lives of people in similar situations. I contend that these novels offer valuable ways of thinking about the roles of narrative in responding to injustice. At the same time as they point toward the limits of fiction as a means of recovering voices, they invite readers into ethical relationships with the real-life people whose experiences underpin the texts. They create foundations for provisional communities based on efforts to assert responsibility toward lives too numerous to count and too multifaceted to grasp. Such efforts provoke vulnerability because they invite readers to reconsider how they fit into the varied social structures that shape their lives. As Jean-Michel Ganteau and Susana Onega argue, vulnerability of this kind lies at the heart of an ethical response to stories of injustice.[95] It is a foundation for critiquing existing power structures and forging new connections with others.

In chapter 4, I continue to probe how fiction can offer ethical responses to marginalization and injustice. I strive to complicate the commonly held view that ethical responses to life stories rest on striving to grasp the subjectivity and experiences of the individual, and by extension recognizing the humanity of people whose humanity was denied by their persecutors. I argue that this view downplays the ways lives exceed stories, the circumstances and discursive frameworks that affect how life stories circulate, and the structural conditions in which those stories take shape. In this chapter, I take up several of Warner's short stories that deal with witnessing, either through characters testifying to their experiences or characters struggling to understand the experiences of others. These stories seem to ask readers to recognize the suffering and resilience of the characters. However, I contend that Warner complicates efforts to read them as tales of self-revelation. As in the previous chapters, I analyze narrative strategies that challenge presumptions of understanding on the part of readers. I suggest that by complicating responses that centre on recognizing the identities and experiences of the characters, Warner encourages readers to look beyond the bodies on the page toward the social structures that underpin the stories. She invites readers to consider what roles they play in those social structures and how they are connected to real-life people whose life stories are most vulnerable to being ignored.

With chapter 5, I turn back to Warner's non-fiction and the question of how to write about people who have been "othered" without claiming a form of analytic authority denied to them. I focus on Warner's three encyclopedic studies of myths and fairy tales: *From the Beast to the Blonde: On Fairy Tales and Their Tellers* (1994), *No Go the Bogeyman: Scaring, Lulling, and Making Mock* (1998), and *Stranger Magic: Charmed States and the Arabian Nights* (2011). These are among Warner's best-known and most frequently taught books, which makes them a valuable site to analyze how her non-fiction responds to the ethical quandaries involved in writing about marginalization and injustice. On a literal level, the three texts are studies of stories rather than studies of people or cultures. Yet they all depict people or groups that have been "othered" (excluded or defined as alien), from the female fairy tale tellers left out of masculinist literary histories to the Arab cultures that produced the *Arabian Nights*. To undertake scholarly work about processes of othering can risk presenting the people who have been "othered" as objects of knowledge, figures to be explained by the academic.[96] I argue that the eclectic style and anecdotal structure of Warner's studies offer one means of responding to this quandary. With their digressions, asides, and incongruous juxtapositions of detail, these studies resist claims to narrative closure. They hint at a desire to know more and a suspension of argument or even reason as an organizing principle. They resist the certainty of a place from which the writer is "sure of being able to begin to speak," to borrow a formulation used by Anne Dufourmantelle to describe Derrida's conception of hospitality.[97] I contend that, much like Warner's early journalism and life writing, these books invite a reading practice that resists certainties about other people and cultures. This kind of reading practice offers a potential foundation for challenging us-versus-them rhetoric and unjust socio-cultural hierarchies. Such challenges are particularly important in a period when us-versus-them rhetoric is being inflamed across Europe and North America, from debates on immigration to secularism laws in France and Quebec.

The coda provides some closing thoughts on the insights that Warner offers into the power and limits of narrative. It echoes Warner's optimism about the capacity of narrative to connect people across boundaries created by cultural differences, unjust hierarchies, and histories of mistrust. It simultaneously insists that telling and reading stories can only be a first step in connecting people to one another. Even at their most transparent, stories capture only fragments of lives, framed through the perspectives of the writer, available discursive frameworks, and conventions that promote the circulation of some stories but not others in a global cultural economy. As the coda shows, Warner's writing calls attention not just to what readers do not know about her characters, but to the work readers must do to understand the structural conditions that shape the characters' lives and the ways those conditions manifest themselves in the real world. The coda points toward future directions in Warner scholarship by considering how these concerns are reflected in her work as a curator and the comments she has made on her novel in progress, provisionally titled *Inventory of a Life Mislaid*. It shows the ongoing importance of her concerns with the power and risks of telling suppressed stories, and it demonstrates the significance of such stories for contemporary efforts to create new communities and connections in a globalized world.

1

Writing across Cultures

Multiple Viewpoints and Openness to Uncertainty in Warner's Early Life Writing and Vietnam Journalism

In *Fiction across Borders* (2010), Shameem Black observes: "Telling stories that are not considered one's own, particularly when the teller approaches these stories from a position of privilege, is often described as a form of invasive imagination." This view is "a powerful and necessary one," but as she points out, the ethics of telling stories across social and cultural differences are complicated.[1] The writer may risk appropriating the lives of an individual or group but simultaneously create connections, probe ethical responsibilities, and examine the limits of her knowledge.

In this chapter I analyze Warner's first book, *The Dragon Empress*, and her Vietnam War journalism as early examples of her negotiation of the risks of appropriating voices from cultures other than her own. Warner published the biography in 1972. She had been fascinated by China since childhood, and a college friend had told her stories about the "dragon empress," Tz'u-hsi, who ruled China as regent for most of the period from 1861 to 1908.[2] The year the book came out, Warner travelled to Saigon with William Shawcross, her first husband. While he covered the Vietnam War for the London *Times*, Warner wrote freelance articles for venues such as the *Times*, the *Guardian Express*, and the *Spectator*. Both her biography and her Vietnam journalism reveal Warner grappling with some of the questions that would form compass points for her writing over the next few decades. She explores how to tell stories about other people in ways that respect their singularity while navigating limitations of space, information, and generic conventions.

These early works strive to combat silencing, albeit in very different ways and with very different stakes. In each case, Warner focuses largely on female experiences left out of dominant narratives. With that said,

The Dragon Empress is not about someone in a position of precarity in the contemporary sense.[3] The biography centres on a woman with enormous power. It is driven by the conviction that "[h]eroines and leaders, rulers and fighters, regardless of intrinsic merit or ability – let alone virtue – were the necessary opponents of history as it was taught" (*DE* vii). By contrast, Warner's Vietnam journalism focuses on the effects of the Vietnam War on civilians, particularly women and children – people often represented in arguments for and against the war, but regularly pictured as silent victims rather than actors or speakers.

In both cases, Warner was writing from the position of a cultural and linguistic outsider. She did assiduous research for *The Dragon Empress*, travelling to the European colonies of Hong Kong and Macau as well as to Taiwan, but she could not go to mainland China because of the travel restrictions in place during the Cultural Revolution. She visited China three years after publishing *The Dragon Empress*, taking advantage of increased movement across the Chinese border even before the end of the Cultural Revolution and the death of Mao Zedong (*DE* xiii). Her access to information was limited to English sources – whether by British writers or in translation – at a time when English writing about China was filtered through a corpus of Orientalist images. Tz'u-hsi's life had already been transformed into myth by Sinologists and diplomats, who built a picture of the empress dowager as a ruthless and conniving ruler using stereotypes of "Eastern" exoticism, deceit, and excess. Warner risked perpetuating an Orientalist legend of a rapacious tyrant even while celebrating Tz'u-hsi as an emblem of female power. Her Vietnam journalism involved writing across cultural and social distance in a different way. Once again Warner was an outsider. She was free to leave any time and return to a home untouched by the conflict. In writing human-interest stories that focused largely on women and children, she was working in a genre that all too often reduced its subjects to passive icons of suffering or mobilized them as rhetorical tools in opposition to the war.

I argue that Warner's biography of Tz'u-hsi and her Vietnam journalism invite readers to consider how the people she represents exceed her representations. First, both the biography and the journalism offer multiple ways of interpreting the people at their centres. The biography depicts Tz'u-hsi as an ambitious ruler as well as a vulnerable young woman in a political structure that gave power almost exclusively to men. It combines an individualistic story about one woman's quest for power with a more collectivist account of the constraints and opportunities facing women in nineteenth-century China. In Warner's journalism, a multiplicity of interpretive lenses works against readings that might otherwise homogenize wartime victims in a faraway country. In both cases, this multiplicity counters the impulse to define the people Warner depicts in any single way. It suggests that Warner can only shed light on fragments of their lives. Second, Warner complicates the illusion of intimacy typically provided by biographies and human-interest journalism. In different ways, both the biography and the journalism remind readers of their distance from the people they are reading about. They question the ability of readers to grasp those people and by extension complicate Warner's ability to "make sense" of them.

I am not claiming that these early works always succeed in avoiding the appropriation or spectacularization of their subjects. To a degree, *The Dragon Empress* bolsters the existing myth of the monstrous empress, casting Tz'u-hsi as a spectacle for the enjoyment of a British reading public. In a foreword written a decade after the first edition, Warner mused that if she were writing the book again she would explore how the myth of "the monstrous and powerful empress" took shape (*DE* xv), but that was not her focus in 1972. It is worth remembering that Warner wrote these texts in the earliest stages of her career, in a period before anyone had begun to theorize the concepts of Orientalism or appropriation. Still, in both cases the distancing effects of the texts and their openness to multiple readings offer intimations of narrative strategies that develop more fully in Warner's later works and point toward the limits of any writer's ability to make her subjects present to readers. These strategies complicate, even if they may not fully undermine, readings that place readers in positions of power or privilege. Thus they create foundations for ethical relationships between Warner's readers and the people and cultures she writes about.

THE ELUSIVENESS OF THE SUBJECT IN *THE DRAGON EMPRESS*

The Dragon Empress picks up on a goal Warner expressed as a student journalist and editor of the Oxford student magazine *Isis* when she developed a special issue titled "Women." She strove, she proclaimed, to showcase "women who did something in their own right and not in the traditional roles of puppet or muse."[4] The biography reflects this desire for models of female achievement. It presents a woman who was chosen as a concubine at age sixteen and then became a fabled despot. But in writing *The Dragon Empress*, Warner faced two interrelated challenges. The first was telling Tz'u-hsi's life story without bolstering a myth shaped by Orientalist tropes. The second was constructing her own vision of Tz'u-hsi without reducing a complex life to an object lesson on the capacity of women to wield political power. I argue that by presenting multiple ways of reading the empress dowager, alongside suggestive gaps in the text, the biography resists claiming to account for her life. The book unsettles the illusion that it is bringing readers close to the enigmatic protagonist and hints at the impossibility of capturing Tz'u-hsi on the page.

The stories that circulated about Tz'u-hsi prior to Warner's biography (and, indeed, are still told today) presented her as ruthless, deceitful, and larger than life. She was characterized by excess in her exercise of both power and desire. Tales of her supposed affairs circulated wildly. For British readers, the most influential images of the "dragon lady" were shaped by Sinologist Edmund Backhouse and journalist J.O.P. Bland. In *China under the Empress Dowager: The History of the Life and Times of Tzu Hsi* (1910), Backhouse and Bland created a titillating vision of a corrupt ruler. They combined Orientalist tropes with "an ancient Chinese literary tradition of vilifying fallen emperors, empresses, and concubines."[5] Though they argued that Tz'u-hsi was not the "savage monster" portrayed in some stories, in the same breath they described "her childish lack of moral sense, her unscrupulous love of power, her fierce passions and revenges."[6] They constructed a ruler "addicted to pleasure, and at one period of her life undoubtedly licentious after the manner of her Court's traditions."[7] In Backhouse's autobiography, he claimed that the empress dowager initiated a torrid affair with him when she was nearly seventy.[8] Hugh Trevor-Roper showed in 1976 that Backhouse's autobiography was filled with invented stories, and he questioned the authenticity of key sources for *China under the Empress Dowager*, developments that Warner would acknowledge in her preface to the second edition of *The Dragon Empress*.[9] *The Dragon Empress* is far more sympathetic to Tz'u-hsi than Backhouse and Bland were. Still, even while challenging many of their claims, Warner relied on their biography as a key source.

Warner cannot be faulted for drawing on sources whose accuracy was later called into question. She was in the company of most or all British writers who addressed this period of Chinese history between 1910 and 1976. In the words of Sterling and Peggy Seagrave, every British writer who wrote about Tz'u-hsi before Trevor-Roper's revelations took Bland and Backhouse's vision as a foundation, creating "a skewed picture of imperial China in the half-century preceding its downfall."[10] It is worth noting that even in the twenty-first century, Tz'u-hsi's life story remains subject to uncertainty. Seagrave and Seagrave, who wrote their own biography of the empress dowager in 1992, cast her as an innocent dupe.[11] Jung Chang's 2013 biography depicts her as a proto-feminist emblem.[12] Popular sources still present Tz'u-hsi as a tyrant and monster.

A website for "Beijing Tours," for instance, describes her as a "venal and selfish woman" who showed finesse at murdering her rivals.[13] The case of Tz'u-hsi still hangs, to borrow a phrase from Warner's foreword to the 1993 edition of the biography (*DE* viii). With the facts of Tz'u-hsi's life subject to continued debate, the line between Orientalist fantasy and historical scholarship sometimes remains blurred.

Warner's "life and times" set out to give the life of the empress dowager a global reach. But Warner had to work out how to represent a life that had already been translated and distorted by her sources – and how to avoid her own distortions. Even good-faith efforts at historical recovery are invariably partial. While they may give visibility to previously overlooked experiences, they can also subordinate those experiences to the researcher's interpretive lens. This is not just an issue of accuracy but one of power relations. To publish another person's "life" invariably grants the writer an authority the subject does not share. The writer is the one selecting, framing, analyzing details, and ultimately presenting the work to the public.[14] These concerns have a long history in the study of biography and life writing, particularly since the late twentieth century, as scholars have deconstructed "the supposedly secure limits of selfhood and auto/biographical expressions of selfhood."[15]

Warner's version of Tz'u-hsi sometimes echoes pre-existing images of a power-hungry and conniving figure. Yet *The Dragon Empress* hints at the distance between the writer and her subject as well as the inevitable partiality of Warner's portrayal. This is not to suggest that in writing *The Dragon Empress* Warner deliberately sought narrative strategies that would unsettle her authority as a scholar. *The Dragon Empress* is not explicitly concerned with the ethics of representation. It does not experiment overtly with literary form or reflect on Warner's relationship to the material; that kind of reflection is reserved for the prefaces she wrote in the subsequent decades. The book is written with the "distanced, authorial voice" commonly seen in biographies – a voice that typically "provides the illusion that the life actually was as it is presented."[16] Nevertheless, *The Dragon Empress* contains provocative paradoxes and gaps that resist confining the empress dowager within a single interpretive lens.

The Dragon Empress tells the story of a woman who was born "the daughter of a minor Manchu mandarin" (*DE* 1). When the Hsien-feng emperor ascended the throne in 1851, sixteen-year-old Tz'u-hsi was summoned to the Forbidden City with sixty other young women and selected as a concubine. Though initially she held the fifth and lowest rank of concubine, Tz'u-hsi gained the favour of the emperor and bore his only surviving son. Primogeniture did not necessarily determine succession, since the emperor could confer the throne on anyone from the imperial line, but in 1861 when Hsien-feng was dying Tz'u-hsi persuaded him to name his six-year-old son as his successor. Thus, at twenty-six she became empress dowager alongside the late emperor's senior consort, Niuhuru. They "presided in the emperor's stead" at the head of a group of regents (*DE* 73), but Tz'u-hsi had little intention of becoming a figurehead. She steadily increased her power through political machinations. Except for two periods of nominal retirement, when her son T'ung-chih and later her nephew Kuang-hsu became emperors, she spent most of her adult life as regent, presiding "at the very heart of affairs, from the Dragon Throne itself" (*DE* 118).

On one hand, Warner recounts the life of Tz'u-hsi as a quest narrative. In this way she tells the kind of story that Carolyn Heilbrun would later challenge feminist historians to write in *Writing a Woman's Life* (1988). Warner also broadens the images of female achievement prominent in the 1970s, when many of the texts at the core of the women's liberation movement tied female agency to collective political resistance.[17] She focuses on a woman who identified her desires without hesitation and fought for them at every turn. In her account, Tz'u-hsi's life was shaped by ambition. For Warner, the fight for power does not make Tz'u-hsi a heroine – she was too cruel, and her oversights were too costly for China – but it makes her a model of determination. Warner attributes Tz'u-hsi's achievements to effort and skill rather than circumstances. She depicts Tz'u-hsi "forc[ing] her way" to the bedroom of the dying emperor and proclaiming, "Here is your son," when she feared the emperor would confer the throne on someone else (*DE* 68–9). In her account, Tz'u-hsi indulged corruption among the court eunuchs because "as soon as she entered the Forbidden City in 1852, she understood that these her servants were her most useful tools" (*DE* 23). Tz'u-hsi befriended Niuhuru, the Hsien-feng emperor's consort, because she had a knack for "instinctively attaching herself to success" (*DE* 19). This narrative challenges a tradition of writing about powerful women as if their power came to them unbidden.[18] In Warner's account, Tz'u-hsi consolidates power not just through luck, but through strategic machinations.

But Warner tells multiple and even contradictory stories, of which the individualistic quest narrative is only one. She weaves a tale of autonomy on one hand and vulnerability on the other; a legend of a wicked empress and a fable about creative responses to political constraints; a masculinist vision of power set against a broader exploration of self-invention. I am not claiming that this combination of narratives can account for the complexities of the empress dowager's life, but rather, that the proliferation of narratives tacitly admits none can adequately define her.

If Tz'u-hsi's machinations make her as much a villain as a heroine, Warner also depicts a very different kind of agency, one marked by creative efforts at self-authorship. Tz'u-hsi's creativity makes her a role model, albeit a flawed one, for female readers. In depicting other aspects of the empress dowager's life, Warner often passes judgment on her faults (she was naïve and impressionable; she was callous and even cruel to her attendants). Yet she describes Tz'u-hsi's creative achievements without comment, as if to let them speak for themselves. Warner notes that the empress dowager invented makeups, foods, and games. She concocted a facial spray made from glycerin and honeysuckle (DE 135). She created a board game titled "Eight Fairies Travel across the Sea," which she played with her ladies-in-waiting (DE 143). These acts of creativity reveal determination to expand her opportunities and even to build new social possibilities and cultural practices. Warner's Tz'u-hsi not only seizes the limited power available within existing strictures, she extends those limits, manipulating conventions to forge new opportunities for self-realization. Here she is not just a power-hungry tyrant but a woman with a sophisticated understanding of the cultural economy in which she lives, striving to carve out space for her desires within the limits of the Forbidden City.

Furthermore, while Warner has critiqued *The Dragon Empress* for privileging a single woman in power above the question of women's interests (DE vii), the book offers a complex portrait of female rights and constraints in nineteenth-century China. When Warner introduces Tz'u-hsi as "the daughter of a minor Manchu mandarin," she emphasizes how much a father's status shaped the prospects of a young woman, in contrast to her own desires or actions. She explains that mothers and mothers-in-law could wield "tyrannical powers" in a household but "a daughter had no voice in the decision of her future" (DE 15). She points out that women in nineteenth-century China seldom received any formal education, that Tz'u-hsi must have been self-taught, and that concubinage offered one of the few opportunities for increased socio-economic status. Thus, if Warner uses Tz'u-hsi to illustrate the capacity of women to achieve power, she undermines the idea that all women have to do is fight for it. She shows how Tz'u-hsi's achievements were enabled and constrained by the social structures of late-nineteenth-century China. She suggests that Tz'u-hsi's machinations were necessary tools for a woman who wanted to be anything other than a figurehead, pawn, or glorified servant in the imperial court. She also complicates the individualism of the quest narrative, albeit just slightly. On one hand, Warner says little about Tz'u-hsi's relationships and attributes most of her alliances to political strategy. On the other hand, in showing how Tz'u-hsi's freedoms were bound up with those of Niuhuru or the eunuchs, and acknowledging the loneliness Tz'u-hsi must have felt as she rose to power, Warner points toward the ways in which people's lives and worlds are shaped by others. By offering varied ways to read the empress dowager, Warner provides a vision of selfhood as multiple, subject to metamorphosis, and ultimately resistant to the confines of any single narrative.

The silences of the biography also hint at the impossibility of Warner or her readers gaining a complete picture of Tz'u-hsi's life. This is a narrative strategy that I trace throughout this book, as I explore varied silences within Warner's writing and the ways they gesture towards what lies outside the scope of her texts. *The Dragon Empress* offers a panoramic view of nineteenth-century China, in the tradition of a "life and times," but provides only occasional glimpses of Tz'u-hsi's thoughts, feelings, or speech. Warner's tone remains highly unemotional. In other writing from the same period, she constructs far more intimate portrayals of her subjects. For instance, in 1974 she wrote a feature for the *Sunday Times Magazine* on IRA member Rose Dugdale, on trial for a major art heist. The *Sunday Times* feature offers readers a strong sense of its subject's presence. Readers hear Dugdale's "deep, pleasant" voice and see her "fasten the judge with her pale blue eyes." Warner's discomfort is palpable when Dugdale gives a courtroom speech that is "excruciating to hear" because it is so "laboured, repetitive and disjointed."[19] These descriptions reflect the idea of biography as portrait, a metaphor that indicates "empathy, bringing to life, capturing the character."[20] By contrast, *The Dragon Empress* keeps readers at a much greater distance from its protagonist. Some of that distance is the inevitable result of unavailable information. Compounding Warner's lack of access to Chinese documents, Tz'u-hsi was very private, and "the world she lived in was uniquely designed to hide her behind many layers of court ritual and etiquette."[21] Still, Warner's Tz'u-hsi remains notably elusive in contrast to the richly drawn portraits of the imperial court. The effect is to highlight the gap between the life of the empress dowager and the access afforded to readers.

As the biography unfolds, the empress dowager keeps receding from view. Warner describes the ceremony for choosing a concubine, but says almost nothing about Tz'u-hsi's life over the next three years except that she studied Chinese classics in the imperial libraries and probably persuaded a scholar-official to tutor her. Warner explains that at age twenty Tz'u-hsi bore a son and was raised to concubine of the second rank, and then Tz'u-hsi's story pauses as the book turns to the Opium Wars and the Taiping Rebellion. Warner takes up Tz'u-hsi's story several years later, at the point when the emperor died and Tz'u-hsi and Niuhuru were named empresses dowager and regents. At this exciting moment, Warner returns to foreign affairs and Tz'u-hsi recedes from foreground to background once more. Readers get little sense of Tz'u-hsi's day-to-day life until Warner reaches the period of her first retirement, in 1889. Granted, all biographers have to make "hard decisions" about gaps in information, and it is not uncommon to fill in those gaps with social context.[22] In the words of celebrated biographer Hermione Lee, "[b]iographies are full of verifiable facts, but they are also full of things that aren't there: absences, gaps, missing evidence, knowledge or information that has been passed from person to person, losing credibility or shifting shape on the way."[23] Warner's oscillation between the biographical subject and her social context also makes sense in the context of a "life and times." Still, the tendency to retreat from Tz'u-hsi's life at the moments of greatest suspense makes the gaps in the narrative conspicuous and undermines the sense of intimacy that typically marks biography. It distances readers from the ruler the book seems to hold out to them and reminds them of the limits of their ability to grasp her world.

When readers seem to come closest to Tz'u-hsi, the sense of proximity is invariably brief. Early in the book, for instance, Warner offers a physical portrait of the young concubine: "As a young girl, Tz'u-hsi had long eyes, a broad forehead and a firm, rounded chin which was to develop later into quite a jowl. But these heavy features were enlivened by an alert and vivacious expression and a smile that flashed across her face with winning suddenness" (*DE* 7). This description offers a rare moment of intimacy. Warner's account of Tz'u-hsi's vivacious expression and flashing smile invites readers to imagine themselves in her presence. However, Warner moves from this vividly individualized sketch to descriptions that rest on custom rather than personal characteristics or behaviour. She depicts Tz'u-hsi's "delicate well-shaped hands and nails that she grew four inches long on her third and little finger, as the snobbery of otium demanded." She comments on the hair that was never cut and the white makeup that Tz'u-hsi wore "[l]ike all Manchu girls" (*DE* 7). The young woman with the sudden smile fades out of focus beside the richly delineated customs of the court. On the next page, Warner observes that "[a] poem survives which celebrates Tz'u-hsi's beauty, but it was written by a flatterer who never saw her," and in any case, "descriptions of beauty rarely conjure a face precisely" (*DE* 8). Here she not only calls attention to what readers do not know, she undermines the sense of insight offered by her earlier description, itself unable to "conjure" Tz'u-hsi in any complete way. As the passage continues, she moves back to the sumptuary customs of the court. On one hand, she offers a detailed visual image of the young concubine, especially her makeup, jewels, and clothes. On the other hand, she devotes more space to cultural practices than personal attributes or preferences.

Warner's attention to visual detail paradoxically underscores the limits of her access – and the access of readers – to Tz'u-hsi's life. *The Dragon Empress* is filled with rich visual descriptions. The book opens with a dramatic image: "Walls within walls within walls not only encircled the Middle Kingdom, but contained each city, and within each city each quarter, and within each quarter each palace and each mansion" (*DE* 1). The first extended description of Tz'u-hsi focuses on the spectacle of a prospective concubine entering the Imperial City: she crossed the palace moat "attired in the finest robes and jewels her family could buy or borrow," and then she passed into "the Imperial City and the maze of halls and pavilions, temples and living quarters, pagodas and garden retreats of the Purple Forbidden City beyond" (*DE* 15). Warner's frequent references to the "maze of halls" and the "labyrinthine apartments of the … Emperor" (*DE* 15), coupled with long, winding sentences that echo these labyrinthine structures, may hint at her ability to bring readers into an inner sanctum otherwise outside their reach. At the same time, the visual focus of these images offers a reminder that Warner and her readers are observing from a distance. While the biography may let readers imagine themselves in Peking (modern Beijing), it gives them only the access that might be available to tourists (if tourists had been allowed into the Forbidden City). The contrast between the vivid sights and the absence of interiority exposes the ways Tz'u-hsi, as an individual with a multifaceted identity, eludes the reader's gaze.

Many of the most vivid and memorable scenes are characterized by uncertainty, emphasizing how much readers do not know. For instance, Warner offers several possible versions of Tz'u-hsi's first summons to the emperor's bed. The emperor's stepmother, who had chosen her as a concubine in the first place, might have suggested her to the emperor. Alternatively, "the eunuchs, begged by the impatient girl, may have recommended a meeting; or, as the storytellers say, Tz'u-hsi was singing to herself in her clear, animated voice … when the emperor passed her pavilion and ordered the sweet singer to his side" (*DE* 29). The most vividly drawn images – whether the singing concubine or the impatient girl pleading with the eunuchs – add drama to the book but conspicuously offer readers little knowledge about Tz'u-hsi.

The closing chapter highlights the open questions that surround so many of the major episodes in Tz'u-hsi's life. The chapter focuses on two deaths: that of Tz'u-hsi and that of her nephew, the Kuang-hsu emperor, who died the day before her. Warner recounts the lunch Tz'u-hsi ate before she died ("her favorite dish of clotted cream and crab-apples") and the valediction in which she recounted the major events of her rule (*DE* 225). But the dramatic focus falls on the death of the emperor and the question of whether or not Tz'u-hsi poisoned him. If death stories often provide readers of biography with a sense of closure,[24] this one does the opposite, both by subordinating Tz'u-hsi's death to the emperor's and by emphasizing the uncertainties that surround their final days. Warner gives several potential explanations for the emperor's death. Tz'u-hsi might have had him poisoned because she opposed his reformist ideals. Eunuchs might have poisoned him independently because his planned reforms threatened their financial security. The emperor might have died naturally, since he had suffered from health trouble since childhood.[25] Ultimately Warner exonerates Tz'u-hsi, arguing that there is little more than speculation and gossip to link her to the emperor's death. On one hand, with this conclusion Warner claims the authority to pass judgment on conflicting stories. On the other hand, she gives readers only negation as a means of understanding her protagonist. She does not offer a tale of loyalty, or hatred, or inward desire for the emperor's demise; she only points to what Tz'u-hsi (probably) did not do. The uncertainties of the chapter leave readers grappling with the elusiveness of the protagonist. I am not suggesting that this is a weakness of the biography; much the opposite. While conventional biographies promise "an understanding of the subject's life" that readers see as "accurate and reliable,"[26] I contend that uncertainties in Warner's text tacitly acknowledge the limits of the biographer's ability to represent her subject and the reader's ability to grasp her. This is doubly important in the case of a woman vilified by the legends that circulated (and still continue to circulate) about her.

The epilogue emphasizes the elusiveness of the empress dowager. Warner moves past Tz'u-hsi's death and funeral to an incident twenty years later when bandits attacked the mausoleum where she was interred. They plundered her jewels and flung her face-down on the ground with her clothes partially torn off. Warner closes by quoting the commission of enquiry charged with reporting on the matter: "Very gently … we turned the Jade Body on its back. The complexion of the face was wonderfully pale, but the eyes were deeply sunken and seemed like two black caverns. There were signs of injury on the lower lip" (DE 229). The scene calls attention to the traces through which historians reconstruct the past, such as bodies, tombs, photographs, and written reports. Here, the reader's view of Tz'u-hsi is mediated by the description of her body provided by the commission and reproduced by Warner. (In fact, one more layer of mediation intercedes: Warner's endnotes show that the quote from the commission comes from a book on the emperor P'u-i, who succeeded Kuang-hsu as the last emperor of the Ching dynasty.) The closing lines emphasize the time, space, and historical documents that separate readers – and Warner – from Tz'u-hsi.

On the surface, it might seem like Warner's portrayal of Tz'u-hsi reflects Virginia Woolf's approach to characterization, conveying character through "the tone of a voice, the turn of a head, some little phrase or anecdote picked up in passing."[27] Indeed, *The Dragon Empress* characterizes Tz'u-hsi through scattered details and anecdotes. Readers see her in her flower-shaped jewels and her "Manchu slippers with the central raised heel … embroidered and beaded and decorated and sewn for her in their hundreds" (DE 135). They hear Tz'u-hsi's pride in her ability to rise to challenges: "I must say I was a clever woman, for I fought my own battles and won them too" (DE 30).[28] Yet the effect is very different from the impressionistic characterization in Woolf's *Orlando* or "Mr Bennett and Mrs Brown." In *The Dragon Empress* Tz'u-hsi seems almost like a secondary character beside the tapestry of Chinese domestic and foreign affairs. The details convey social and economic networks more than character traits or personal experiences. On one hand, items like Tz'u-hsi's jewels and slippers can "open into stories" and evoke imagination, as Warner has said about the power of objects in discussions of her novel in progress, *Inventory of a Life Mislaid*.[29] On the other hand, these details function as screens in two respects.[30] Even as they present images of the imperial court a century ago, they screen out the empress dowager, hiding her from view. They do not let readers presume to understand her inner life.

From a point of view concerned with the appropriation of lives and cultures, this is a somewhat uneven book. Some of the imagery invites accusations of cultural tourism and Orientalist spectacle. An early description of Peking enumerates the sights available to visitors: "flags announcing their wares streamed in a typical Peking breeze; beggars in organized gangs buttonholed passers-by; rope dancers twirled and spun … pedlars shuffled past carrying yoked paniers of sweets and needles and tea and toys and rice cakes and paper patterns and donuts and fans" (DE 2). The description replicates tropes of "Eastern" excesses and feeds desires for the exotic domesticated for consumption by the European traveller. Like Backhouse and Bland's biography, Warner's portrait of the empress dowager herself sometimes evokes images of "Oriental" deceit and excess. She describes Tz'u-hsi as "a gourmet of astonishing voraciousness" who had fancy breads baked for her "[i]n spite of the quantities of tribute rice exacted from the farmers and sent from the south to Peking" (DE 142). She proclaims that Tz'u-hsi was "extravagantly generous, after the manner of all Chinese," but used her "generosity" as a weapon, giving enemies extravagant gifts that required them to beggar themselves by returning the favour or else lose face (DE 144). She presents a woman who "played the subtle instrument of court intrigue with a sure touch" (DE 65), who was often "unscrupulous" in her dealings (DE 109), and who could plot with a "scalpel's accuracy" (DE 158).

Yet while the biography occasionally replicates Orientalist tropes, it also unsettles "the sense of mastery that writing about others is often said to afford."[31] This rejection of claims to cognitive mastery is important because "[a]dmitting one's inability to inhabit the perspectives of others" can form a foundation for ethical relations across cultural and social divisions.[32] Such admissions can reject positions of privilege that link the power to interpret and evaluate other people to assumptions of cultural and political superiority. In this way they can enable an openness to the lives of others that strives to respect both what one understands and what exceeds one's understanding.

"CRUSHED BUTTERFLIES" AND "POOR LITTLE BASTARDS": SUBVERTING STEREOTYPES OF VICTIMHOOD IN WARNER'S VIETNAM COVERAGE

Warner's Vietnam journalism, similarly, invites readers to acknowledge the limits of their ability to grasp the lives of other people. Like *The Dragon Empress*, her war journalism seemingly enables a broad English readership to cross cultural and geographical distances, though in a very different setting. Instead of the Forbidden City in the nineteenth century, she takes readers to a developing country during a protracted war. She could easily have replicated a common journalistic lens that presented civilians in distant wars as passive embodiments of suffering. Yet Warner's responses to the war are far more complex.

In later writings, Warner has commented on how difficult it was to make sense of her position as an outsider in the face of the suffering caused by the war. She was on Route 1, the road that led to Trang Bang, when the South Vietnamese air force conducted the napalm strike emblematized by Nick Út's famous photograph of Phan Thi Kim Phúc screaming as her skin burned. Warner witnessed the effects of the bomb firsthand. Decades later she mused, "as I stood there looking, waves of different feelings came over me all at once: horror at my helplessness (I had nothing with me even to cover a baby in that state, let alone do something medically useful), shame at my position as a foreign visitor, a voyeur out to find and see these terrible events."[33] Her Vietnam journalism does not discuss the bombing in detail, though she has drawn on the attack in some of her later fiction.[34] Yet her journalistic coverage explores how to write about lives vastly changed by war without simply engaging in voyeurism.

In "The Bitch Route 13," published in the *Spectator* in 1972, Warner asks how to cover a war from an ethical standpoint and whether that is ever fully possible. The war correspondents, she writes, "are – and they recognise it – living off the sufferings they describe."[35] She emphasizes the contradictions of their position. The press corps put themselves in danger to cover the war, and many are traumatized by the pain they witness. She describes one journalist shouting as he ran down the road after the napalm bomb on Route 1, "crazed … in fury and grief."[36] At the same time, she reflects, "the central irony of the indisputably courageous and vital coverage of the Vietnam War" is that "[n]o matter how bitterly opposed to the war a journalist might be, it really is against his interests for the war to calm down."[37] Though here she speaks of the journalists in the masculine third person, she recognizes that these observations implicate her as well. In a later reflection on her time in Saigon, she modulates consciously from "they" (the journalists) to "we."[38] "The Bitch Route 13" implicitly asks the questions Arthur and Joan Kleinman put as follows: "To what uses are experiences of suffering put? What are the consequences of those cultural practices for understanding and responding to human problems?"[39] Her war coverage tacitly probes the implications of the journalist's rhetorical choices not just for antiwar protests and policy-making, but for readers' broader understandings of their relationships to the people in Vietnam.

In this respect Warner's Vietnam articles contrast starkly with human-interest journalism that defines its subjects through their suffering – a common trend in Vietnam War writing, in both the US and the UK. As early as 1962, Susan Sontag notes, "[t]he color photographs of tormented Vietnamese villagers and wounded American conscripts that Larry Burrows took and *Life* published … fortified the outcry against the American presence in Vietnam."[40] Vietnamese women were often presented as passive victims in American press coverage, reduced to "examples of the consequences of war."[41] The same is true in British broadsheets. Of course coverage of the war was highly varied, but many British news articles from this period presented civilians solely as suffering victims to be saved by Western aid initiatives. A photo caption from a March 1968 *Guardian* article reads, "(Above) Napalm and (below) fragmentation bombs. Men, women, and children, suffer alike. They desperately need your aid."[42] A 1972 *Guardian* photo depicts a line of women photographed from the back, with the caption, "South Vietnamese women hurrying to board a landing barge evacuating them from Tan My island, seven miles east of Hue. A woman who collapsed while waiting to board is ignored by her fellow refugees."[43] The women appear as an anonymous mass incapable of helping themselves or one another. Set alongside an article on tension in Washington as "Nixon plans his next move," the photo presents the women as little more than illustrations of the cost of war. The use of war journalism to mobilize anti-war sentiment and condemn human rights abuses should not be downplayed or overlooked. Yet when people are reduced to icons of suffering "to mobilize support for social action," the complexities of experience are simplified and distorted.[44] Such writing all too often works "by differentiating between the reader and the others."[45] This kind of representation subordinates its subjects even (and perhaps especially) when it aims to protect them.

Warner's Vietnam journalism occasionally echoes representations of distant suffering that turn their subjects into passive victims. "Poor Little Bastards of Vietnam" features a photo of a baby in a cage-like crib. Beside the photo, Warner offers a graphic description: "babies doze on bare plastic with heavy stiff rags for nappies; the two-year-olds' thin bodies erupt in boils." She writes of children "in an ill-vented dormitory under a communal mosquito net" where some suffer from incontinence and "[e]ach morning one shrinks from the reek."[46] These descriptions would be at home in a strand of journalism that presents suffering bodies as illustrations for an anti-war argument. But ultimately Warner refuses to define her subjects through the privations or violence of war. As in *The Dragon Empress*, she tells many stories at one time. In this way she acknowledges the complexities of Vietnamese lives and experiences of conflict. She does not claim to grasp the people in Vietnam as objects of knowledge.

While Warner tells a story of exploitation and vulnerability, she also provides a complex portrait of survival strategies. For example, in "The Crushed Butterflies of War," she explains the economy of prostitution in Saigon before the advent of martial law in 1972. "Bar girls" spent time with GIs in exchange for the purchase of "Saigon tea," and the women shared the proceeds with the bar. Sometimes the women simply sat and flirted with the GIs; if a GI bought enough, a woman might spend the night, but they "always reserved to themselves the prerogative to refuse."[47] Warner's description emphasizes the agency of the women even if their work reflects economic vulnerability and limited options. Whereas Western journalism from this period often uses stories about Vietnamese prostitution to exemplify displacement and economic need,[48] Warner depicts a complex interplay of vulnerability and resistance strategies.

Moreover, far from presenting Western readers as saviours, Warner emphasizes local decision-making and social networks. In "Poor Little Bastards of Vietnam," she details Vietnamese responses to the needs of war orphans. She describes a Vietnamese teacher who "transformed a kindergarten classroom [in Hoi Duc Anh orphanage] into a marvelous panorama."[49] She quotes approvingly from an aid worker who suggests that the Vietnamese middle class adopt war orphans, as Korean families did after the Korean War (though she acknowledges that adoption is uncommon in Vietnam and this strategy would require changing mindsets). She writes of a Vietnamese nurse who runs a malnutrition unit in a Catholic charity centre. Whereas spectacles of distant suffering often abstract away social networks, Warner calls attention to collaboration, not just in official organizations but also in informal relationships. She presents three women who live together and care for eight children, some theirs and some children of acquaintances, and "all help each other."[50] When Warner calls on Western readers to intervene in the crisis, she urges them to contribute to sponsorship schemes, an intervention that leaves the executive work to the Vietnamese.[51] While exhortations to intervene in violence can separate the reader who has the power to act from the "victim" who needs rescue, Warner shows how Western political action has contributed to the problem of abandoned children but does not suggest that her readers have the power to solve it. Her multifaceted stories ironize the titles of the articles. The people she depicts emerge as far more than "poor little bastards" or "crushed butterflies of war." They cannot be characterized easily, if at all, and certainly not just as vulnerable figures to be pitied by Western readers.

Warner's Vietnam articles hint at the limits of readers' ability to interpret the people they depict by undermining the illusion of proximity frequently offered by human-interest stories. This point comes across most clearly in "The Crushed Butterflies of War." At the centre of the article is a thirty-five-year-old woman named Tra Kim Anh, who conceived her son in a liaison with an American GI. In some ways this is a classic human-interest story. It depicts a mother trying to care for her children in the face of adversity. She leaves her son with another family and keeps her daughter with her while she works as a bar girl to support them both. On one hand, the article seems to bring Anh close to readers. Warner depicts Anh sitting with her at a "fly-blown table" and laying a photo of her ex-lover on the surface. The scene presents Anh in close-up, the physical proximity of the two women a seeming metaphor for the ability of journalism to cut across geographical and cultural distances. Yet Anh is described in even less detail than the GI in the snapshot. Her "bleak smile and white teeth" offer readers less purchase than the absent GI, "[s]nub-nosed and fresh-faced in his crisp uniform," who grins up at them from the photo.[52] The fly-blown table, a detail that seems to place readers in the room with the two women, could be almost anywhere. I am not arguing that Warner depicts Anh as inherently beyond her understanding because of cultural or experiential differences. Rather, by unsettling the illusion that she is bringing readers close to her subject, she points toward the limits of the journalistic article as a means of translating Anh's life for the British reading public.

Warner also depicts Anh's power to mediate her story. Two moments in the article demonstrate respect for the silences of the Vietnamese woman, emphasizing that she is not just a "native informant" but a storyteller who chooses what to share and what to withhold. Warner explains that Anh's former lover has stopped sending money, "but now, as Anh writes no English, and has never written to him, she can't or won't communicate."[53] The openness to varied possibilities in Warner's phrase, "she can't or won't," encodes recognition that Anh can choose what to communicate not just to the GI but also to Warner. The motives behind her silence remain outside the scope of the article. Later, Warner calls attention once again to Anh's power to decide how much of herself to share. Warner recalls, "When I asked her what she thought of Americans, she said it was hard for her to say. During the Tet offensive of 1968, she explained, she had been living with one GI when her mother had been killed by another. So it was hard to say."[54] Her repetition emphasizes Anh's refusal to pass judgment – or perhaps more accurately, her refusal to articulate a judgment to Warner, the British reporter. In both of these passages, Warner shows that neither she nor readers can "read" Anh's story in any complete way. To adapt a phrase from Wendy Kozol, here Warner hints at the "complex worlds and subjectivities" of Anh and other Vietnamese civilians, "both articulated and unarticulated to the [reader]."[55]

In structure, too, "The Crushed Butterflies of War" hints at the multiplicity and complexity of the life stories Warner strives to tell. The article leaps from one scene and topic to another. It starts with the complicated relationships and social hierarchies connecting one of the American GIs and his Vietnamese counterparts. It moves to the babies abandoned by GIs and the mothers who "work the bars" to support their children, then to Warner's conversation with Anh, and back to the Vietnamese soldiers. This fragmented structure suggests that the story Warner tells is not fixed or finite. Instead, to borrow a formulation from Julie Salverson about ways to tell stories about violence, it is "an open [story] that changes and carries with it the possibility of reformings and retellings."[56] Warner shows that the story (or stories) in the article could take many possible directions. One of the most conspicuous changes in direction appears in her discussion with Anh. From Anh's insistence that "it was hard to say" what she thought of the Americans, the scene jumps to a new proclamation: "'I was going to America,' she added, brightening, 'but the papers are very complicated.'"[57] This abrupt shift highlights Anh's role as a storyteller, actively choosing one topic over another, and creates what Salverson might describe as "a space or 'gap' … that holds the circle of knowing open and … prevents steering a straight line through the story."[58] It invites recognition that Anh might tell her story in different ways at different times, and the same is true of all the people Warner interviews.

In contrast to images of war that both atomize their subjects and define them through suffering, Warner's Vietnam articles resist appropriating her subjects "to mobilize moral sentiment and collective action."[59] Warner tells multilayered stories, exploring forms of exploitation as well as resilience and personal struggles alongside social networks. Moreover, as in *The Dragon Empress*, Warner intimates that she is only portraying fragments of complex local worlds. Her Vietnam articles call attention to the ways her informants frame and limit the stories they tell her. In this way she complicates the "asymmetry of power between the comfort of spectators in their living rooms and the vulnerability of sufferers on the spectators' television screens" (or the pages of their newspapers).[60] It is not proximity or affect that brings about ethical relations here.[61] Rather, these articles ask readers to probe their responsibilities in the face of the situations on the page, but they do not grant readers the power to fix those situations or even to grasp them in full.

CONCLUSION

Warner's biography of Tz'u-hsi and her Vietnam journalism confront very different risks of appropriation. The first risks reducing a complex life story to a myth that trades in Orientalist stereotypes even while constructing an emblem of female power. The second risks transforming people with varied life experiences into icons of victimhood. Both lenses would spectacularize people and cultures already subjected to tropes that present them as distant, exotic, and different. Yet the biography and the journalism resist the illusion that they can account for the lives of the people they depict. They forgo the pleasures of intimacy that often drive biography and human-interest stories, and they hint that the people they portray exceed any interpretive framework they could offer.

Writing across cultural differences in ways that purport to account for a person's life and social context can simplify and domesticate the unfamiliar, consolidating privileged identities and intercultural hierarchies. On the other hand, representations that refuse illusions of cognitive mastery, such as *The Dragon Empress* and Warner's Vietnam articles, can do the opposite. They can oppose the privilege that ties knowledge and judgment of others to social and cultural domination. Even if the ways they resist claims to knowledge are fleeting and partial, they have the power to "alter the character of the public sphere"[62] by inviting openness to lives that cannot be easily pinned down.

In chapter 2, I build on this point about the importance of interpreting other people's lives with openness to what lies outside one's understanding. I move from Warner's early life writing and journalism to her early fiction. With this shift, I turn from a focus on strategies for writing about real people to dramatizations of fictional characters trying to understand the lives of others. I suggest that like *The Dragon Empress* and Warner's Vietnam articles, her early novels explore ways of interpreting the lives of other people across geographical distances and unequal power relations. They push readers to resist presumptions of understanding and cultivate open-ended efforts to imagine other people's lives.

2

Role Models and Parallel Lives

Identification and Imagination in In a Dark Wood, The Skating Party, *and* The Lost Father

Warner's early novels may not seem like obvious sites to explore the ethics of writing about other people or the risks of appropriating voices. *In a Dark Wood* (1977) and *The Skating Party* (1982) are realist family dramas with upper-class English protagonists. It is not until *The Lost Father* (1988) that Warner's fiction starts to bear witness to silenced voices in a sustained way. Even then, the novel tells a story about her own family: her mother's parents, aunts, and grandparents. However, all three novels dramatize questions about how to interpret other people's lives across social differences. As I noted in the Introduction, by "social differences" I mean distinctions between groups that affect relations of power between them, such as race, socio-economic class, and geography. I argue that Warner's portrayals of characters interpreting one another's lives have important implications for the ways she invites readers to respond both to the characters in the novels and to people outside the texts.

Warner's three early novels ask whether identifying with other people's experiences of silencing can create solidarity in the face of social differences. I am using "solidarity" to refer to a sense of unity based on common purpose or experience coupled with an affirmation of the other person's rights and needs. I argue that these novels show how identifying with another person can reaffirm existing hierarchies when that identification ignores differences of power and privilege. At the same time, they hint that identification across social differences can create a foundation for ethical connections when it enables a person to give up their initial presumptions and undertake open-ended efforts to imagine someone else's life.

Theories of literature concerned with connecting people across differences frequently link literature's ethical potential to its capacity to evoke identification, the feeling that someone else is fundamentally like oneself, and empathy, the sense that one shares another person's feelings.[1] As I observed in the Introduction, a humanist ethics of reading holds that both identifying and empathizing with seemingly distant characters can help readers develop greater sensitivity toward real-life people whose experiences may seem equally distant.[2] This conviction can be heard regularly from teachers of literature, though it is subject to debate. On one hand, empirical research shows that empathizing with literary characters does not necessarily lead to empathy with real people or to pro-social behaviour.[3] On the other hand, there are some persuasive links between empathy and identification in reading, attitudes toward marginalized groups, and active efforts to support people across differences of race and class.[4]

Despite the widespread hope that identifying with other people can undermine social and cultural divisions, the effects of identification are complicated. As feminists of colour and anti-racist scholars have shown, acts of identification can ignore and reify differences, particularly when comparatively privileged people blithely identify with people in more vulnerable positions. The consolidation of the women's liberation movement based on shared female experiences downplayed structural inequalities based on race, nation, class, and sexuality.[5] Presumptions of sameness that come from identification can uphold existing hierarchies when they devalue the real wants and needs of a person or group. They can contribute to the "colonization of psychic space" – the affective harm caused by oppression – when they deny the oppression a person has gone through, because that denial undermines a person's ability to make their experiences meaningful.[6] Moreover, presumptions of sameness can prevent a person from recognizing their own roles in the power structures that shaped another person's situation.[7] Thus, for many theorists identification is "at best a weak form of engagement and at worst a violent one."[8] From this perspective, identifying with someone else subordinates that person to one's own psychological needs for the purpose of consolidating the self. This view echoes Freud's construction of identification as an act of erasure. For Freud, in identification "the object that we long for and prize is assimilated … and in that way is annihilated as such."[9] In Freud's work this assimilation is an inherent attribute of identification, but from an ethical perspective the most trenchant critiques of identification focus on its capacity to exacerbate unequal power relations.

At the same time, acts of identification have the potential to engender new conceptions of community and challenge oppressive hierarchies. Identifying with another person across differences of race and class can help prevent the reification of such differences into immutable identities. Such "cross-identifications" can combat dominant ideologies that present subject positions like race and class as natural or unchangeable boundaries.[10] Moreover, although identifying with suffering or marginalization can make it easy for a person to ignore their position in the social structures that led to that suffering, it can also do the opposite. Identifying with suffering can elicit a sense of connection in the face of geographically or temporally distant events. It can transform privileged readers by making them aware of their privilege.[11] Identifying across social differences may drive privileged subjects to "a radical transformation in consciousness" that leads not only to "greater understanding and compassion" but to new recognition of the ways one's social positioning affects others "within transnational hierarchies of power."[12] Thus while identification can be appropriative, it can also combat social divisions.

In this chapter, I argue that *In a Dark Wood*, *The Skating Party*, and *The Lost Father* offer provocative insights into the ways acts of identification across social difference can harm and connect. In all three novels, female protagonists identify with other women subjected to marginalization. For instance, the narrator of *The Skating Party*, a Cambridge lecturer struggling to be recognized as more than the wife of a professor, identifies with a young woman in Palau whom her husband wrote about years earlier during his anthropology fieldwork. She sees the young woman as a symbol for the ways she herself feels limited by patriarchal expectations. The narrator of *The Lost Father*, a British historian and curator writing a memoir about her mother's family, finds inspiration in the life of a great-aunt who lived in Mussolini's Italy. I contend that the novels expose the potential violence of acts of identification that deny a person's formative experiences. Yet they suggest that identification can promote solidarity when it engenders ongoing imagination and resistance to the closure that comes from claims to knowledge or understanding. This solidarity is not founded on what is already shared, but on what Sara Ahmed describes as "the *very work that we need to do* in order to get closer to others": a process that is always singular, fluid, and unfinished.[13] The ongoing imagination envisioned here may be difficult or even impossible to instantiate – as an act without end, it is perhaps better defined as an ideal than a goal – but it offers a valuable source of connection in the face of difference.

IN A DARK WOOD AND THE PITFALLS OF SEEKING PARALLELS BETWEEN STORIES

Warner's first novel, *In a Dark Wood*, is carefully patterned, with storylines echoing and refracting one another. It maps the struggles of its characters onto a variety of literary models, and the characters often see one another's lives as parallels for their own. The novel tempts readers to endorse the ways the characters identify with others, but it also raises questions about the accuracy and consequences of those identifications. The novel hints that for acts of identification to create connections across social differences, such acts must lead people to question their understandings of those they identify with and the webs of relationships that link them.

The dangers of facile identification are dramatized most vividly in a scene belonging to a minor subplot. Teresa Namier, a wealthy British actress, plays a starring role in a modernized version of the 1949 musical *South Pacific*, set in Vietnam. She talks grandly about the importance of the show, her voice shaking with emotion as she tells her husband, "We tell it like it is … all about the bargirls exploited by the GIs … Leaving them with coffee-coloured babies. Perhaps we could adopt one, darling" (*IDW* 248). Her grandiose claims enrage her daughters and photojournalist son-in-law, who argue that the musical transforms violence into kitsch and trivializes the bloodshed in Vietnam. Teresa's superficial identification with the women in Vietnam betrays her lack of interest in the complexities of the war. Yet while the scene critiques her reduction of suffering to spectacle, it illustrates the power of identification to make people feel responsible for faraway others. Much of Warner's Vietnam journalism is driven by the same concern Teresa expresses for the women impregnated by overseas troops (though without the saviour complex). This shared concern suggests that the compassion created by identification should not be dismissed out of hand. In fact, even in its portrayal of the kitsch musical, the novel capitalizes on the power of identification. When Teresa's daughter Paula visits a rehearsal and feels horrified at "this charade … [that] was supposed to be Vietnam," the text invites readers to identify with Paula's discomfort. The scene is focalized through Paula, her views expressed through free indirect discourse and her emotions visceral, as "a wave of hysterical laughter" vies with a feeling of "sickness" (*IDW* 124). Of course, not all readers identify with the same aspects of a text, and identification is influenced by many factors, but it is commonly held in narrative theory that focalization and intensity of emotion can encourage identification and empathy.[14] If readers identify with Paula and share in her critique of her mother, that identification invites them to take broader responsibility for critiquing the reduction of violence to kitsch and to ask how they should respond to stories of war. It turns readers into witnesses, albeit distant ones, to the bargirls in Vietnam invoked by Teresa and to women in other, unnamed sites of war. Thus, while the scene shows how the feelings of closeness promoted by identification can be superficial, it also hints that identification can promote new ethical relations.

The interwoven plotlines at the centre of the story extend this examination of the relationships between identification and solidarity. Paula's uncle Gabriel, a Jesuit priest and scholar, struggles with his faith and sexuality. In his effort to define himself and his spiritual beliefs, he identifies with two figures: the lost pilgrim in Dante's *Inferno*, who features in his recurring nightmares, and a fictional missionary named Andrew da Rocha, whose biography he is writing. In a second plotline that dramatizes acts of identification across socio-cultural distances, Gabriel, Paula, and Paula's father travel to Sicily when Gabriel's Jesuit order charges him with assessing the visions of three girls who claim to have seen the Virgin Mary in an olive grove. Both Gabriel and Paula interpret the visions of the three girls in Sicily through their own desires: Gabriel's need for faith and Paula's search for models of self-expression.[15] *In a Dark Wood* shows that identifying one life story with another can overlook the particularities that make a life unique and the social, political, and cultural contexts that shape it. The novel suggests that identification with other people may be most valuable as a source of solidarity when it is an ongoing, uncertain process and not one that stems from assumptions of commonality.

The dangers of appropriative identifications receive their most sustained treatment through the character of Gabriel. Gabriel superimposes the struggles of the fictional missionary, Andrew da Rocha, onto his twentieth-century London life. His closeness to the missionary becomes a source of distance as his perception of the connections between them shapes the ways he imagines the man and takes him ever further away from da Rocha's historical context. But the plotline about Paula's response to the girls in the olive grove, though it comprises only a brief section of the novel, offers a more complex vision of the potential interplay between appropriation and solidarity in acts of identification.

Paula idealizes the girls in the olive grove even though she has no religious beliefs. Much as Gabriel uses the story of Andrew da Rocha to define himself, Paula seeks validation through the girls. She wishes for "a feminine ideal" to help her determine who she wants to be.[16] Here, a paradoxically twinned identification and idealization give rise to a perception of commonality that alleviates her loneliness and seems to undermine geographical and cultural boundaries.[17] "Fascinated" and "impressed" (*IDW* 125), Paula casts the young visionaries as models for her own life, both as victims of patriarchal power and as emblems of resistance to silencing. Her response illustrates the role played by fantasy "in the articulation of both individual and collective identity."[18] Her admiration for the girls, whose testimony turns them into public figures, echoes feminist discourses that idealize women projected "into masculine public space where they experience the pleasures and dangers of transgressing social and sexual boundaries."[19] Her admiration simultaneously creates a fantasy of female agency within domestic (and feminized) space, since despite their newfound fame the girls live at home under the rule of their parents in a conservative Catholic community. Paula's construction of the girls offers her a model for developing voice both within and outside traditional gender roles and creates a potential foundation for a female community with the power to call those roles into question.

The text invites readers to identify with Paula in her identification with the girls, even though it ultimately troubles that invitation. At one point, Paula, her father, and her uncle discuss the three young visionaries over dinner at a village restaurant. Again, free indirect discourse and emotional intensity encourage readers to share her feelings, even if reader identifications cannot be entirely predicted in advance. Warner describes Paula's emotions more vividly than those of the other characters. Tears come to Paula's eyes and she chokes on her words as she tries to express her sympathy for Maria Pia, the leader of the three girls (*IDW* 212). Paula insists that like herself, "the girl here" is "probably fed up too and she didn't want to be alone either. So she saw something else, something fabulous, which she used to stop the separateness, the unconnectedness" (*IDW* 212–13). Her identification with Maria Pia becomes a means to assert her own subjectivity. Feminist theory has long associated coming to voice with the development of the self. By connecting herself to Maria Pia, Paula enacts a vicarious coming to voice that contrasts with her own struggle for articulacy, illustrated by her vague language and frequent hesitations. For readers, too, identification with Paula and by extension with the girls in Sicily offers a vicarious coming to voice and enactment of solidarity toward the voices of other women. If "the articulation of experience (in myriad ways) is among the hallmarks of a self-determining individual or community,"[20] then hearing and validating Maria Pia's speech, in contrast to the male authorities who question her testimony, is a foundational step in constructing communal bonds. For readers who are drawn to identify with Paula, the text extends an invitation to participate in the process of constructing a female community across boundaries of age, language, class, and geography.

While the novel tacitly critiques Gabriel for dismissing the young visionaries due to his own crisis of faith, it never critiques the sincerity of Paula's response to the girls. Yet in a book that thematizes the ways people instrumentalize the lives of others for their own self-definition, it is noteworthy that Paula's identification with Maria Pia minimizes important differences between them. Maria Pia remains vulnerable to religious authorities seeking to pronounce on the validity of her claims. She is far more constrained than Paula, whose age, relative independence, and position in a wealthy household mean that her freedoms do not depend in any simple way on male authorization. On the other hand, the respect accorded by the villagers to Maria Pia's visions gives her the connectedness that Paula still longs for. Paula's identification with the girl illustrates that "from one angle, identification contributes to empathy and the bridging of difference. From another angle, it stands opposed to recognizing the other: the self engaged in identification takes the other as fantasy object, not as an equivalent center of being."[21] Paula "reads" Maria Pia for her own purposes, much as Gabriel reads the missionary da Rocha, even if she aligns herself with the girl. She reduces Maria Pia to the characteristics she is seeking in her own life. Moreover, Paula's identification with the girls is based on judgment – validation and admiration of their outspokenness. As such, it echoes the power structures that give Gabriel and the Jesuit church the authority to judge the girls' testimony. Thus while Paula's act of identification seems like a means of creating connections, it also forecloses understanding.

The novel offers readers an alternative way of responding to the three girls, one that involves ongoing imagination and interpretation. The text does not provide a singular corrective to Paula's view of the girls in the grove. Instead, multiple voices describe the girls, their families, and their relationships to the village. Each account is incomplete and shaped by its own biases, suggesting that no single narrative can adequately capture the girls. The chorus of voices invites both curiosity and imagination. In the scene at the restaurant described above, a group of fishermen describe Maria Pia's family history, explaining that she was born out of wedlock when a priest seduced her mother and disgraced both parties. Even then, their insights only extend to "what everyone knows, but will not say" (*IDW* 210), the tale of an affair that acquired the status of legend and the ability to account for a woman's entire life. The novel invites deeper curiosity by alternating the men's statements with Paula's halting efforts to express her feelings. Her speech is both immediate and idiosyncratic: "I can feel this sand. I can feel it there. I want to stop feeling alone. I want to feel people, things, like I can feel this" (*IDW* 212). This affective, sensory self-expression contrasts starkly with the story offered up to "explain" Maria Pia and her mother. The juxtaposition invites readers to wonder about the emotions and desires of the mother and daughter, beyond the tale of thwarted love told by the fishermen. Of course, the characters cannot have "real" emotions or desires outside the confines of the text, because they are textual constructs; yet readers can still imagine how the women might feel and how they would respond to the fishermen's tale. Thus the novel creates space for readers to undertake the kind of open-ended imagination that eludes the protagonists. It suggests that such imagination can underpin deeper forms of solidarity than identification predicated on shared experience, because it instantiates an ongoing, active process that centres the other person rather than one's own needs.

The conclusion of the novel offers one more vision of identification associated with openness to uncertain, multifaceted stories. Paula's uncle Gabriel is killed in a homophobic attack while he is walking on the heath near his home, and the other characters are left wondering what led him to the heath and what roles they might have played in his death. Paula, who blames herself for encouraging Gabriel to take late-night walks on the heath, meets a young man named Oliver, a secret object of Gabriel's affection, who confesses that he had also encouraged Gabriel to walk there. Paula and Oliver tell each other only snatches of their relationships with Gabriel, but through these fleeting narratives they become sources of insight and comfort for one another. The novel ends with Paula and Oliver kissing as Paula reflects that "she wanted to look at Oliver, and remember Gabriel" (*IDW* 266), and Warner hints at a sexual encounter to come. Paula identifies with Gabriel as she initiates a tryst with the man he was attracted to. This is not an identification based on perceived sameness but a tacit declaration of the desire to be like her uncle, to share in a small element of his experience. By tying Paula's act of remembrance to the kiss, a prelude to a relationship in its infancy, Warner suggests that Paula's commemoration is just beginning. It is the initial stage in a continued act of memory that involves reinventing her view of Gabriel as she comes to learn more about him through Oliver. The effort to expand her understanding of her uncle rests on imagination because it focuses on an aspect of his life that he never shared with her. Her commitment to that imagination forms the foundation for a new and complex web of relationships with responsibilities both to Gabriel's memory and to the young man who makes himself vulnerable to her by sharing his own feelings of guilt over Gabriel's death.

Thus the novel shows how acts of identification predicated on sameness can ignore differences, but it also expresses optimism about forms of identification that lead to ongoing curiosity and openness to multiple narratives. It hints that continuous effort to imagine a person's life can create a deeper solidarity than presumptions of shared experience and give rise to new understandings of the relationships that bind one to that person.

IDENTIFICATION AS A SOURCE OF SOLIDARITY AND DIVISION IN *THE SKATING PARTY*

Warner's next novel, *The Skating Party*, once again explores the roles of identification and imagination in creating solidarity across social differences. Fantasies of identification make the protagonist, Viola Lovage, feel connected to women in very different social positions from her, but also lead her to ignore her complicity in the oppression of other women and her own marginalization. As in *In a Dark Wood*, a more complex vision of solidarity emerges not through the behaviour of the characters but through the potential alternatives offered to readers. *The Skating Party* invites readers to embark on open-ended acts of imagination that elude the protagonist: to imagine the motives, drives, and social contexts shaping the lives of the women Viola identifies with and real people in similar positions.

On the surface, *The Skating Party* has a simpler plot than *In a Dark Wood*, though it too is highly patterned. Like *In a Dark Wood*, the novel focuses on an upper-class academic family, this time in Cambridge. The plot covers a single day: a skating party organized by an anthropology professor named Michael Lovage for his students, colleagues, and friends – including his wife, Viola, and his student and mistress, Katy. The present-day storyline is interspersed with flashbacks to the early days of Michael and Viola's courtship, Michael's anthropological fieldwork in Palau, Micronesia, and the development of Michael's affair with Katy. Much like *In a Dark Wood*, the novel refracts the family drama through several storylines. It draws parallels between Viola, Katy, and a young woman in Palau who is condemned as a witch during Michael's fieldwork trip for seducing a man of lower caste. It maps the present-day love triangle onto the Greek myth of Phoenix and

Amyntor, and through the name of the protagonist and the setting on Epiphany, the day after Twelfth Night, it invokes Shakespeare's *Twelfth Night*. With these echoes, the novel invites readers to interpret varied plotlines through one another, and by doing so, to endorse the characters' acts of identification with one another. However, the acts of identification in the text wreak their own violence, and the parallels between stories ultimately fall apart. The novel ultimately provokes a different kind of reading, attuned to the systems of power that shape the characters in differential ways. In this way, it calls on readers to consider how they are implicated in systems of power that both connect them to and divide them from others (within and outside the diegesis).

On one hand, the novel depicts mutual identification between women as a strategy of resistance toward misogynistic pressures. For Viola and Katy, mutual identification marks a refusal to be divided by rivalry for male attention and a means to redefine what seem like personal pressures as part of a gender-based system of marginalization. The two characters exemplify women's fight for legitimacy in the British universities of the 1960s and 1970s. Viola joins the faculty of Cambridge at a time when colleagues are still debating the appropriateness of women's membership in traditionally male colleges, and "the wife of a don, let alone a member of the teaching faculty, [is] meant to be dowdy and plain" (SP 8). Her frustration recalls Warner's descriptions of Oxford in the late 1960s, when women were still a species apart in the eyes of many undergraduates and a fellow student could proclaim that he never expected her to amount to serious scholarship because she was "just a pretty thing in a mini skirt"[22] Katy, a Classics student in her own short skirts, faces similar prejudices, as Michael thinks of her as a child and potential admirer rather than a young scholar. Despite the women's rivalry for Michael's affections, their shared struggle forms a fragile bond between them. Viola looks at Katy with a combination of apprehension and understanding. Watching Katy at Michael's skating party, she realizes, "I like you, you funny, tense, fierce girl" (SP 144). With this sympathy, she undermines the way patriarchal constructions of female rivalry position the rival "as 'the other woman,' not a subject interesting in her own right."[23] Katy's identification with Viola becomes a source of strength. It drives her to take responsibility for her choices in a way she previously resisted, and it gives her the confidence to question her affair with Michael (SP 143).

The two women's identification with one another emerges not just as an emotional instinct or defense mechanism but as a rebellion against the roles in which Michael's affair has confined them. Still, that identification overlooks important differences between them. Katy does not think about the ways her affair might harm the older woman. For Viola's part, identifying with Katy lets her participate in the social construction of women as a group but also subsumes the individual to the collective, like Paula's identification with Maria Pia in *In a Dark Wood*. The brief sense of sisterhood that connects Viola and Katy obscures Katy's youth, her doubled vulnerability to Michael as a student involved with a professor, and Viola's willingness to manipulate Katy – ultimately, Viola sends her son Timothy to distract Katy by seducing her. The sexual rivalry between them and their differential positions within that framework preclude any simple alliance and complicate a straightforward narrative of shared experience.

The novel further illustrates the potential violence in fantasies of collective identity through the seeming parallels between the two women and the "witch" Viola and Michael encounter in Palau ten years earlier. During Michael's fieldwork trip, he discovers to his great excitement that he and Viola will get to see a traditional ceremony called a ghost dance. As the ceremony unfolds, they witness a young woman being accused of witchcraft because a man of lower caste has fallen in love with her. She is sentenced to starvation at a local temple unless she admits to having enchanted her lover. The novel seems to align Viola, Katy, and the "witch" in Palau through parallels in plot and language as well as Viola's identification with the girl. Michael thinks of Katy and the "witch" in the same terms. All three women are stripped of control over their relationships by men of greater age and social power, and they are simultaneously idealized and devalued on account of their attractiveness. Yet the apparent parallels between the characters disguise a tale of colonial legacies, class privilege, and what it means to be an ethical witness.

Viola reacts to the accusation and sentencing of the "witch" with fury. She is unwilling to define the girl, as Michael does, as a prop in an anthropological discovery. She secretly brings the girl food, willing her to defy her captors, though the girl never touches Viola's offerings. This rescue mission offers Viola a way to distinguish herself from her husband. At the same time as it aligns her with the accused girl as a victim of patriarchal oppression, it casts her as a protector and saviour. It turns her into an activist, unwilling to stand by and watch injustice, in contrast to Michael, who insists that they cannot intervene.

This episode of the novel positions readers in ambiguous ways. Viola's "rescue mission" in Palau makes up the second chapter of the book. It takes the form of a flashback in which she draws her seven-year-old son into a game of make-believe as a ruse to get close enough to the girl to leave her a package of food. In the transition from chapter one to chapter two, the number of characters shrinks, the pace quickens, and suspense heightens, all narrative strategies that can promote intimacy and identification.[24] The scene is focalized through Viola, and the strategy behind her make-believe game is made clear to readers but not to the other characters. The chapter begins with Viola reflecting that she used the make-believe game "to conspire with Timmo against the priests' power in the island" (*SP* 13). The structure makes it her story, according her a narrative authority that might otherwise accrue to Michael, the anthropologist whose fieldwork brings the family to the island. If the scene persuades readers to identify with Viola, then it allows them to imagine that they, too, would respond to the girl's oppression with creativity and resourcefulness. Like *In a Dark Wood*, the text invites female readers into a collective – one that simultaneously identifies them with the "witch" (taking her side against patriarchal oppression) and distances them from the "witch" (as agents of resistance rather than victims).

However, if readers identify with Viola's response to the "witch," that identification makes them complicit in what is fundamentally a colonizing move. Viola's response to the unnamed girl, despite her conviction that they both suffer from patriarchal injustice, is predicated on the girl's inability to save herself. It replicates a familiar colonial narrative of white visitors "saving brown women from brown men," as Gayatri Spivak famously puts it in "Can the Subaltern Speak?"[25] Warner's version simply accords a white European woman the power traditionally claimed by white men. If Viola's reading of the drama in Palau is an act of self-authorship, it denies self-authorship to the girl at the temple and casts her as a victim in need of rescue. It is only later, when Viola is looking for models of agency in the face of oppression, that she proclaims, "They wanted to starve her into submission and she turned it into a hunger strike" (*SP* 145). Even at that point, her recognition of the agency of the girl has a flattening effect. The initial portrait of the "witch" as a passive victim conforms to the image of the "average" third world woman as "ignorant, poor, uneducated, tradition-bound," a critique Chandra Mohanty levelled at Euro-American anti-colonial feminist writings in 1984, two years after the publication of *The Skating Party*.[26] The revised portrait of the girl's strength simply maps her onto Viola, in line with Western feminist self-representations characterized by "control over their own bodies … and the freedom to make their own decisions."[27] Viola asserts her rebellion either by denying rebellion to the nameless girl or by casting the girl as a mirror for her own rebellious desires.

To read the girl in Palau as a symbol for Viola – or to identify with both women as opponents of patriarchal oppression – ignores the social hierarchies that give Viola, the wife of the visiting anthropologist, the right to watch the ghost dance as spectacle and choose whether or not to turn away. Her indignation confirms her privilege to pass judgment without facing consequences like the exclusion the girl would risk if she refused the terms of her confinement. Moreover, it ignores the cultural and political history of the archipelago. Palau has a fraught history of colonial rule. The country was part of the Spanish East Indies in the nineteenth century. It was administered by Germany and then Japan in the early twentieth century, and from the 1940s to the 1980s it belonged to the UN Trust Territory of the Pacific Islands under American administration. This history involves its own violations. In the decades leading up to the publication of *The Skating Party*, the US carried out devastating nuclear tests in the region alongside a campaign of violence and intimidation against Palau's anti-nuclear movement. The customs studied by Michael belong to an Indigenous culture that had to confront missionaries and colonial occupation. The novel does not mention this history, but it nonetheless inflects Viola's efforts to save the girl. Her intervention in the ritual contrasts with her (and Michael's) silence about historical and ongoing injustices in the region.

The novel does not offer an overt critique of that response. Nor does Warner criticize it when she talks about the novel in interviews. On the contrary, Warner echoes Viola's accusation that Michael appropriates the girl's story to build his reputation as an anthropologist. In a 1992 interview with Nicolas Tredell, she explains that Michael uses the girl "to endorse his own principles."[28] Warner likens Michael to politicians and historians who appropriate the story of Joan of Arc for their own ends, a phenomenon she analyzes in her study *Joan of Arc: The Image of Female Heroism* (1981). The novel draws Viola in a far more sympathetic light than Michael, and I may be reading against the grain by arguing that it invites readers to critique Viola's identification with the "witch." Yet I contend that by showing the characters' fluid and contradictory levels of power and privilege, the novel creates space for readings different from the one Viola constructs.

On one hand, it is easy to adopt Viola's point of view and map her onto the "witch" in a reading that risks promoting a "flattened historical sensibility," to borrow a phrase from Megan Boler.[29] The colonial history of Palau is never mentioned. The seeming connection between the two women places them in an unmoored, fantastical "anytime" or "anyplace." Readers can get caught up in what bell hooks labels "a consumer cannibalism that not only displaces the Other but denies the significance of that Other's history through a process of decontextualization."[30] If readers focus on the lives of the main characters – which, indeed, the plot and character-building make it easy to do – they can ignore the social and historical context of the episode in Palau. This is particularly true since the majority of characters from Palau remain unnamed, most conspicuously the "witch." They are given fleeting physical descriptions – a baseball jersey, a tortoiseshell comb – in contrast to Warner's detailed accounts of the fashion, makeup, and features of the Cambridge students and faculty in the present day. From this angle, one could argue that Warner uses a postcolonial island as little more than background for a British family drama. As such, the novel is vulnerable to hooks's critique of texts that make people of colour into "backdrop, scenery for narratives that essentially focus on white people."[31]

On the other hand, I contend that Warner's portrayal of the "witch" is more complicated. The young woman in Palau is subordinated very differently by Michael in his role as academic expert and by the men who sentence her to starvation, and both are very different from the marginalization faced by Viola in her Cambridge teaching position and adulterous marriage ten years later. Moreover, recurrent, fleeting references to the "witch" invite readers to wonder about her motives and desires. Though she is always seen through the eyes of the other characters, who reduce her to symbols in their own versions of the family drama, the unnamed woman haunts the text. Yet if ghosts call on the living to remember them, the recurring figure of the "witch" calls on readers to imagine her outside the terms offered by the other characters' descriptions.

The text also appeals to readers to think about the marks of the past on the present, including the colonial history that it does not address directly. One way is by presenting the long-ago trip to Palau as a source of insight into Michael's and Viola's present-day lives. Another is through Viola's work as an art historian. Throughout the novel, Viola struggles to identify the subject of a set of Renaissance frescoes found in the bathroom of an apartment in the Vatican. They turn out to be scenes from the Greek myth of Phoenix and Amyntor, and (as I will explain below) they operate as a symbol for the present-day family drama. The novel's insistence on the value of decoding the frescoes, and the contemporary relevance of the Greek myth, points toward the ongoing effects of the past on the present. For readers, this insistence on the links between past and present may act as a spur to curiosity about the histories in Palau that remain outside the boundaries of the text – both the histories of the fictional characters and the real-life history of the country. The novel offers readers the opportunity to engage in acts of imagination that the characters do not undertake: to imagine the broader context of the judgment handed down to the "witch," the reasons for her refusal to confess to witchcraft, and the history of her community. It invites an unbounded effort at cultural and historical understanding, unbounded because readers cannot imagine "the" story behind the girl's refusal (that story does not exist within the confines of the text) and because the narratives involved in the real-life history of Palau are infinite.

The relationship between the main storyline and the novel's mythic sources promotes ongoing imagination as well, inviting readers into open-ended analysis of that which does not fit the interpretive paradigms the novel seems to offer. In this way *The Skating Party* evokes a vision of witnessing similar to Kelly Oliver's notion of "infinite response-ability," an ongoing responsiveness to the stories of others, as a source of solidarity across space and time.[32] At the novel's climax Viola begs her son Timothy to distract Katy from Michael's attentions, and Michael walks in on Timothy and Katy having sex. As Michael rages, his colleague Wilton, an elderly historian, tells Viola not to give the scene a second thought because the battle of "[o]ld wolf, young wolf" is such an old story. "Forgive the pedantry of an old man," he says, "but Homer is so beautiful, and the story of Phoinix one of the most beautiful of all" (*SP* 172; spelling as in the original). The parallels in plot are clear. Like Viola, Amyntor's wife importunes her son Phoenix to seduce his father's concubine. When Phoenix carries out his mother's wish, Amyntor curses him with childlessness, breaking the family line. But once again, the novel invites reflection on the limits of a reading that equates the two stories.

Wilton's comment reduces a tale of anger and grief to spectacle. Though Viola takes his words as an attempt to spare her embarrassment, they cast her as a type found again and again in literature. In fact, they echo the blithe pronouncement of *In a Dark Wood*'s Teresa that Jerome's rivalry with a younger editor is just a battle of "Old Wolf, Young Wolf" (*IDW* 146). Wilton's statement, like Teresa's, ascribes an essential nature to the story and its characters: mother/wife, concubine/lover, son, and patriarch. Yet the novel in its detail shows that "[t]here's an illusory sameness established by referring to a category of person … as if it never changed."[33] The meanings of the terms "mother," "wife," "mistress," and "husband" themselves have transformed over the intervening millennia. Experiences of motherhood can hardly be considered universal in light of the vast differences in social and political situations of mothers across the globe, such as differential access to fertility drugs or differential resources allocated to parents.[34] "[E]ven across a specific slice of time, motherhood as 'female experience' effectively does not exist; it is always constituted within, and in turn constitutes, multifaceted social locations."[35] In *The Skating Party*, despite the seeming parallels between Viola and the wife of Amyntor, motherhood and marriage have very different meanings for the two women.

In Homer's story, Amyntor's wife is defined by her position as a betrayed woman who uses her son for revenge against her husband. Once Amyntor discovers Phoenix's transgression, his wife recedes into the background. In Warner's tale, the women exert more complex claims to agency, and they take on multiple roles. Viola acts as a surrogate for Michael when she takes her husband's side and criticizes Timothy and Katy for having sex, a move that simultaneously restores her to parental authority and condones her husband's infidelity. Her charade is metaphorically an act of cross-dressing, in an echo of her namesake from *Twelfth Night*, or even a form of "double drag." According to Warner, double drag often functions as a means of disrupting social norms as well as a survival stratagem, a performance of gender that uses the tools available within existing social codes.[36] When Viola sides with her husband in response to Michael and Katy's encounter, she acts out the role of the jilted male lover, but she simultaneously adopts a conventional female role, the wife who supports her husband even when he cheats on her. She emerges as a parallel for both Amyntor's wife and Amyntor. And if assigning Timothy to sleep with her husband's lover makes Timothy her proxy, enacting both distraction and revenge on her behalf, then Viola is Phoenix as well. If the parallel between the stories implies that there are only limited roles for men and women in a patriarchal culture, *The Skating Party* ultimately suggests otherwise: to identify one mother or one mistress with another is to overlook the multiplicity of roles available within these seemingly unified categories as well as the fluidity and multiplicity of the self. As the parallels between plotlines loosen, the novel anticipates Judith Butler's claim that women must be "self-critical about the processes that produce and destabilize identity categories," and about what they gain and lose by identifying with other women.[37]

The painting on the bathroom wall tacitly calls attention to this need and hints at a conception of solidarity based on ongoing questions rather than shared experience. Wilton's allusion to the myth catalyzes an academic breakthrough for Viola, and she suddenly realizes that the Renaissance frescoes she has been struggling to identify tell the story of Phoenix just like the events unfolding in her home. Yet a whole section of the painting deviates from the story of Phoenix. This ambiguity suggests that "Viola's reading represents just one possibility that makes immediate sense to her because there is a direct connection to her own personal experience."[38] The fourth wall of the bathroom is taken up by an image of Amazons that disappears from the novel when Viola finds an interpretation that fits neatly into her life. Initially Viola asks herself, "why the Amazons on the north wall? No Amazon story she knew intertwined with Homer's story of sexual revenge … Does the son who is cursed become an outcast, the companion of other outcasts, the anomalous woman, the unmated mother?" (*SP* 173–4). These unanswered questions both connect and divide the frescoes and the contemporary scene. Viola may see herself as an outcast, filling the anomalous role of "the unmated mother," but she remains part of a respected academic family, arm in arm with her husband as the novel draws to a close. She may be an Amazon rescuer, holding Michael upright as he falls against her in his emotional frenzy, much like Katy comforts Timothy after Michael's outburst. But the strength of the two women is very different from that of the warlike Amazons, especially with the women's collusion with traditional forms of femininity. A reader may develop one confident reading of the Amazons or another. Yet the novel invites a multi-perspectival effort at interpretation, one that involves continued imagination rather than the closure of a solution, and that ongoing imagination offers a model of how to read other people as well.

Like Paula's solidarity with the visionaries in Warner's previous novel, the tentative moments of solidarity between the women in *The Skating Party* stem from acts of identification based on perceptions of shared experience. But these characters' assertions of solidarity risk collapsing very different places and times and flattening multifaceted figures into monolithic stories. I argue that through its depiction of the complex power relations between the characters – which the characters themselves overlook – the novel enables readers to read differently from those characters. It suggests that solidarity does not call for blithe identification with someone else but for ongoing engagement with the multiple stories of a person's life. This engagement involves an effort not only to understand the other person but also to re-imagine the self. It situates both parties within intersecting webs of relationships that may be characterized both by shared experience and by unequal positions within systems of power.

It is worth noting that the novel's subversion of the parallels between storylines sits uneasily beside some of Warner's comments in interviews. She encourages readers to probe the intertwined storylines in all three of her early novels for their similarities. In a 1992 interview with Nicolas Tredell, she comments that she was initially uncomfortable with the relationship between plotlines in her novel *Indigo* because they did not map straightforwardly onto each other, whereas in her earlier novels the parallels between storylines were unambiguous. She quotes Frank Kermode saying that in *The Skating Party* the plotlines overlap too closely, and she acquiesces to his criticism, musing that "they match exactly."[39] She implies that this is true of *In a Dark Wood* as well. These comments are belied by crucial differences between her seemingly parallel storylines. They hint at unreconciled tension between her desire to trace shared experiences, on one hand, and recognition of the dangers of oversimplistic identification, on the other. They suggest that the varied ways in which her early novels complicate bids for identification between women – and invite more open-ended efforts to imagine one another's lives – may not always reflect deliberate authorial strategies.

OPEN-ENDED IMAGINATION AS AN ACT OF WITNESS IN *THE LOST FATHER*

The Lost Father marks a shift in Warner's fiction. It is the first of Warner's novels undertaken as a deliberate act of witness, a commitment to the memory of people who have passed away. The novel is a four-generation family saga based on the history of Warner's mother's family, who belonged to the working classes in the southern Italian region of Puglia, then immigrated to the US and subsequently England. Forging a British counterpart to the American immigrant novel, Warner sets out to imagine the stories of a group of people largely excluded from historical records, a goal that also shapes her next two novels, *Indigo* and *The Leto Bundle*.

Unlike Warner's previous two novels, *The Lost Father* reflects overtly on the fantasy involved in recovering overlooked histories. The narrator is a historian named Anna Pittagora, who is writing a fictionalized memoir about her maternal family, much like Warner herself. Anna's project is driven largely by identification with her great-aunt Rosa. Her identification serves as a tool for self-fashioning as well as a source of solidarity with the dead. The woman she constructs through her research and imagination becomes a role model and exemplar of courage. While Warner acknowledges that the fantasies that emerge from desire can appropriate the experiences of others, she presents them as potential sources of transformation. *The Lost Father* joins *In a Dark Wood* and *The Skating Party* in suggesting that identifications that lead to ongoing imagination may underpin cross-generational and cross-cultural solidarity. Moreover, the novel suggests that for Warner, bearing witness to silenced or ignored stories through fiction is a task that can never be complete. No single narrative – or finite collection of narratives – can ever bear witness to an experience in full.

The Lost Father is based on careful research. Yet while the novel strives to combat historical silences, it acknowledges that efforts at historical recovery are always constructions themselves. Warner has talked about how closely her mother's family's migrations echoed general trends: "the exact time that they attempted to emigrate to America, the time they came back, the time they went again, all these were peaks on the graph."[40] She was excited when she learned that 1913, when her family left Puglia, marked a spike in Italian emigration. While doing research at the New York Center for Migration Studies, she discovered that her grandfather was one of seventy-nine professionals and her great-uncle was one of ninety-three musicians. Looking back on that moment, she reflects, "the knowledge that the characters whom I am trying to recreate … were part of such an exodus gave me one of those shivers that I count as the most intense pleasures of the act of writing."[41] Despite the work she put into historical accuracy, Warner frames the book with scenes in which Anna, the narrator, questions her understanding of her family's history. With this self-reflexiveness, the novel joins a corpus of historiographic metafictions written in the same decade by writers including Salman Rushdie, Jeanette Winterson, Angela Carter, and Toni Morrison.[42] Warner shares the commitment of these writers to stories that have been left out of dominant histories alongside their recognition that novels and histories striving to redress historical erasure never truly recover the past.[43] Yet *The Lost Father* does not simply offer a postmodernist commentary on the subjectivity of historical records. The novel explores the ways acts of identification shape historical narratives. It implies that while identification can distort, it can also be harnessed to defamiliarize social and political structures and inspire new ways of thinking about one's connections to other people.

The desire for ancestors to identify with drives Anna's memoir, the text within Warner's text, even as Warner emphasizes that those ancestors are an imaginative construction, a reinvention rather than a recovery. *The Lost Father* joins the work of novelists such as Maxine Hong Kingston and Louise Erdrich in "recomposing 'the book of memory'" by commemorating ignored female experiences.[44] It also resonates with Helen Barolini's 1979 epic *Umbertina*, itself a four-generation family saga and "[t]he first novel by an Italian American woman to explore, in depth, intergenerational female relationships in an Italian immigrant family."[45] Despite the title, *The Lost Father* is fundamentally a novel about lost mothers. Warner draws inspiration from two "lost" fathers: her maternal grandfather, who supposedly died from a bullet wound sustained years earlier in a duel, and the initial hopes inspired by Mussolini, "the imagined ... figure of authority" that many welcomed as a potential saviour after years of economic and political instability.[46] Yet the Pittagora mothers form the core of the story. They hold their family together and use creativity to combat economic constraints. Warner's narrator, Anna, shares Barolini's hope that if she could understand "the strong woman of the house" then "maybe I could figure out something about myself. What I wanted to know about myself is what *all* women wanted to know about themselves at that particular time."[47] For Anna, telling the story of her mother's family produces a female genealogy with models of inspiration. Thus, like Warner's earlier novels, *The Lost Father* illustrates the power of imagination to bring a community into being. The text invites readers to identify with Anna in her search for self-definition, both through the familiarity of a common struggle and through the sense of immersion provided by first-person narration and highly sensory descriptions. By extension, readers are offered an entry into the community constructed by Anna's novel (and Warner's own), an opportunity to imagine themselves as part of a line of women who respond to adversity with creativity and strength.

The Lost Father enables readers to make common cause with Warner and her memoirist-narrator, commemorating female forebears as an act of resistance to the exclusions of patriarchal histories. *The Lost Father* depicts women's bids for limited agency, small victories, and moments of tacit courage. Anna's great-grandmother, Nunzia, carries out feats of domestic creativity as she beats egg whites to mold her hair into curls and mixes flour and water to stiffen the collars of her husband and sons. Nunzia's daughter, Maria Filippa, runs her household after the death of her husband, and she combines superstition with ruthless pragmatism, much like Sycorax in *Indigo*. Anna's great-aunt Rosa, overlooked by her parents and neighbours because she has neither beauty nor charisma, insists on her desires, like the women in much of Warner's early work, from the empress dowager Tz'u-hsi to Paula in *In a Dark Wood*. Nunzia's domestic strategies, Maria Filippa's superstitions, and Rosa's flirtations all constitute traditionally "feminine" means of self-expression as well as forms of resistance to powerlessness. To borrow a formulation from Lila Abu-Lughod, with these images Warner gives her mother's family "credit for resisting in ... creative ways the power of those who control so much of their lives," without projecting onto them a political consciousness outside of their experience or overlooking their acts of resistance as apolitical.[48]

It is tempting to claim that in the name of historical recovery, the novel seeks to "narrate and preserve authentic female experience," as

Ruth Jenkins writes of Kingston's novels.[49] However, *The Lost Father* emphasizes the fantasy endemic to the construction of these role models. It shows that readers who identify with the women's bids for agency are not simply joining a heritage of female resistance but bringing one into being. At the end of *The Lost Father*, Anna realizes that her story about Rosa's quest for romance and sexual awakening is a projection of her own desires. A cousin gives her an old newspaper clipping about clashes between trade unionists and squads working for the estate managers, and she starts to imagine Rosa as a revolutionary: "a heroic Rosa, a fighter who had broken free" (*LF* 276). Much like Paula's view of the young visionaries in *In a Dark Wood*, Anna's new narrative projects her great-aunt into a public space traditionally reserved for men, where her voice transgresses political and social boundaries. Moreover, just as Paula's identification with the visionaries and Viola's identification with the "witch" in Palau overlook the differences between them, Anna's identification with Rosa's romantic disappointments and her new vision of Rosa the revolutionary both flatten out her portrait of her great-aunt. These identifications also reflect the class differences between her and Rosa. If Anna is driven to tell Rosa's story because Rosa kept no records, her freedom to write the book invites readers to ask, following Gayatri Spivak and Rey Chow, whether any representations are ultimately free of class privilege.[50] Yet Anna's multiple stories suggest that the fantasies created by projection are not fully separable from the kind of ongoing imagination that can enable ethical relationships. Such fantasies can turn the process of identification from a presumption of sameness into a creative act, a means of imagining new relationships into being.

Warner's narrator, Anna, acknowledges that she is "trying to piece … together" her family's past from her mother's "scraps of memory" (*LF* 137). The phrase links her efforts as a writer and historian to the feats that her mother, Fantina, achieves with the scraps in her sewing basket. It offers a reminder that she is producing a compilation, an art object like a collage or quilt. Her memoir is an ongoing process, a labour of love. If Anna's narrative, like Warner's, recovers the Pittagoras from historical obscurity, it can only bring them to life as long as it gives rise to a continuous act of memory. Rewriting the story – from sexual awakening to revolutionary awakening – marks a commitment to continuous imagination as Anna strives to envision the elements of her great-aunt's life that lie outside her frames of reference.

An epigraph to the novel from a poem by Czeslaw Milosz encapsulates the desire for faithful representation alongside devotion to an ongoing form of witness that rests on multiple, fluid narratives.

Faithful mother tongue
I have been serving you.
Every night, I used to set before you little bowls of colours
so you could have your birch, your cricket, your finch
as preserved in my memory.[51]

In Milosz's poem the "faithful mother tongue" modulates into the speaker's "native land," but the epigraph also implies that the novel serves a lineage of mothers. The novelists (both Anna and Warner) take over their mothers' devotion to "serving" their families, this time with "little bowls of colours," the details that make their ancestors' lives vivid. These details conjure a sense of authentic experience and pay tribute to the homes the women built. *The Lost Father* is crammed full of sensory images: visual – the angle of a sister's head; auditory – "a sister's footfall on the scoured stairs"; and olfactory – "the nursery smell of clothes boiling in the copper cauldron on the stove" (*LF* 3). The descriptions are lavish. Anna exults in the extravagance of southern Italian wisteria, which "would need only a hundredth, a thousandth of the perfume it expended to attract enough bees to cross-fertilise the whole of the province" (*LF* 5). The visual bleeds into the tactile, as in the present-day section, when woolly light "wraps[s] the house in its grey muffler" (*LF* 6). A silent mother tongue, these "little bowls of colours" evoke Fantina's "native land" and the environment in which she, like Warner's mother, was shaped as she grew up.

These images seem to present the characters' material experiences as metonyms for the lives of Warner's ancestors. They signify loyalty and love, as Anna (in the diegesis) and Warner (outside the text) carefully paint every detail. Yet the lavishness of the images emphasizes their status as literary constructions rather than artifacts of the past. As the novel depicts the light "spattering" the Pittagora courtyard and the "grey muffler" that wraps around the adult Fantina's home, it offers the Pittagora women not memory but figures of speech. The "little bowls of colours" formed by Warner's sensory descriptions express a desire to make the past present for readers, but they undermine any single vision of that past. Anna cannot keep from revising her manuscript: "'[T]he morning splashed' – no, maybe 'spattered' is the better word"; "What's a good name for Baked Alaska Ninfania-style? How about a Theda Bara? … No, I know, a Pola Negri!" (*LF* 4). These shifting descriptions mark a resistance to fixity that signals not just a poststructuralist insistence on the subjectivity of memory but a willingness to keep re-imagining the past. Anna's identification with her great-aunt gives rise to curiosity, wonder, and openness to multiple, fluid narratives.

The text embodies this commitment to multiple narratives through its open-ended conclusion. As Anna starts to reassess her great-aunt's life, readers are reminded that the story they have just read is a fiction within a fiction. However, Anna's uncertainties do not push readers to reject the story she has told, like the "a-ha" moment when the reader of a mystery learns the truth and rejects a previous conjecture. While Rosa's story may be the product of Anna's imagination, the vividness with which it is drawn does not let readers dismiss it easily. Instead, Anna's questions about how to tell her great-aunt's story invite readers to hold onto multiple versions of that story at once and to engage in their own creative practice by imagining how else Rosa's life might have unfolded.

Thus, *The Lost Father* ties identification to ongoing imagination as a form of ethical witness. Anna's identification with her mother and great-aunt leads her to keep re-imagining their lives in a way that creates not simply fellow-feeling but ethical responsibility. She lays claim to the task of keeping their legacies alive even if she must continually construct those legacies anew. Anna's continuous efforts to imagine her mother's life are associated with love and proximity. Anna and her mother discuss the memoir while Fantina cooks a Sunday roast and knits a sweater for Anna's son, gesturing "with the bobbly end of a knitting needle" and laughing "softly, your head still bent over your knitting" (LF 273). Warner emphasizes the connection between Anna and the great-aunt she never met as Anna muses, "I had tried to be with Rosa, when I put down, *Rosa in the apartment by the curtain at the window willed her eyes to see the scene unfolding*" (LF 270; italics in the original). Toward the end of the novel, Anna's search for information leads her to a family reunion with a group of cousins she has never met. Her memoir, accurate or not, becomes a source of interpersonal connection. The second-person address of the frame tale, in which Anna speaks directly to her mother, emphasizes the way her imaginative efforts connect her to her mother and her mother's family.

Much like Derrida's conception of absolute hospitality, Anna's ongoing imagination marks an ethical commitment that can never be complete; it can only be infinitely renewed. When Anna takes on the lives of her mother's family as the topic of a memoir, she declares herself responsible for their legacies and welcomes them as part of her life. By re-imagining, again and again, the lives of her ancestors and the ways they connect to her own, she lets go of the ability to put limits on their relationship to her. She also opens herself to potential transformations to her self-definition and worldviews. As she considers different histories for her great-aunt and different points of connection between them (from sexual awakening to revolutionary ardour), her imaginative act drives her to reconsider her assumptions about who she is and what is important to her.

Anna's identification with her mother and great-aunt calls to mind Carolyn Pedwell's account of empathy "as translation." Anna keeps translating her mother and great-aunt into new contexts and new characters in a process that is "relational, imaginative, [and] incomplete." Her imagination forms a foundation for "transformative (though unpredictable) modes of connection."[52] A line near the end of the novel hints at the unpredictability of these connections. Anna goes from reflecting on the history she wants to imagine, her "family romance," to contemplating her mother's reaction. "I couldn't refuse your feelings," she reflects; "they leaped towards me like the tongue of a flame along a fuse" (*LF* 265). This line intimates that Anna's identification with her mother may lead to something unexpected and indefinable. The explosion created by "the tongue of a flame along a fuse" may be destructive or beautiful or generative, as when loggers use explosives to clear logjams or builders clear space for new constructions. Yet it inevitably creates a transformation. *The Lost Father* suggests that Anna's efforts to imagine her mother's family have the power to transform her by giving her a new understanding of the webs of relationships that encircle her, an understanding itself subject to continual change.

Warner's portrayal of Anna's changing perceptions of her task shows that if *The Lost Father* strives to tell a story left out of history books, this is a process that can never be complete. Moreover, this process is not just a matter of creating well-rounded and vivid characters so that readers can imagine themselves into the lives of Warner's southern Italian ancestors. By highlighting the partiality and incompletion of her story, Warner invites readers to join her in a process of continuous imagination aimed not just at the characters on the page but at the uncountable people whose lives form the basis for those characters.

The novel extends readers a twinned invitation and charge. It asks them to bear witness to the lives of the characters as metonyms for the broader phenomenon of Italian immigration to the UK and US. Yet since the characters cannot fully embody that past, for readers to stand as witnesses to Warner's ancestors and an entire generation of fellow immigrants requires imagination outside the scope of the text. It involves a commitment to memory that cannot be discharged. The novel encourages readers to assert solidarity with the immigrants whose lives inspired the text. Moreover, it invites them, like Anna, to consider how people they do not know might have created foundations for their own lives. Thus the novel creates a foundation for ongoing effort to understand one's complex and shifting relationships to the lives of others.

CONCLUSION

The identification that can lead to solidarity, these novels imply, is not simply a humanist one based on characteristics common to all people. Nor is it based on the constructions of shared identity that underpin identity politics, where people are bound together as women, or women of colour, or LGBTQ+, etc. Taken together, these novels suggest that identification can engender deeper solidarity when it leads to continued efforts to imagine the life of another person and the conditions they face. This optimistic view of identification is especially provocative in the present academic climate, where empathy and identification are sometimes seen as superficial responses to inequality.[53] Warner's novels suggest that identifying with someone else in ways that lead to ongoing imagination may unsettle deeply held narratives about our relationships to other people and spark new commitments to those around us.

It is worthwhile to interject a cautionary note about responses to other people based on identification and imagination. When people project their own feelings onto images of others, particularly in situations that involve marginalization or suffering, they can short-circuit ethical engagement by reading others as stand-ins for themselves. Moreover, to celebrate the power of imagination in bearing witness to people's lives, as distinct from information-gathering and historical analysis, risks de-emphasizing the need to think critically about the historical and social structures that shape those lives. Joanne Lipson Freed, in a discussion of traumatic histories, offers the salutary warning that imaginative reconstructions of the past can be self-serving. They can provide a sense of connection to that past, but they can also deflect ethical responsibility.[54] Still, Warner's novels maintain optimism about the power of identification that leads to ongoing imagination. Taken together, *In a Dark Wood*, *The Skating Party*, and *The Lost Father* suggest that continual efforts to imagine another person's life can engender ethical commitments deeper than presumptions of sameness and underpin reconsiderations of one's own position within the social structures that bind one to others. The novels invite readers to initiate such open-ended imagination not just with respect to the characters but in relation to real people in similar situations, such as working-class

Italian immigrants to the UK and US – people too numerous to delimit or name.

In the next chapter, I expand my analysis of the ways Warner's fiction invites commitments to imagining the lives of people subjected to silencing or marginalization. Turning to her novels *Indigo* and *The Leto Bundle*, which are commonly read as efforts to "give voice" to colonized people, immigrants, and refugees, I argue that Warner highlights the fictionality of her narratives and the limits of her ability to "give voice" to other people. Her novels simultaneously evoke and unsettle empathy toward her characters in ways that promote recognition of the distance between the fictional text and the experiences of the people who inspired her fiction. Thus the novels acknowledge that fiction cannot undo violence at the same time as they show how fiction can drive people to assert responsibility toward those who have been treated unjustly.

3

Unsettling Stories

Disruptions of Empathy in Indigo *and* The Leto Bundle

In 2002, fourteen years after publishing *The Lost Father*, Warner gave one of the Amnesty Lectures in Human Rights at the Oxford Sheldonian Theatre. She commented that since the 1980s, many women writers had used negative capability "to give muted subjects their voice."[1] John Keats developed the concept of negative capability in a letter of 1817 to his brothers. He defined it as the ability to remain "in uncertainties, mysteries, doubts, without any irritable reaching after fact and reason."[2] For Keats, negative capability was the highest possible achievement for a writer, a willingness to give up a sense of self in order to tell someone else's story. In a letter of 1818 to Richard Woodhouse, Keats elaborated, "A Poet is the most unpoetical of any thing in existence; because he has no Identity – he is continually … filling some other Body."[3]

Warner praised Toni Morrison, Louise Erdrich, and Maxine Hong Kingston as exemplars of negative capability and models for her own writing, especially *Indigo* and *The Leto Bundle*. She implied that like these writers, she sought to "give voice" to stories that had been widely ignored or forgotten.[4] Yet the lecture took an immediate turn as Warner delved into the hazards of that desire. The idea of the writer's negative capability, she acknowledged, ignores the role of the writer in shaping her text. Far from envisioning herself as a conduit for the voices of others, Warner probed the intractable dilemma of recounting histories that must be remembered without claiming to speak for the people who lived them.

Warner's Amnesty Lecture admitted that a writer cannot give up her voice to tell someone else's story, much as she might wish to. As deconstructionist ethics warn, no one can fully grasp the life of another person; we are all other to one another in our singularity.

The understanding and representation of other people are doubly fraught when they hinge on suffering. Trauma studies hold that pain can never be fully conveyed to another person and by extension can never be adequately represented in literature or art.[5] While postcolonial scholarship has challenged this view,[6] there are certainly barriers to the understanding and expression of pain. Warner's Amnesty Lecture illustrated this difficulty through Aeschylus's classical Greek play *Prometheus Bound*. In Warner's words, pain drives Io, transformed into a cow and harried by a gadfly, to an "[e]xcess of language" that cannot express her grief but spills "out beyond control, beyond organisation."[7] Suffering, as Warner acknowledged, cannot be easily translated to the page, nor can complex lives that involve suffering as well as resilience, strength, and creativity. The commitment to opposing erasure cannot obviate the impossibility of recovering muted voices through fiction.

Moreover, to combat injustice through evocative portrayals of suffering can reaffirm that injustice by distracting from social and historical relations of power. "History can be lost to view when it's personified in a suffering subject," as Warner explained in her Amnesty Lecture.[8] Responding to the emotional impact of one person's experience can make it easy to overlook the stories of others and the social structures that cause suffering. Sympathetic accounts of oppression – and sympathetic responses by readers – proclaim an alliance not necessarily borne out by further action. They can thus serve as what Eve Tuck and K. Wayne Yang, drawing on Janet Mawhinney, call "moves to innocence," tacit refusals of culpability that obscure the work needed to redress injustice.[9] People can lay claim to moral authority by empathizing with oppressed groups:

> like pilgrims kissing the wounds of the crucified Christ, contemporary political subjects seek to touch these springs of sympathy, and apologists – by consenting and yielding and admitting wrong – strive to reach the same condition of pathos, and consequently partake in the currency of merit.[10]

Like politicians apologizing for injustices that occurred before their time, novelists and readers who empathize with persecuted victims may envision themselves as virtuous and innocent. Nevertheless, Warner proclaimed in her Amnesty Lecture, "If history is an agreed fable, as Voltaire said … then any initiative to change things must begin with stories."[11]

In this chapter, I analyze how Warner's novels *Indigo* and *The Leto Bundle* explore this quandary. Much like *The Lost Father*, with its fictionalization of Warner's maternal ancestors in southern Italy, both novels re-imagine the experiences of people too long ignored by political policies and historical documents. Yet I contend that while *Indigo* and *The Leto Bundle* invite readers into the lives of silenced characters, the novels call attention to parts of their lives that remain untold. In an echo of Warner's biography *The Dragon Empress*, important pieces of the characters' histories form conspicuous gaps, and their perspectives are often absent. Thus both novels point out that the lives that inspired them resist representation in fiction, a problem that Warner explored in *The Lost Father* through Anna's struggle to memorialize her mother's family. The novels do not simply insist on the singularity of all people. They point toward "the limits of the fictional form to traverse distances of time and space that are also, inevitably, differences in power."[12] They create constant tension between the illusion of intimacy and the absent voices of the characters. In this way they hint at the impossibility of redressing the violent erasures of political practice or mainstream historical discourses through fiction.

Both *Indigo* and *The Leto Bundle* undertake a more complicated task than available criticism acknowledges. The two novels have received far more critical attention than any of Warner's other books, *Indigo* especially, because they lend themselves to postcolonial and feminist analysis. Scholarship on both novels typically focuses on the ways they "restore" speech to the marginalized. Steven Connor, Carolyn Cakebread, and Chantal Zabus, among others, focus on the ways *Indigo* enables previously silenced figures to talk back.[13] Connor accords *Indigo* a prominent place in his survey *The English Novel in History: 1950–1995*. While he discusses how novels such as J.M. Coetzee's *Foe* (1986) explore the limits of their ability to reproduce "the voice of the other," he takes for granted that *Indigo* "sets out to restore the voices that are suppressed by *The Tempest*." Even as he acknowledges that for Warner this task can never be complete, he contends that the novel's central goal is to create space for those voices rather than to undertake an "ethically sustained disruption."[14] Rebecca Weaver-Hightower, similarly, sees *Indigo* as providing a "vision of the vanquished," in a phrase drawn from historian Nathan Wachtel, and giving them "a face, a name, and finally, a voice equal to the European colonialists'."[15] But while Weaver-Hightower praises texts that question "if it is ever possible to get beyond our own perspective to experience that of another," she does not see *Indigo* asking this question; for her, *Indigo*'s chief project is to "help us imagine how ... gaps in the historical record could have been filled."[16] Siân Harris describes *Indigo* and *The Leto Bundle* as creative interventions into forgotten histories, ways of "making space" for those overlooked by historical records.[17] Similar lenses underpin scholarly work on *Indigo* and *The Leto Bundle* by Richard Todd, Eileen Williams-Wanquet, and Milada Franková.[18] Yet the two novels provoke unease about their ability to recover marginalized voices. They foreground the quandary that "'getting' someone else's story is also a way of losing the person as 'real,' as 'what he [or she] is,'"[19] a problem particularly important for novels that reflect on real-life injustices. This tension aligns Warner with writers of diverse backgrounds and styles, from Caryl Phillips to J.M. Coetzee, who use fiction to combat silencing while refusing authority over the stories of those who have been silenced.[20]

Both novels pose fundamentally unanswerable questions as they strive to imagine how the people they commemorate might have told their own stories. The silenced people whose lives inspired the novels are innumerable. They include the Indigenous people of seventeenth-century St. Kitts, the victims of napalm bombing in the Vietnam War, and the inhabitants of mid-1990s Sarajevo, along with refugees and single mothers throughout history. Many of these figures are doubly inaccessible due to the absence of records from their points of view. Moreover, even when a person tells the story of his or her life, the narrative can never fully express the history behind it, "as though the tellability of one's story were a finite, measurable thing."[21] Consequently, the novels reflect Warner's description of fiction as an "open-ended and ambiguous terrain" that does not have to offer certainties but only "to bring the issue[s] to life in some way."[22] In this process, they challenge readers to question their ways of reading literature as well as reading other people.

MARINA WARNER, CARIBBEAN NOVELIST? WARNER'S COMPLEX RELATIONSHIP TO COLONIALISM

Indigo strives to imagine the colonization of the Caribbean from the perspective of the Indigenous inhabitants at the same time as it tacitly points toward Warner's inability to recover the stories of the colonized. The novel takes its inspiration from Warner's father's ancestors, who were among the first colonial governors in the British West Indies. Thomas Warner arrived on the island of St. Kitts, then known as Liamuiga, in 1623. There he established "the first of the British holdings of Empire."[23] A long line of Warners grew up in the West Indies, like many English planter families, ending with Marina Warner's paternal grandfather, Sir Pelham Warner. Born in Trinidad, "Plum" Warner became a famous cricketer who first played for the West Indies and then captained the England team. In 1904, he won the Ashes, one of the most prestigious trophies in British sports. "He was a national hero," Marina Warner writes in the *London Review of Books*, and he and her grandmother were "the Posh and Becks of their day."[24] While Plum never lost his attachment to his birth country, in Marina Warner's eyes "he was the pattern of an English gentleman."[25] Plum was proud of his imperial heritage, and he passed his pride on to his son Esmond. Hanging over the mantelpiece of the family home was a copy of the charter that named Sir Thomas governor of the West Indies.[26] But it was only when Marina Warner's father went to Trinidad in the 1960s, to sell the last vestiges of property owned by the family, that she learned she had West Indian relatives. Her grandfather had never admitted that a history of intermarriage gave the Warners West Indian ancestry. In an interview with David Dabydeen, she explains, "I think I was very shocked when I first discovered that my family had these West Indian connections, not shocked, stricken. It had never been part of the story that we were telling ourselves."[27] *Indigo* arose from the desire to retrieve "[her] family's Creole past, gainsaid, erased."[28] The novel served as a rebellion against her father alongside a form of "reparation and examination of conscience."[29] In this respect *Indigo* is very different from *The Lost Father*, which offers a tribute to Warner's mother, an act of filial piety.

Indigo maps the colonization of Liamuiga onto Shakespeare's *Tempest*, turning the "foul hag" Sycorax into a Carib wisewoman and casting Caliban and Ariel as her adopted children. The novel intertwines magic realism with Caribbean spiritual beliefs and provides a realist portrait of colonialism and slavery. Warner's Sycorax saves Caliban's life by cutting him out of the womb of a dead African woman thrown overboard from a slave ship; she names the baby Dulé, and he is later renamed by the British settlers. While Dulé is a child, Sycorax takes in Ariel, a young Arawak woman brought to her island by a group of settlers. In the present day, a second plotline centres on the descendants of Kit Everard, a fictionalized rendition of Thomas Warner. Warner develops two twentieth-century characters based on Shakespeare's Miranda. The first, who inherits the name of Shakespeare's heroine, identifies with a Caribbean heritage embodied by her nanny, Serafine. Yet she is torn between the desire to embrace her Caribbean roots and the need to fit into her resolutely British family, emblematized by her grandfather "Ant" Everard, the novel's version of Plum Warner. Only with difficulty can Miranda redefine herself as a descendant of Sycorax, Ariel, and Serafine. Meanwhile, Miranda's "sister-aunt" Xanthe, child of Ant Everard's second marriage and six years younger than Miranda, feels little connection to the Caribbean and makes her fortune in Liamuiga's tourist industry. Between them, the two women represent a spectrum of affiliative choices open to Marina Warner as a descendant of British colonists and illustrate the difficulties of forging female communities in the face of divisions of race and class.

At the same time that *Indigo* re-reads Shakespeare's *Tempest*, the novel re-reads a history of Caribbean *Tempest* revisions. The play has occupied a central place in Caribbean literature since George Lamming's 1960 essay "A Monster, a Child, a Slave," which reads Caliban simultaneously as a symbol of the Caribbean intellectual and an emblem of the ways colonial discourses presented colonized people. Lamming drew on a growing corpus of New World readings of *The Tempest*. At the turn of the twentieth century, Nicaraguan journalist Rubén Darío and Uruguayan philosopher José Enrique Rodó inaugurated a tradition of anti-colonial *Tempests* by comparing the greed and aggression of the United States to Caliban's violence.[30] Simultaneously, Sidney Lee initiated "[t]he Americanization of *The Tempest*" in Anglo-American scholarship by reading the play as a commentary on the New World.[31] Of course, as Elmer Edgar Stoll impatiently complained in 1927, "There is not a word in *The Tempest* about America."[32] But the play was first performed in 1611, two years after the *Sea Venture* was wrecked by a hurricane off the coast of the Bermudas on the way from Plymouth to the English colony in Jamestown, Virginia. William Strachey's 1610 letter *The True Reportory of the Wracke* is generally accepted as a source of inspiration for the opening scene.[33] Ariel mentions flying to "the still-vex'd Bermudas,"[34] and the name "Caliban" is an anagram for "canibal," a word with a fraught history in the colonization of the Caribbean. When Columbus first arrived in the Antilles, Indigenous inhabitants told him that the people of one of the islands were called *canibales* or *caribes* and they ate human flesh (assuming Columbus understood them correctly). Gradually the assumption that Caribs or Cannibals ate humans transformed into a definition of "cannibals" as a common noun for people who ate human beings.[35] Most trenchant from a postcolonial viewpoint is that Prospero takes over Caliban's island and enslaves its only inhabitants, justifying his authority on the basis of his generosity and their ingratitude. Hence, fifty years after Darío and Rodó adopted Caliban as a symbol of imperial power, Octave Mannoni's *Psychologie de la colonisation* (*The Psychology of Colonization*) re-cast Caliban as a colonized subject; and with Lamming's seminal essay, Caliban came to embody the "developing cultural self-assertion" of the Caribbean.[36]

Indigo pays tribute to a history of Caribbean *Tempests* and other Caribbean literature. Warner has written in several essays about the influence of her Caribbean precursors. She praises Caliban's "many, varied and powerful metempsychoses" in the work of Roberto Fernández Retamar, Derek Walcott, Kamau Brathwaite, Gloria Naylor, and David Dabydeen.[37]

She singles out Lamming's *Tempest* novel *Water with Berries* (1971) and Aimé Césaire's play *Une Tempête* (*A Tempest*, 1969) as inspirations for *Indigo*.[38] She draws on a broader tradition of Caribbean writing as well, acknowledging C.L.R. James's *Beyond a Boundary* (1963) as a source of insight into the connections between empire and cricket,[39] selecting an epigraph from Walcott's 1990 long poem *Omeros*, and modelling Serafine after the wisewoman and voodoo practitioner, Christophine, in Jean Rhys's *Wide Sargasso Sea* (1966).[40] *Indigo*'s magic realism reveals the influence of Caribbean writers Alejo Carpentier and Gabriel García Márquez, both writers she has praised.[41]

Despite this legacy, *Indigo* is not a straightforward example of Caribbean or postcolonial literature. Race has long been at the centre of debates over what counts as Caribbean fiction. In the 1970s, Kamau Brathwaite argued that *Wide Sargasso Sea* was not a West Indian novel despite its Jamaican setting and Creole heroine because Jean Rhys belonged to the West Indies's white colonial elite. He maintained that given the structure of race relations in the West Indies, white Creoles could not meaningfully identify with the West Indian spiritual world.[42] Acutely aware of the association between race and authenticity in the Caribbean, Warner has admitted that she felt presumptuous in writing *Indigo*. At the same time, she has argued, "if speaking is left to those who are justified by oppression in the past and in memory, then in one sense one part of the story has been written out of it."[43] Her insistence on her right to tell a Caribbean story echoes the arguments of Evelyn O'Callaghan, Denise deCaires Narain, and Elaine Savory that reading white Caribbean writing alongside Black Caribbean literature can provide a more nuanced glimpse into the roles played by race in Caribbean culture.[44] While Warner does not have the same personal connection as Rhys, *Indigo*, like *Wide Sargasso Sea*, is at home in a corpus of fiction that explores the complex legacies of Caribbean colonialism.

Warner pays homage to Caribbean precursors such as *Une Tempête* and *Water with Berries* by casting Caliban as a Black revolutionary. But she resists the Caribbean focus on Caliban and Prospero, and instead she gives pride of place to Miranda, Ariel, and Sycorax. Like all of the works analyzed in chapters 1 and 2, *Indigo* reveals Warner's devotion to stories of female experience left out of dominant narratives. In the words of Chantal Zabus, she "provides the Daughter's plot and thus forces a reconsideration of the doubly colonized subject – woman."[45] She also challenges the bleakness of Lamming's and Césaire's *Tempests*. Lamming's modern-day *Tempest* is set in a forbidding London, its doors exuding "the solid, leaden feel of gates."[46] In Césaire's play the pig-nuts and jays' nests that connect Caliban to his island have disappeared. By contrast, Warner's Miranda redraws her environment through sketches, magazine articles, and fashion statements, illustrating the potential for individuals to effect social change. By writing back to Lamming and Césaire, Warner situates herself in dialogue with them and defines the Caribbean *Tempests* as cultural touchstones in their own right. To use a phrase that John Thieme adapts from Edward Said, she replaces the "filiative relationships" of the British literary canon with "affiliative ones."[47]

She constructs similar affiliative bonds with a corpus of Caribbean women's fiction. Warner writes Sycorax and Serafine into what Brathwaite and O'Callaghan call "the grandmother tradition,"[48] exemplified by Rhys's Christophine and the legendary Nanny of the Maroons, who helped to establish a community of runaway slaves in eighteenth-century Jamaica.[49] Sycorax and Serafine join the women of *The Lost Father* in providing models of strength and courage to a younger generation. Sycorax passes on forbidden knowledge and controls fertility through magic, much like Rhys's Christophine. In Serafine, that magic is transformed into stories. Serafine adopts the teaching role of the "grandmothers" as she tells Miranda about Liamuiga. However, Warner complicates a line of descent from Nanny and Christophine to Serafine. Serafine inculcates conservative values in Miranda. She passes down the family romance of Kit Everard, who first colonized the island, in an echo of the Warner family romance that glorified the imperial project. In this way she brings to mind the Jamaican servants described by Michelle Cliff in *Abeng* (1984), "[s]ome of [whom] were called Nanny, because they cared for the children of other women, but [who] did not know who Nanny had been."[50] As these literary traditions converge in Serafine, they simultaneously demonstrate respect for Warner's Caribbean precursors and expose the ways individual lives exceed narrative models.

Of course, the primary narrative challenged by *Indigo* is the colonial account of St. Kitts. While restoring Sycorax and Caliban "to power, value, and presence,"[51] *Indigo* rewrites the traditional story of Sir Thomas Warner. In the seventeenth-century section, Kit Everard sets sail for the twin islands of Liamuiga and Oualie with a company of settlers. One of their first acts on Liamuiga is to set fire to Sycorax's home, aiming "to smoke out the enemy" as a precursor to trade (*I* 130). Sycorax is badly burned, and Ariel agrees to help the colonists in exchange for Sycorax's life. Gradually she becomes Kit's mistress, echoing the real-life story of Thomas Warner, who had several children with a woman from Liamuiga before marrying an English woman. Ariel joins the many women in Warner's earlier fictions, such as *The Skating Party*'s Viola, discussed in chapter 2, who struggle to gain autonomy through complicity with patriarchal frameworks.

History books distort the story of Sir Thomas's first wife, argues Warner in her essay "Siren/Hyphen, or, The Maid Beguiled."[52] She enters an ambiguous world of legend through the *Histoire Générale des Antilles* (*General History of the Antilles*), written by a missionary named Jean-Baptiste du Tertre between 1667 and 1671. In Du Tertre's version, in 1625 or 1626 a Carib woman named Barbe warned the English colonists on St. Kitts that the Indigenous people were planning to ambush them. Her warning, he claims, was motivated by her love for Sir Thomas, and it gave the settlers a chance to launch their own attack. As Warner points out, Du Tertre's story interweaves fact and romance, echoing the tale of Pocahontas and John Smith as well as Cortés and his interpreter Malinche. There may never have been any warning, and the story may simply be an invention to justify the settlers' attack on the islanders, but Barbe "merges with the historical Madame Ouvernard [Sir Thomas's real-life mistress] in the folklore of Empire."[53] In retelling her story, *Indigo* picks up *The Lost Father*'s exploration of the intersections between historiography and fantasy. Warner re-imagines Barbe's supposed treachery. The Caribs in *Indigo* plan a rebellion against Kit Everard and his settlers, but Ariel, in the role of Barbe, has no loyalty to the English. On the eve of the rebellion she tries to poison Kit. Her plan fails; he guesses at the impending attack; and history books proclaim that she raised the alarm "out of the great love she bore the founder of the island" (*I* 225). Where the historical records obscure the values and intentions of the Carib woman, *Indigo* gives them pride of place, like *The Lost Father* does for Warner's mother's ancestors. Yet unlike *The Lost Father*, which opposes the tyranny of Mussolini on behalf of people who lacked the political or economic power to defy him, here Warner depicts the islanders fighting for themselves.

Indigo satirizes the ways colonial records denied the reality of the islanders. Much like John Smith in Virginia, Kit pretends his presence on Liamuiga is temporary. He builds gun emplacements in the stockade around his settlement and tells Tiguary, the island chief, that the holes are there just "[s]o the chickens can pop in and out" (*I* 175) – almost exactly the claim made by the real Thomas Warner to the Carib chief of St. Kitts.[54] Kit's strategic answers show that the settlers can only hold onto their identity "by denying the substantiality of other worlds, other words, other narratives," as Peter Hulme writes of the colonization of Virginia.[55] So too does the transformation of Dulé into Caliban. After a battle between colonists and islanders, Kit's men imprison Dulé and slit his hamstrings "[b]y due process of law" (*I* 200). As Dulé hobbles around the settlement, the men "call him 'cannibal,' seeking to undo the power of his monstrousness by naming it" (*I* 201). Kit prefers "the lisping usage of the children, Caliban" (*I* 201). The scene parodies the way European settlers equated Caribs with cannibalism, an act that crystallized "the encounter between Europe and America [as a battle between] civilization and savagery."[56] When Kit renames Dulé, at once an act of vilification and infantilization, he too produces monstrosity so that he can control it.

In contrast, *Indigo* portrays the islanders' views of the colonists. Sycorax and Tiguary refer to Kit and the settlers as "tallow men" and "shellfish people" (*I* 99), inverting Shakespeare's descriptions of the fishlike Caliban. Ariel observes that Kit looks like a river fish, his skin dappled like scales or "a kind of pale and hairy fruit" (*I* 139). The imagery parodies the exoticization of the islanders by the colonists. In the present day, too, Warner turns the naming power of the imperial centre on itself. The novel opens with Serafine telling Miranda about a king – a possessive, rich man like Miranda's grandfather – who claims not to remember Liamuiga, his homeland. The king re-enacts the colonial project in miniature as he denies the riches of the island while inwardly wishing that he could "go there and take it for himself" (*I* 8). Like Ariel's descriptions of Kit, Serafine's pointed fairy tale asserts her right to define her home.

Warner's portrayal of the islanders asserts the same right. Whereas *The Lost Father* is filled with sensory details of the Pittagora household, the fictional version of her mother's family, the seventeenth-century chapters in *Indigo* are filled with animals, plants, and leaves, even though they mean nothing to the colonists. Sycorax gathers "bay and sedum, mangrove and aloe, jumbie tobacco and tamarind, cinchona bark and soursop" (*I* 81–2). She is attended by vervet monkeys, porcupines, agoutis, and caveys. By contrast, when Kit Everard writes home about the island, he describes a generic paradise: "its marvellous bounty, its plentiful springs and well-watered pastures, its salt ponds and forest arbours where gay birds fly and trees bear abundantly" (*I* 151). His near-biblical language echoes the "[t]ravellers, traders, administrators, settlers, [who] 'read' the strange and new by drawing on familiar books such as the Bible."[57] For her part, Sycorax has a practical relationship to the island. She makes dyes out of indigo, a crop that eventually becomes central to the colonial economy. Her work with indigo illustrates her autonomy, though it also hints at the difficulty of women's lives on the island. Though Warner does not mention it, working with indigo often causes lung damage, and the fermented plants used in the dyeing process exude a terrible odour. Sycorax's indigo may represent the best of limited options because it provides a measure of independence. Against the imported judgments of the settlers, who reduce the island to a virgin land ready for conquest, the novel demonstrates the complexity of the islanders' lives.

The structure of the seventeenth-century section replaces the islanders at the centre of their history as well. The novel undercuts the idea of the "New World" through a family chronicle that starts before Sycorax and her people meet the settlers.[58] The chapters on Liamuiga begin with Sycorax rescuing Dulé and progress through her adoption of Ariel and the birth of Ariel's child. While this account is shaped by colonialism, opening with the dead slaves and proceeding until the islanders lose control of Liamuiga, Warner continues past that moment and describes slaves praying to Sycorax after her death. She concludes the seventeenth-century story with Shakespeare's famous line, "The isle is full of noises," echoing her earlier statement that "Sycorax is the source of many" (*I* 77, 213). In Shakespeare's play, those noises are produced by Ariel under Prospero's command; here, the sounds of the isle remain under the control of the islanders. Sycorax remains the fulcrum of the story, and the mythologies of the Caribs and slaves are sustained even though they mean nothing to the colonists.

With this story, Warner strives to expiate her family history, "an enterprise that so resembles Prospero's theft."[59] She "historicise[s] the mythical" by providing "a plausible, complex prehistory" for Shakespeare's marginal figures and the islanders reduced to myth by European histories.[60] She simultaneously expresses uncertainty about this goal. While Warner admits that she wanted to hear the voices of Caliban, Ariel, and Sycorax in their island,[61] *Indigo* questions its capacity to restore presence to the long-dead Caribs and Arawaks. At the same time as the novel reveals Warner's effort to create spaces for the stories of her Indigenous Caribbean ancestors, it hints at the barriers to recovering those stories.

DISRUPTING THE ILLUSION OF VOICE IN *INDIGO*

Indigo repeatedly calls attention to its status as a story. It builds on *The Lost Father*'s emphasis on its fictionality in ways that are both subtler and more continuous. The novel's allusions not only invoke European and Caribbean precursors but also foreground layers of mediation. In this way *Indigo* resists "crude" empathy, as Bertolt Brecht labels empathy that focuses on the way the empathizer would feel in a given situation rather than the complexities of the other person's life.[62] Through the interplay of evocative imagery and distancing effects, *Indigo* echoes *The Lost Father* in acknowledging the impossibility of capturing the lives that inspired the fiction.

Throughout the novel, vivid descriptions create the illusion of presence. Sycorax, making indigo dye, turns "blue-black as a damson when it's picked and fingers leave shiny marks on the maroon-purple skin underneath" (*I* 90). She smells of the lemons and limes that she rubs on her skin to ward off insects (*I* 93). Sensory details impart a sense of bodies close enough to smell and touch. This semblance of immediacy produces a "provocation, call, and response that bind … reader and text," a phrase Adam Newton uses to explain the power of narrative.[63] Sycorax lends her voice to this call when she shouts to her gods, Adesangé and Manjiku, "HEAR ME NOW" (*I* 212). Her cry, receiving no response from the gods, reaches out of the text as a demand to readers. Yet the novel invites readers to ask what it means to "hear" its characters. In the interplay between Sycorax's apparent presence and her status as a fiction, *Indigo* redefines listening as hearing the resistance of life stories to storytelling. Sycorax's plea asks readers not only to hear the words on the page but also to "listen," through a state of openness, to what the text cannot say. It does not just point out the inevitable subjectivity of storytelling but calls on readers to recognize how a history of colonialism and colonial records have left the lives of the Caribs and Arawaks out of reach.

Warner presents the islanders as authors when she rewrites the song that Shakespeare's Ariel sings to comfort Ferdinand in *The Tempest*. She distributes Ariel's song among the voices of the drowned men and women thrown overboard from a seventeenth-century slave ship: "'The sea … would make us food for fishes' … 'Grit for oysters' … 'Bonemeal for vines' … 'From our carcasses, the melon and the gourd'" (*I* 82–3). These images cast the slaves as poets, telling the story of their death. The slaves emphasize their fertility; instead of ossifying into coral and pearls, like Ferdinand's father Alonso in *The Tempest* and Xanthe later in *Indigo*, they turn into melons and gourds. Their chorus creates a sense of abundance, their voices multiplying as their bodies mutate. This profusion alludes to the abundance of stories that underpin the scene. Its source is J.M.W. Turner's painting, "The Slave Ship," inspired by a ship whose captain threw a hundred and thirty-two dying slaves overboard in 1781 because the ship's insurance covered death by drowning but not by illness. In her 1994 Reith Lectures, Warner mused that Turner painted the slaves as disembodied limbs, with one leg and several hands breaking the surface of the water. She reflected, "Turner was always more interested in the weather than in people."[64] The contrast between *Indigo*'s images of abundance and Turner's bodily fragments emphasizes the limits of Turner's vision. But far from claiming to encompass the experiences of the slaves, *Indigo* illustrates the futility of trying to pin them down in narrative. Like their transforming bodies, which cannot be caught or held, the lives of the slaves evade the grasp of readers.

Whereas María José Chivite de León claims that *Indigo* uses fiction to retrieve identities forgotten by history,[65] Warner resists the comfort of assuming that fiction can renew the lives of the dead.

The stylized diction of Warner's most marginalized characters hints at the impossibility of giving them voice. Even when the Caribs and Arawaks seem to speak directly to readers, Warner's narrative style conspicuously overlays theirs. When Dulé, Sycorax's adopted son, urges his mother to fight the settlers, his vocabulary and syntax are formal: "Curse them, Mother. Use your arts, change their condition with your skills; alter their shape, as only you know how. So that they learn to fear us and do not stay. They use our water and eat our substance, they're not welcome" (*I* 102). The islanders' grammatical correctness contrasts with the speech of the novel's more enfranchised characters and the naturalistic dialogues of Warner's earlier novels. Xanthe speaks in the accents of her time: "So how's London? It must be the holidays – how's your ma? And Feeny? Go on, tell. I want all the news" (*I* 234). Her conversations are riddled with slang: "if poss" (*I* 280), "come a cropper" (*I* 272), "you've gone Afro" (*I* 281). The formal language of the islanders calls attention to the necessary role of the author in creating characters and the lack of historical documents from the Indigenous people of St. Kitts. Given the speed and extent of the destruction wreaked by the colonists, and the inability of Western people to read any Indigenous texts that might survive (such as stone and wood carvings), the only surviving documents are the ones produced by the colonial powers.[66] Even the most respectful visions of the islanders' lives are inevitably shaped by those sources.

The novel illustrates this difficulty through its absences. As in Warner's earlier novels *In a Dark Wood* and *The Skating Party*, conspicuously flawed descriptions of characters from the viewpoints of others provoke readers to ask how those characters might have described their own experiences. For example, in a seemingly objective description of Serafine's relationship with her employers, Miranda's father and grandfather, Warner writes,

> Serafine Killebree loved Anthony Everard, Kit's father, even more than she loved Kit himself, and could find nothing to reproach him with, not even her own long exile in the cold maze of the Old Country. Before Xanthe was born, she was often lent to Miranda for the night. (*I* 50)

The remark shows how easy it is to re-interpret someone else's experiences for one's own benefit. It sounds like something that the Everards might say to one another. Serafine would presumably not think of herself as being "lent," and it is not quite true that she "loved Anthony Everard … and could find nothing to reproach him with." She reveals a more nuanced relationship with Miranda's grandfather when she parodies his friends while telling stories to Miranda, "puffing out her chest and her cheeks and swaggering a little" (*I* 6). Though her criticisms remain veiled, they create a sense of dissonance when read against this portrayal of her love. She hints at a history of loss when she tells the story of a fairy tale princess from Liamuiga. "She longs – " Serafine states, and breaks off and taps her chest, as if she were discussing her own longing (*I* 8). Later in the novel, Miranda reflects that Serafine left a daughter on Liamuiga long ago, but Serafine does not talk about her and Miranda does not know the circumstances (*I* 221). Like Serafine's feelings about Ant Everard, her separation from her daughter forms a source of suspense that is never resolved. Her untold stories become ghostly presences that haunt the novel, a strategy that recurs in *The Leto Bundle* and Warner's later short stories.

As Warner's sources interweave, they undermine straightforward interpretations of the characters. The resulting disorientation warns against reducing unfamiliar stories to familiar storylines. As in *In a Dark Wood*, *The Skating Party*, and *The Lost Father*, apparent parallels turn out to be misleading. Xanthe, *Indigo*'s selfish golden girl, calls to mind haughty fairy tale princesses punished for their arrogance, such as Toute-Belle, who rejects twenty husbands and dies over the corpse of her groom in Marie-Catherine d'Aulnoy's seventeenth-century tale "The Yellow Dwarf" (*BB* 252–3). In this context, Xanthe seems to deserve her ignominious death. With her much-admired blonde hair and taste for sexual conquest, Xanthe also resembles Circe, the mythical witch who turns Odysseus's crew into a herd of pigs and transforms the legs of her rival, Scylla, into dogs. This connection aligns Xanthe with Sycorax, for Circe might have inspired the name "Sycorax."[67] Xanthe shares the ruthlessness of both witches. She is impervious to emotion, "like a tablet of costly, scented soap … [with] no purchase on her smoothly milled and creamy surfaces" (*I* 272); Zabus describes her as "a Barbie doll version of Miranda."[68] Her snobbery makes it easy to be unsympathetic when she drowns, rowing toward her husband, in the midst of a coup on Liamuiga. Indeed, Ángeles de la Concha muses that as Xanthe sinks into the underwater pearl beds, she is "splendidly mummified by the riches she had cherished."[69] But Xanthe's role as a symbolic descendant of Circe and Sycorax, an embodiment of female power and sexual knowledge, calls into question the poetic justice of her death. When Xanthe is transformed into pearl, she becomes one of the primary resources of seventeenth-century New World trade. By suggesting that the island's resources are finally returning to the island, the scene reduces her to a commodity, just as her father does throughout her youth by standing guard over her virginity and chasing away her suitors. Xanthe's death draws attention to the compromised and contradictory nature of her power. As the parallels between *Indigo*'s characters and their literary models crumble, Warner insists on the individuality of her characters, and by extension, the singularity of the people whose stories she fictionalizes.

The novel's magic realism disrupts assumptions about genre as well. While *The Lost Father* pays tribute to Warner's mother's family through sensuous images, *Indigo* makes the islanders' ways of life vivid through the lushness and magic of the island. Nonetheless, Warner challenges the notion that magic realism can reflect a pre-colonial way of being, as Alejo Carpentier claimed when he coined the phrase "*lo real maravilloso*" (the marvelous real) in the prologue to his 1949 novel *El reino de este mundo* (*The Kingdom of This World*). In her essays, Warner rejects the idea that magic realism offers "an authenticity of Otherness stamped Indian, or Latin American."[70] *Indigo* inverts the exoticism of *The Kingdom of This World*, where the overabundance of the natural world shades into the brutal excesses committed by human beings as if immoderation were endemic to nineteenth-century Haiti. Warner undermines the image of an Indigenous ontology. The novel depicts Liamuiga as "a place of beauty and exotic abundance, but these are presented as the fruit of labour and experience."[71] Warner describes Sycorax experimenting with the properties of leaves and grass before observing, "nobody on Liamuiga had ever become such an expert sorceress" (*I* 109). Sycorax is a pragmatist; she provides clients with the nail clippings of small animals to wish pains on their enemies but also offers them poisonous tree sap "for a more direct approach" (*I* 125). Her pragmatism connects her to the women in *The Lost Father*, cleaning furniture with cigarette ash and learning domestic remedies that seem almost as magical as Sycorax's spells. When Lisa Hopkins commented, in a 1994 interview, "The magic realism elements in *Indigo* are very strong," Warner protested, "they're not very strong magic realism things. It's meant to be quite realistic ... Sycorax is meant to be practical, not really magical, I'm afraid."[72] Far from using magic realism to depict a collective worldview, Warner's combined genres, with realism, fairy tale, and magic realism jostling for primacy, call attention to her story's status as a story.

The ambivalences of the closing chapter reflect *Indigo*'s opposition to historical silences alongside the limits of the novel's reach. On the surface, the novel offers a happy ending evocative of a traditional fairy tale. Miranda marries a Caribbean man named Shaka who plays Caliban in a theatrical production of *The Tempest*, and together they name their first child Serafine, affirming a shared cultural legacy. To borrow Edward Said's terms, with this union the novel expands "the overlapping community between metropolitan and formerly colonized societies."[73] Zabus persuasively reads the birth of the young Serafine as a sign of hope for a future in which England will be "peopled by little Feenies."[74] But Warner reminds readers that there are no little Feenies as Serafine tells one last story, ending with the moral, "To look for yourself in little, it's dangerous" (*I* 402). Serafine's double-edged comment celebrates the interracial union of Miranda and Shaka, but also encodes a rueful acceptance that she is still caring for other people's children, not for the daughter "who she left in Enfant-Béate long, long ago" (*I* 221). The new baby only carries on her legacy metaphorically. Thus, whereas Marta Sofía López complains that "the ending of *Indigo* is tainted by self-complacency,"[75] the seemingly conventional reconciliation calls attention to the continued imbalances in the Everard family. Serafine's position in this happy ending calls to mind the compromised nature of the endings in traditional fairy tales. As Iona and Peter Opie point out, fairy tales tend to restore social order.[76] The lowly people who gain stature are often aristocrats previously humbled by magic. Snow White is a princess; the Frog Prince is a prince. The social structures that caused their suffering remain unchanged. In *Indigo*, the ambiguous ending illustrates that stories of reconciliation can help people forget ongoing inequalities, obscuring the injustices they set out to commemorate. *The Leto Bundle* echoes this point, exposing current abuses alongside historical wrongs but questioning the capacity of fiction to do justice to suffering.

THE DISPOSSESSED AND THE "CONTACT ZONES OF HISTORY": SCENES OF EXILE AND IMMIGRATION IN *THE LETO BUNDLE*

Much like *Indigo*, *The Leto Bundle* confronts readers with past and present injustice. The novel calls on readers to respond to Leto's experiences with sympathy and anger at the same time as the text foregrounds its fictionality in a reminder that the issues it dramatizes exceed its confines. Warner spent eight years writing *The Leto Bundle*,[77] and she has described it as her most ambitious novel.[78] It is certainly the most politically driven, "its starting point … the mystery that nations are founded on the persecuted."[79] It is also highly intertextual, like all of Warner's novels. *The Leto Bundle* is built on the Greek myth of Leto, a Titaness who incurs the wrath of Hera when she is impregnated by Zeus. In revenge, Hera consigns her to exile, so that no land will grant her refuge to give birth to her children. After nine days of labour, Leto eventually bears twins, Artemis and Apollo, on the floating island of Delos. In Warner's novel, Leto is once again a single mother and refugee. A modern-day variation on Virginia Woolf's Orlando, she is successively reincarnated from the Hellenistic period to the twentieth century. In the present day, a museum curator named Hortense Fernly finds a tomb containing a bundle of mummy wrappings that tell Leto's story. Leto's life intersects with Hortense's when Leto reappears as an asylum-seeker in Enoch, the novel's London – a reference to Enoch Powell, a Conservative British MP whose notorious 1968 "Rivers of Blood" speech accused immigrants of destroying Britain. The novel responds to tightening immigration policies across Europe over the last two decades of the millennium. It is quite prescient in its depiction of the treatment of refugees, a fact that Warner has acknowledged with a mixture of pride and regret.[80] She wrote about Leto and her children being placed in detention centres even before the British government first announced the creation of "dispersal centres" for refugees. In this context it seems appropriate that the novel is far more pessimistic than *Indigo*, in spite of the fantastical lifespan of its protagonist.

As in *Indigo*, in *The Leto Bundle* Warner creates evocative depictions of suffering, but she also reminds readers that Leto is a fiction, and her story is just one imagined version of the lives of people persecuted or imprisoned for seeking refuge. Pregnant and isolated, Leto is exposed to die in the desert in the fourth century and again centuries later outside a medieval stronghold. She becomes a stowaway on a nineteenth-century naval ship and finally a refugee from a village bombarded with napalm. Seeking asylum in the 1990s, she finds Britain filled with pressure "to keep the country sealed against ... well, opportunists and imposters" (*LB* 315; ellipses in original), as state policies stigmatize refugees as criminals. As Warner notes in her essay "Castaway on the Ocean of Story," Leto's impossible journey offers "a way of giving voice to a woman of our time, a refugee such as we see every day, in the streets of our cities and, above all, on our TV screens."[81] Leto's repeated assaults emblematize the vulnerability of many contemporary refugees. Nevertheless, if *The Leto Bundle* gains much of its force from the suffering of its heroine, her story remains at a remove from readers, like the stories of the islanders in *Indigo*. Even within the diegesis Leto's experiences are textual, written on the wrappings of a mummy on display at the Museum of Albion. *The Leto Bundle* introduces the mummy, in transit to the museum, before Leto herself, and frames the chapters about Leto's past with scholarly notations about manuscript provenance, authorship, and translation. These frames undermine the suspension of disbelief that lets readers imagine characters as real people. They invite readers to recognize the distance between the fictional heroine and the many, diverse stories of real-life refugees.

Leto's namelessness has a similar effect. Early in the novel, Hortense, the curator, explains that "Leto" means "Lady" in the language of the fictional Near Eastern region where the mummy wrappings were found (*LB* 31). Leto eventually adopts the name Ella Outis, which is also a cipher. "Ella" means "she" in Spanish and Italian (with variants in many languages) and "Outis" is an Ancient Greek word for "no one." In calling herself "Outis," Leto echoes the ruse in Homer's *Odyssey* in which Odysseus outwits the Cyclops by calling himself "no one." When the Cyclops shouts that "no one" is bothering him, his fellow Cyclopes assume he does not need their help, and Odysseus escapes from the cave of the Cyclops unscathed. Odysseus takes the name in irony, since his cleverness in moments of danger ensures his reputation, but Leto adopts it to avoid notice. Her anonymity links her to Dulé, who loses his name in *Indigo*, and alludes to the ways single mothers and refugees are ignored in public discourses. At another level, her namelessness signals the tenuousness of efforts to give life through narrative. It reflects Warner's insistence that "[t]he book is really about how someone is seen" more than about Leto herself.[82] The novel leaves its heroine "almost waxen, pressed out by Fate into different shapes,"[83] in much the same way that media outlets and policy-makers press vulnerable groups into their own narrative models. This focus on the ways people are seen by others aligns the novel with Warner's portrait of colonial discourses in *Indigo* as well as her depictions of characters who oversimplify others in *In a Dark Wood* and *The Skating Party*.

While *The Leto Bundle* replaces Britain's dispossessed at the centre of the nation's history, it is not through "negative capability," or efforts to inhabit the body and psyche of the protagonist. Instead Leto remains a symbol. Her symbolic status simultaneously draws attention to the ways in which she is defined by others and hints at the diverse people whose stories exceed the text. She becomes an emblem of fertility, embodying the power of strangers to foment change, and she is adopted as a figurehead by Kim McQuy, founder of an organization called History Starts With Us, or HSWU. Halfway between madman and visionary, Kim often voices principles that Warner expresses elsewhere, in her essays and lectures. When Kim sees the mummy on display at the museum of

Albion, he insists that Leto has survived across eras – which, of course, she has. In an e-mail to Hortense, the curator, Kim exclaims that Leto is:

> always in time present cutting across ours that's always going by so she's of all time of our time or put it another way she's a story and stories have a life and a time all of their own[.] (*LB* 139; extra spaces in the original)

The spaces in the e-mail, as if Kim were gasping for breath, intimate that Leto represents a change that is only beginning and that he cannot put into words. Her generative ability takes tangible form when she hatches her twins from eggs. Here Warner fuses the myths of Leto and Leda, two stories sparked by the rapacious sexual appetite of Zeus. In the well-known myth, Zeus rapes Leda while in the form of a swan, and she gives birth to two sets of twins: the semi-divine Helen and Pollux, and the mortal Clytemnestra and Castor.[84] In many versions the children are born from eggs, and as Warner explained in her 2001 Clarendon Lectures, eggs are widely accepted symbols of "origin and potentiality."[85] In *The Leto Bundle*, Leto takes on the same transformative potential as she slips from one lifetime to another. To Kim, she illustrates the ways "[n]ewcomers, the stranger who walks into town, the creatures who inhabit other worlds … drive history and stories and films and … curiosity" (*LB* 94; 2nd ellipsis in original). Kim's descriptions of the importance of strangers and his vision of immigration as "the blending of spices and herbs and fruits of the earth" (*LB* 24) echo Salman Rushdie's essay "In Good Faith" and Primo Levi's novel *The Periodic Table*, as well as Warner's final Reith Lecture, "Home: The Famous Island Race."[86] Warner returns to the same imagery in *Stranger Magic*, where she locates the magic of strangers in their ability to catalyze hybrid cultural forms. *The Leto Bundle* prefigures *Stranger Magic*'s portrayal of "the contact zones of history" as "areas of mingling and interfusion … a process of Creolisation" (*SM* 26). Leto represents the dual extremes of globalization: the vulnerabilities entrenched by the flow of people and capital across national boundaries alongside the potential for new stories, perspectives, and traditions. Yet her status as a symbol of transformation serves as a reminder that she is a textual construct, standing in for the experiences of countless people.

The responses of museum visitors emphasize the transformative power of the marginalized alongside Leto's status as a textual construct. The museum initially displays the bundle in a conventional exhibit, cordoned off from crowds and publicized through mailings and online advertisements. Then the mummy is sent for exhibition abroad, angering museum-goers who find an empty dais where they expected the mummy and its cartonnage. Even before the disappearance of the bundle, visitors reject standard museum etiquette, bringing votive offerings and prayers written on scraps of paper. They adopt the role of "resisting readers," in the terminology of Judith Fetterley,[87] declaring Leto a symbol of their struggles and not simply a historical artifact. As the museum staff members resist their efforts to sacralize the site, the novel parodies colonial regimes that turned sacred sites into sources of prestige and reproduced them in postage stamps and textbooks.[88] The museum functions as a repository of imperial treasures rather than a means of perpetuating memory, for "[t]o aim at the perpetuation of memories means, inevitably, that one has undertaken the task of constantly renewing, of creating, memories."[89] The ethos of the museum contrasts starkly with the archive of ephemera in *The Lost Father*, where Anna salvages toys and stickers to preserve cultural practices. But the visitors turn the exhibit into what Pierre Nora famously labelled "*lieux de mémoire*," sites of memory that "block the work of forgetting" with their "capacity for metamorphosis, an endless recycling of their meaning."[90] Reading the museum against itself, visitors transform it into a source of living memory, much like the islanders in *Indigo* who pray at Sycorax's grave. Through their reactions to Leto, they insist on the right to narrate their own lives alongside the stories of the imperial centre. They maintain a creative power that the imperial centre cannot diminish. At the same time, their creative responses to the Leto bundle serve as yet another layer of mediation separating readers from the protagonist. In these scenes, readers encounter Leto as a symbol of the museum-goers' self-expression rather than a character with her own hopes, dreams, or fears.

The ways Kim and the museum-goers "read" Leto are celebratory, even empowering. She becomes an "active, animating, inspiriting agent," a role that Warner ascribed to Zeus in her Clarendon Lectures.[91] Yet these celebratory portraits have their own dangers. Reading strangers as agents of change or symbols of fertility de-emphasizes the vulnerability migrations can involve as well as the varied survival strategies used by migrants. As Patricia Yaeger argues, the translation of people into tropes substitutes the lightness of rhetoric for the weight of bodily dignity.[92] Still, Warner does not respond to this dilemma by trying to "enflesh [Leto] as a realist protagonist in the tradition of the great nineteenth-century social novel."[93] Instead Leto remains a figurehead, her inner life perpetually out of reach.

THE PROTAGONIST AS FIGUREHEAD AND THE LIMITS OF EMPATHY

The documents in the mummy wrappings that depict Leto's experiences foreground her status as a fiction, like Anna's memoir in *The Lost Father*; but whereas *The Lost Father* often lets readers forget that it is telling a story within a story, *The Leto Bundle* keeps alluding to Leto's textuality. The narratives are produced by several different hands. The earliest text is by the scribe of a fourth-century priestess; the next is by a medieval monk. The fourth-century manuscript "braids disparate strands of mythology ... to enhance the status of the sanctuary" where it was written (*LB* 33), and the tale echoes Aeschylus's tragedies and the infancy gospels. Leto's laments – "Why did he let it happen like this?" "I'm cursed" (*LB* 29) – call to mind Io, in Aeschylus's *Prometheus Bound*, wailing, "Are there any in all this suffering world / Who endure what I endure?"[94] and Anna, in the Book of James, crying, "Woe to me, who begot me? / For I was born as a curse."[95] The priestess's text exalts suffering, just as these models do, and emphasizes her misfortunes above her survival strategies. Her narrative hints at its own limits when it portrays Leto criticizing pelicans that sacrifice themselves for their young because "a weakened or dead mother was no good to anyone" (*LB* 9). The comment reveals a stoical attitude suppressed by the rest of the priestess's manuscript. In the nineteenth-century chapters, written in the style of an imperial romance, archaeologist Giles Skipwith defines Leto as "Wonderful priceless raw material – a treasure above rubies! ... a key to a puzzle, the greatest puzzle – the human mind" (*LB* 209). He objectifies Leto as an anthropological tool and tries to map her the way he would map other artifacts, reminding himself that "deciphering the signs can't be done hastily but has to be approached slowly, patiently" (*LB* 194). In each case, Leto's story reflects the desires of the person who records it, much like the Everards' descriptions of Serafine in *Indigo* reflect their own needs.

In the novel's contemporary sections, which are not framed by museum documents, it seems as though readers must encounter Leto unmediated by the interpretations of other characters. Even in the twentieth century, though, any identity Leto seems to have is imposed by others. At one point, singer Gramercy Poule hires Leto as a housekeeper. The two women have met before: in an earlier scene Leto, working as a hotel maid and prostitute, rescues Gramercy when Gramercy is locked out of her hotel room. Leto gives her a massage in return for her tip and then steals her tights and sandals. When Gramercy later hires Leto under the name Ella Outis, Gramercy renames her "Nellie," saying, "It feels right to me, do you mind?" (*LB* 338). This seems like an act of generosity, bestowing a name on an effectively nameless woman, but Gramercy's gesture recalls slave-owners renaming their slaves. Asking Leto to repeat the massage from the hotel, Gramercy proclaims, "'*I* know who you are, and that's what I wanted, that's what I want.' Her voice went whispery and she plucked at Nellie's sleeve: 'Use the downstairs shower when you've finished here and then, please, Nell darling, give me your special treatment again!'" (*LB* 339). By invoking the history that connects the two women, Gramercy confines Leto in a role she might wish to transcend. Leto's many pasts, from mythological Titaness to Victorian stowaway, belie Gramercy's declaration that she knows Leto.

Kim's rhetoric, too, enables him to ignore the details of Leto's experiences. For him, the Leto bundle represents "everyone who's ever been driven from home, who's been stolen away or beaten out ... she's Persephone and dozens and dozens of young women who've been raped – not least Europa ... She's Hagar and Mary and ... well, she's Leto" (*LB* 95; final ellipsis Warner's). Kim's examples illustrate what he fails to notice: "dozens and dozens of young women who've been raped" all have different stories to tell. His sympathy calls to mind Viola and Paula, in Warner's earlier novels, flattening out the lives of other women in the effort to assert their solidarity. When Kim meets the real-life Leto, he subsumes her to his vision of a new Albion, just as he does with the bundle in the museum. Adopted as a child and searching for his biological mother, Kim turns out to be a contemporary incarnation of Leto's son Phoebus, but he never imagines that the refugee-housekeeper in front of him might be his mother. While Leto is wondering whether Kim could be her son, Kim is "acting the defence counsel," asking about her application for asylum (*LB* 373). In Kim the "defence counsel" is an unsettling echo of Skipwith's prideful role as protector. His reaction, much like characters' unsatisfying descriptions of others in Warner's earlier novels, provokes efforts to conjure Leto's story from her own point of view. As Gayatri Spivak writes of J.M. Coetzee's *Disgrace*, another novel concerned with the potential violence of recuperative narratives, *The Leto Bundle* offers a "rhetorical signal to the active reader, to counterfocalize," to develop an alternative reading.[96] This effort, however, can only be provisional, like the open-ended imagination encouraged by Warner's early novels. As I noted in chapter 2, characters have no experiences or perceptions beyond the text, since "novels, unlike histories, do not report on events that have happened but bring them into being."[97] It is impossible to imagine a fictional character's "own" story, so the questions raised by the text remain boundless.

Warner never portrays Leto defining herself. Like readers, she has only questions: "if she could not remember, who was she?" (*LB* 176). Even when Leto briefly takes on the role of a storyteller, the novel calls attention to the artifice of her voice, like those of the islanders in *Indigo*. This conspicuous artifice is particularly surprising in light of some of Warner's assertions about the importance of speech patterns as tools for holding onto cultural identities. In a 2016 essay titled "Those Brogues" in the *London Review of Books*, she writes that speech patterns can be ways of maintaining identity in a new place, "of not losing altogether the places of your past even when you've been dislocated." Equally important, she notes, they enrich that new place. Vocal "marks of identity" are one way in which migrations reshape the nation-state: "like a tune, like a blow-in species of flower, like a story, speech patterns are no respecters of borders."[98] In this essay, she echoes the language of *The Leto Bundle*'s Kim McQuy about the creative influences of migrants. But Leto's speech patterns, which betray Warner's characteristic style, emphasize the distance between this single fictional character and the innumerable migrants she represents.

At one point, bound for the city of Enoch in the nineteenth century, Leto tells her children a story about a stranger who once rid Enoch of flies and leeches. When the city refused to pay him, he destroyed everyone except the children, who treated traders and labourers fairly forevermore. Metal insects sucked the marrow from the bones of the city's men "until they were sucked as dry and friable as the last withered leaves rustling on the twigs of winter trees" (*LB* 221). Leto's story depicts the victory of the persecuted. She changes the genre of her life from romance to fairy tale and translates herself from victim to author. As she speaks, she takes on the role of *Indigo*'s Serafine and the storytellers in *From the Beast to the Blonde*, who impart morals through their tales. But Leto is only partly a storyteller. Like the speech of the islanders in *Indigo*, Leto's words carry Warner's intonations. When Leto's son, Phoebus, interjects, "And then suddenly, what?" (*LB* 219), Warner reinforces the link between herself and Leto. The working title for Warner's 1996 libretto, *In the House of Crossed Desires*, was "Then Suddenly," after a little girl asked her to tell one of those stories "where it says, 'Then suddenly' lots of times."[99] Leto's burst of creativity highlights "the unified authorial self who controls the parcelled body of the narrative" in contrast to the "dispersed and scattered" protagonist.[100] It foregrounds Warner's role in creating, rather than simply representing Leto, and points out that any effort to read Leto is itself a creative act.

Thus, if Leto's plunges through space and time signify her transformative power, they also give physical form to the ways she outstrips the narratives of others, and the single mothers and refugees of history outstrip the imaginative capacity of any author or readers. As symbols of excess, her reincarnations connect her to Serafine, whose unspecified age makes her seem almost immortal, and Sycorax, her spirit preserved in the saman tree that grows above her grave, as well as the many figures in Warner's short stories whose metamorphoses make them impossible to characterize. Spilling over temporal and spatial boundaries, Leto, Sycorax, and Serafine all provoke readers "to imagine the unimaginable," a phrase Mike Marais uses of J.M. Coetzee's *Disgrace*, and in that process, to be "invaded and possessed by that which exceeds [their intellectual frameworks]."[101] The transformative skills of the characters and the strength symbolized by the saman tree on Sycorax's grave represent the power of Warner's novels to transform readers who open themselves to "an alterity that cannot be instantiated or negated."[102]

Leto's torments, too, challenge the imaginative capacities of readers. Leto endures terrible violence. Her ordeals are overwhelming and uncontrolled, punctuated with "broken roaring and grunts and curses and maulings and beatings" (*LB* 61). Yet her experiences also seem unreal, particularly the most horrifying ones. In the twentieth century, as Leto and her children head towards the bombed-out city of Tirzah, they are caught in a napalm explosion. The scene is based on the napalm bomb on the road to Trang Bang, where Nick Út photographed Phan Thi Kim Phúc. In *The Leto Bundle*, Leto's daughter Phoebe replaces Kim Phúc. The violence of the bomb is graphic; her skin is burned off her body. Yet as images accrete, the body at the centre moves further and further away. The sheer mass of imagery underscores the difficulty of conveying the pain of a person flayed by a bomb. As Elaine Scarry explains, like "unseeable classes of objects such as subterranean plates [or] Seyfert galaxies ... the pains occurring in other people's bodies flicker before the mind, then disappear."[103] Warner filters Phoebe's pain through similes: "She looked like a rabbit skinned by a hunter to spit on a fire"; she shakes with a sound "like a lost bird," amid bodies sprawled "like children playing 'Ring-a-ring-o'-roses'" (*LB* 253). The same lyricism shapes Warner's portrayal of Sycorax after the settlers set fire to her treehouse in *Indigo*. Warner writes, "The fire leapt around her, her edges went black in the firelight" (*I* 131), but then evokes another time and place, "when the volcano also spat flames and rocks into the sky, like the strangers' guns" (*I* 146). In a haunting phrase, she describes "the winding sheet of her bodily agony" (*I* 146), translating Sycorax's pain into sight and touch while suggesting that the only way to imagine someone else's pain is through metaphor. These images hint that an understanding of another person's pain cannot stem from identification, but only from recognition of "something irreducible and different, often inaccessible."[104] In this way they echo the critique of identification and the evocation of open-ended efforts at understanding in Warner's earlier novels.

The torments that Leto and Phoebe endure are relentless, particularly in comparison to *Indigo*, with its hope-filled ending. However, *The Leto Bundle* subverts emotional responses more resolutely than *Indigo*. *The Leto Bundle* calls to mind Susan Sontag's warning that the "imaginary proximity" to suffering offered by television and books enables viewers to imagine that they are not implicated in the violence that causes it. In Sontag's words, "Our sympathy proclaims our innocence as well as our impotence," whereas images of violence should inspire questions: Is this inevitable? Could we prevent it?[105] These questions are particularly salient in the face of contemporary debates about asylum and immigration policies and the conditions faced by immigrants in detention centres in the US, UK, and elsewhere. Warner's imagery invites readers not simply to grieve over the suffering of her characters, but also to take responsibility for the needs of vulnerable people in our own societies.

CONSTRUCTING PROVISIONAL COMMUNITIES

As Patricia Yaeger observes in a 2002 essay titled "Consuming Trauma," "[w]e are obsessed with stories that must be passed on, that must not be passed over." Echoing the close of Toni Morrison's *Beloved* (1987), her words hint at the quandary underlying *Indigo* and *The Leto Bundle*: the histories that inspired these novels cannot be reduced to narrative yet must not be ignored. But Yaeger goes on to muse, "aren't we also drawn to these stories from within an elite culture driven by its own economies: by the pains and pleasures of needing to publish, by salaries and promotions that are themselves driven by acts of publication, by the pleasures of merely circulating?"[106] Even to claim that Warner thematizes the difficulties of representing other people credits her with yet another achievement as a writer. Self-reflexive strategies aimed at probing the failures of writing can reinscribe the writer's authority in a text.[107] As Tamlyn Monson puts it, "[the] *performance* of the impotence of writing, and of the irreducibility of the Other … smacks of achievement and mastery, of *agency*."[108] This may simply be an inevitable paradox for writers who explore the limits of representation. The effort to take responsibility for other people's lives while respecting the elusiveness of those lives is an endless process. With no potential for closure, it cannot be measured by dramatic storytelling or renunciation of narrative control. It can only be a partial success, one that takes shape in the interstices between the acts of writing and reading.

This effort invites readers into a community that links people who need not be present or even living. To borrow a phrase from Geoffrey Hartman, it creates the foundation for an "affective community" that may substitute, "however inadequately, for [an] original and tragically decimated milieu."[109] Of course, readers will respond to this invitation in different ways, since reading "always unfolds in a richly determined context, including the context of the reader's situation and personal history."[110] Yet *Indigo* and *The Leto Bundle* create space for readers to reinvent the frameworks through which they understand other people and open themselves to illimitable stories.

The harvest fair at the end of *The Leto Bundle* dramatizes the community envisioned by these novels. A *faux*-medieval setting that yokes together musicians, scientists, and refugee campaigners, the fair cuts across socio-economic boundaries in the "free and familiar contact" of Bakhtinian carnival.[111] Leto's daughter Phoebe sets up a tent devoted to feng shui and face painting. Inside, multiple spaces coexist: her computer monitor glows "subaqueously" while a tape plays "wooden flutes and gongs from a distant rainforest," and the entire tent feels "like a sea cave" (*LB* 393). Phoebe's computerized feng shui blends the ancient and the modern. So does Phoebe herself, with silver fingernails that she dries with acetone and skin produced by medical grafts. To use Homi Bhabha's terms, the tent and the fair surrounding it are "'in-between' spaces … that initiate new signs of identity, and innovative sites of collaboration, and contestation, in the act of defining the idea of society itself."[112] They enable people to step outside divisive histories and construct new relationships based on openness to the unknown. Yet Warner draws attention to the effort behind the fair's hybridity. If the decorations and displays evoke an earlier time with fewer worries or responsibilities, readers cannot help but notice the reconditioned objects that make this fantasy possible, from Phoebe's computer to the pots and pans used for a mock duel. The work underlying the fair points toward the challenges of forging communities that reach beyond traditional affiliations.

Because the communities initiated by *Indigo* and *The Leto Bundle* depend on the imaginative responses of readers, like the communities invited by Warner's earlier novels, they must be constantly recreated. As Jacques Derrida says of friendship, these communities involve "the indefinite repetition of the inaugural instant, always *anew*, once again."[113] Warner gives shape to this vision through the constantly changing city of Enoch. When Leto navigates the city, her landmarks are transient:

plastic recycling bins, heaps of fruit and vegetables, a charity clothes container – all structures that will be gone by evening. A motorcyclist hits a planter and a shop owner sits him down on a folding garden chair (*LB* 309–13). The instability of these spaces makes them hospitable to the improvisation of new identities, individual and communal, as *Indigo* and *The Leto Bundle* are themselves. Yet entry into the community envisioned by the novels involves vulnerability. No one has a predefined role; each person is a stranger in a place with unfamiliar customs. In a phrase from Judith Butler, a reader who enters this community becomes "resituated irreversibly in a field of others in which one is not the presumptive centre."[114] Entry requires giving up the sense of belonging that communities traditionally offer. Nevertheless, the risk that this engenders is also a source of possibility. It unsettles the binary of self versus stranger. It makes one other to oneself, no longer able to lay claim to previous certainties about one's social position, and by extension questions the "otherness" of people who might seem to be foreign or "strange." It makes it possible to invent new ways of relating outside of models based on shared nationality, class, language, religion, or culture.

CONCLUSION

By responding to injustices done to people they cannot delimit, Warner and her readers can enter a relationship similar to Levinas's concept of being-for-the-other, whereby every person is responsible for limitless others in an ethical obligation that precedes any act or commitment that person might make. Here, they respond to things done by other people and before their lifetime; in Levinas's terms, they answer "for a debt contracted before any freedom and before any consciousness and any present."[115] From the end of the twentieth century onward, Warner's writing becomes increasingly concerned with the need to respond to injustice and pushes readers to reassess the sphere of their responsibilities. She takes responsibility for the stories of others as if, by virtue of being alive, those people appeal to the world to acknowledge them and answer for their needs. As in Derrida's conception of absolute hospitality, she declares herself open to people she cannot name, both because they are too numerous and because in many cases their names have been lost to history.[116] Warner does not take the right to narrate their lives as given. She continually reasserts it – as a contingent right, never fully established – through narrative strategies that attempt to reflect the uniqueness of their experiences. At the same time, Warner recognizes that her fiction cannot, in itself, restore agency to her subjects. If agency involves institutionalized recognition and not just inner strength, then the effort of "listening" at a distance – imagining fictitious lives – can only build agency if it leads to acts of real-world listening that validate the claims of the speakers.[117]

The narrative strategies in both novels are illuminated by a comment Warner made in 2004 after a fire at the Saatchi warehouse in London destroyed a number of contemporary artworks. Writing about the loss in the *Financial Times*, she mused that art stretches people's perceptions and "open[s] up ways of being and understanding."[118] *Indigo* and *The Leto Bundle* map efforts to open her own understanding as well as the perceptions of readers. Like her earlier novels, both works call attention to the needs inflecting the stories people tell about others and challenge readers to critique their modes of interpretation. In keeping with the paradoxical endeavour of narrating lives that remain unencompassable, the characters in both novels embody both excess and absence, and the process of responding to them creates openings for partial, provisional responses. The two novels forge spaces for dialogue without conclusions and communities that can connect and transform their members. In the next chapter, I explore how Warner's short stories about witnessing, similarly, invite partial and provisional responses based on recognition of the ways lives and social contexts exceed narratives and consideration of the roles played by readers in upholding those social contexts.

4

Hearing the Unsaid

An Ethics of Bearing Witness in Warner's Short Fiction

In Warner's 2006 short story "Breadcrumbs," a Palestinian refugee and hospital worker in an unnamed country recounts how she got separated from her children when Israeli soldiers attacked her village. Her tale is met with three tiers of listeners: her colleagues, chatting in the middle of an overnight shift; the narrator, an unnamed patient who listens from her hospital bed; and readers. Maryam's colleagues ascribe to her story the closure of a happy ending. When she describes her reunion with her children, they "sigh and kind of chuckle with satisfaction." Yet her closing line alludes to the ways her experience exceeds narrative closure. She labels her separation from her children a "terrible gap, a gap like an eternity," hinting at the ongoing effects of trauma and the difficulty of putting them into words (*FAH* 195). The serene responses of her listeners ignore a tacit plea to hear what lies outside the sequence of events she has recounted. With the disjuncture between the demands of Maryam's story and the dispassionate reactions of her colleagues, Warner raises the question of what it means to respond ethically to the stories of other people, particularly when those stories centre on marginalization or violence. She calls on readers not just to recognize the suffering and resilience described by the speaker, but to listen for what the speaker does not or cannot say. She asks readers to consider what might be excluded by the discursive frameworks that shape the storytelling context and how they may be complicit in those exclusions.

In this chapter, I analyze several tales of witnessing that Warner has written since the turn of the millennium. By "tales of witnessing," I mean stories that centre on people testifying to their experiences or trying to understand the experiences of others. I argue that Warner's witnessing stories both support and complicate the common view that ethical responses to the lives of other people involve striving to understand who they are and what they have experienced: their losses, their joys, their vulnerabilities, and the forms of agency they wield. In this view, for stories of violence to bring about greater "justice, dignity, and freedom," those who hear them "must take responsibility for the recognition of others and their claims."[1] Within this paradigm, we – all people – bear witness more successfully the more we recognize the nuances of an individual's experience. By acknowledging the experiences of those who have suffered, often in the face of denials by the state and neglect by a global community, witnesses can alleviate what Jill Stauffer calls "ethical loneliness," the loneliness of being abandoned to persecution.[2] But as Maryam's story suggests, witnessing is also about more than that: it involves attention to the conditions of speaking and the things that remain unspoken.

When I interviewed her in 2004, Warner mused, "we have perhaps placed too much trust in the truthfulness in the speaking voice" as an engine for understanding the lives of others. "People love it," she reflected; "they feel absolutely close to the sincerity of the speaker who is reconstructing his or her life."[3] But this feeling of intimacy can drive readers to forget that life stories are doubly partial, both mediated and incomplete. To imagine that even an autobiographical narrative captures a person's life ignores the speaker's silences and the active construction of their story. It also ignores the social and discursive frameworks that enable some speech acts to circulate more easily than others. For example, clear narratives about innocent victims or redemptive journeys from suffering to healing often gain greater transnational circulation than complex portraits of injustice and culpability.[4] Moreover, focusing on the recognition of individual suffering makes it easy to respond to violence with sympathy while evading critical thought about broader social structures. Even when personal stories are used to illustrate broad social situations – for instance, to reveal the human costs of injustice – they can paradoxically decrease attention to those situations. "[T]he ethical imperative toward social transformation" may be "replaced by a civic-minded but passive ideal of empathy."[5]

An ethics of witnessing based on recognition for those that have suffered can reinforce existing injustices. It places the person who bestows recognition in the position of subject and the person who is recognized in the position of object (as the passive construction implies).[6] It can involve listening for what one already knows rather than opening oneself to what might be outside one's previous understanding, as suggested by the morphological components of the term:

re-cognition, the repetition of knowledge.[7] This kind of response can cut the listener off from "the unfamiliar that disrupts what we already know."[8] Yet the disruption of previous knowledge is necessary if listeners are to assess their own implication in suffering and envision "new responses to harms that no preexisting remedy fully comprehends."[9]

Warner's stories of witnessing seem to call on readers to recognize the complexities of the protagonists and their experiences. However, the stories also show how much acts of witness based on an individualized ethics of recognition can fail to see. They call attention to the ways lives can exceed familiar narrative frameworks and to social and discursive conditions that outstrip readings focused on individual lives. In each of these stories, the protagonists undergo transformations that illustrate the fluidity of their identities. These transformations undermine the capacity of readers to grasp the characters and imply that a person can never fully grasp the story of someone else, nor even tell their own story. They remind readers that efforts to reduce individuals to coherent narratives or objects of knowledge are often inseparable from projects of control or domination.[10] They invite readers to "respond to what is beyond our comprehension, beyond recognition, because ethics is possible only beyond recognition."[11] This does not mean abandoning the effort to understand other people, which would reify boundaries between "selves" and "others" and make all "others" irreducibly alien to oneself.[12] Instead, as I have argued in the previous chapters, it involves ongoing effort at understanding coupled with recognition of the inconclusiveness of that effort. Moreover, responding to these stories involves more than striving to understand the body on the page. Warner's witnessing stories invite readers to bear witness to precisely the stories that remain unheard and unseen, and they offer reminders that bearing witness to fictional characters is different from bearing witness to real people. Recognizing the experiences of a fictional character cannot improve justice or engender social change unless it translates into recognition of underlying social conditions and the ways readers are positioned within them.

This chapter starts by exploring witnessing stories from Warner's second and third short story collections, *Murderers I Have Known* (2002) and *Fly Away Home* (2015). I show that the lives of the protagonists exceed the stories they tell about themselves and the narratives other characters develop about them. I argue that the texts call for responses more complicated than recognition or compassion for those characters. Like all of the texts I have discussed in the foregoing chapters, these stories push readers to cultivate an openness to the stories of others – within and beyond the diegesis – that comes from giving up the desire for complete understanding or cognitive mastery. I then turn to three short stories that Warner wrote in response to conflicts in the Middle East. I contend that much like *Indigo* and *The Leto Bundle*, while these stories create space for empathetic responses to the suffering and resilience of the protagonists, they also do more. They invite readers to consider the ongoing effects of structural violence, the social structures that make some kinds of violence more legible than others, and their own positions within those structures.

TRANSFORMATION AS A SOURCE OF UNCERTAINTY IN WARNER'S STORIES OF WITNESSING

Many of Warner's short stories centre on characters who are marginalized or disenfranchised. This marginalization takes many forms, from a young woman institutionalized for ostensible delusions to refugees fleeing conflict in Iraq. The characters are often likeable, and their circumstances frequently evoke sympathy. Yet the metamorphoses of the characters and the resulting ambiguities in the texts preclude any comprehensive account of who they are, much like what H. Porter Abbott calls "the palpable unknown": a narrative effect that immerses readers "in the condition of unknowing."[13] In this way the stories call into question the sufficiency of affective responses such as sympathy or compassion for fictional characters. They invite readers to reassess the interpretive frameworks that shape their responses to others (within and outside the diegesis) and to consider what may be excluded from well-meaning acts of witness.

Warner's short stories "Daughters of the Game," "Out of the Burning House," and "Mélusine: A Mermaid's Tale" do not address mass trauma or widespread human rights violations, but they construct scenes of witnessing in the face of marginalization, stigma, or outright violence. "Out of the Burning House" centres on an aging transgender actor named Louie who struggles with gender identity in a period when transgender experiences are not widely acknowledged. "Daughters of the Game" features a movie stand-in named Fernanda who specializes in sex scenes. She is exploited by the film industry, where her work brings in profits that barely trickle back to her, and she is stigmatized by her local community when they find out what kind of acting she does. "Mélusine: A Mermaid's Tale" turns the mythic sea-nymph Mélusine into a teenage mermaid who is attacked when her boyfriend turns out to be a sea monster. Louie and Mélusine each recount their experiences to a listener they hope will provide a sympathethic ear, and readers are positioned as listeners as well, effectively eavesdropping on their conversations. "Daughters of the Game" positions readers as viewers through ekphrasis, with a vivid description of Fernanda in a movie rape scene that becomes a cult classic and gets cut out of film reels as a souvenir. The stories seem to call on readers to confer recognition on the protagonists in ways that those around them have failed to do, to recognize the complexities of their lives and self-definitions that have been denied by others. But ultimately the texts subvert this kind of reading through the metamorphoses of the characters. The texts remind readers that one cannot recognize the subjectivity of a fictional character in the same way one might recognize the subjectivity of a real person, and moreover, that the fluidity and multiplicity of identity make any coherent reading of a person superficial.

In "Daughters of the Game," Fernanda appears to be doubly mute. She plays a silent rape victim and she is never credited for her role in the scene that becomes famous. She speaks only twice in the whole story. Her unrecognized labour indicts a film industry that treats female bodies as commodities for male viewing pleasure. The story seems to invite readers to combat that silencing by acknowledging not just Fernanda's labour but her agency. The text insists that Fernanda chooses her work freely and that a woman who turns her body into a spectacle does not necessarily make herself a victim. Yet Fernanda's determination "to remain fluid, a woman with many faces" (*MIHK* 61), complicates the desire to read the story through any single lens, even one that collapses the apparent binary between exploitation and agency. This line stymies any interpretation of Warner's shape-shifter. Moreover, the narrative style and structure direct attention away from the protagonist toward a broader social commentary. The story starts out relatively quick-paced, focused on the movement and speech of the characters in close-up. As it goes on, the narrative voice gets more detached, almost journalistic. At the end the focus moves from Fernanda to the uses and abuses of images of violation in the entertainment and advertising industries. The last line is about the use of Fernanda's rape scene in an advertisement for a designer clothing company. The brief illusion of intimacy that connects reader and protagonist is gradually attenuated, and Fernanda remains a stranger to readers, just as she is to the film viewers who do not know they are looking at her.

Similar ambiguities underpin "Out of the Burning House" and "Mélusine." In "Out of the Burning House," Louie recounts a history of theatrical roles in a tale of gendered self-discovery: "[T]hat's me, there, in the picture"; "Here I am in *Cinders*"; "There I was, the real me, the one I'd known was inside me ever since I was a titch and first saw Dame Edna on the telly" (*FAH* 3). Readers are asked to see beyond the aging body in a community care centre and acknowledge "the real me" underneath. "Mélusine" has a very different setting, a fantastical underwater land where myths blend together with contemporary technology, but shares the testimonial structure of "Out of the Burning House." In a bid for sympathy and understanding, Mélusine tells her aunt how she courted a human; when she revealed her mermaid shape so that her lover could "see who I really am," he tried to devour her (FAH 15). Once again, the narrative seems to call for recognition of the complex figure she "really" is, the recognition her lover does not confer. Yet like "Daughters of the Game," both stories invite more complicated responses. Much like Fernanda, Louie takes on a vast range of personae – in this case to escape a confining body, or "the outer casing that was supposed to be my body" (FAH 6). No single role can capture Louie's rich and varied life, as shown by the assertion that if Louie had to save one thing from a burning house, it would be the albums with memorabilia from a lifetime of performances. Like Fernanda, who reflects, "A stand-in had no face, she had a thousand faces" (MIHK 59), Louie is constantly transforming, never settling into any role for long. Furthermore, the tone of Louie's monologue is theatrical, even campy, turning it into a performance rather than an intimate account of experience. "Mélusine," too, distances readers from the title character by presenting her words as a performance. Akin to Louie and Fernanda, Mélusine cultivates varied personae. She is exaggeratedly emotional. She speaks alternately in glum pronouncements and energetic exclamations. As she weeps in the arms of her aunt, the mythical Morgan le Fay, Morgan muses, "Mélusine is a performer, and I was being granted a special, private performance" (FAH 13). Like Louie, Mélusine reveals only a thoroughly mediated image. The changing shapes of all three protagonists illustrate the changeable nature of identity and the complex mediations behind the images people project. In an echo of Warner's war journalism and biography of the empress dowager Tz'u-hsi, they call on readers to look at other people in many ways at once.

It is worth reiterating that a fictional character cannot have a "real" identity beneath the surface or a life story that exceeds the text; a fictional character is constituted by the text. However, as in much of Warner's earlier work, the gaps and ambiguities in these stories call into question the tools that readers use to understand characters. Even to describe Louie as multifaceted and multiply gendered or to characterize Fernanda through a complex interplay of vulnerability and agency is to ignore the many aspects of their lives that the texts only hint at. In addition, Warner implies that to think of the characters' verbal testimonies as windows onto who they are is to ignore the performative element of those testimonies. Thus the stories tacitly critique listening practices that treat testimonies as transparent accounts of reality.[14] They remind readers that life stories, even first-person ones, are always narrative constructions. In doing so, they encourage readers to approach life stories with openness to that which exceeds the telling. They suggest that responses to the testimonies of other people can never be complete; rather, like Kelly Oliver's idea of "infinite response-ability," they must be ongoing and attuned to "what is beyond our comprehension."[15]

Another two stories of witnessing, "The Belled Girl Sends a Tape to an Impresario" and "No One Goes Hungry," illustrate the violence done by claiming to make sense of another person's experience of violence. "The Belled Girl Sends a Tape to an Impresario," a modern version of the Grimms' fairy tale "The Maiden without Hands," centres on a young woman named Phoebe who imagines a strange man removing her hands and giving her bells in return. The story takes the form of a tape that she makes about her life and the loss of her hands; a framing letter from her psychiatrist explains that she has been institutionalized for body dysmorphic disorder and her bells are merely a delusion. Though quirky and lighthearted, "The Belled Girl" is a story of violation on two levels. The loss of Phoebe's hands may symbolize sexual abuse, as I will explain later. That possible abuse is compounded by Phoebe's confinement in a psychiatric hospital where her doctor denies her version of her experiences, evoking a long history of oppression of women by mental institutions. "No One Goes Hungry," a modernization of the Greek myth of Erysichthon, depicts a young woman exploited and eventually prostituted by her father. Overcome by perpetual hunger like the mythical Erysichthon, Mr Grindop uses Lucie as bait to attract customers, first for a software package and eventually for her body. As he grows larger, Lucie gets thinner and thinner, until she becomes a virtual reality girl and vanishes altogether. Both stories align readers with characters who bear witness to the women's experiences. "The Belled Girl" interpellates readers as the addressees of Phoebe's taped message and the psychiatrist's framing letter. (Within the text, the addressee is a theatre producer who uses drama as a therapeutic tool.) "No One Goes Hungry" pushes readers to identify with the first-person narrator, an Eastern European academic visiting a US college town, who tries to understand what is happening to Lucie. As the narrator wanders around town striving to make sense of his surroundings, he becomes a guide for readers, who move through that space by virtue of his perceptions.

Like the short stories I discussed above, "The Belled Girl" and "No One Goes Hungry" seem to ask readers to recognize both the vulnerability and the agency of their female protagonists. The stories make it easy to sympathize with the women and admire their resilience. However, the stories also complicate these responses by hinting at the violence done by the male narrators in trying to establish who the women are and what they are going through. In "The Belled Girl," the psychiatrist's explanation of Phoebe's illness undermines the credibility of her narrative, effectively removing the conditions in which she might be heard. In "No One Goes Hungry," the narrator's efforts to understand Lucie are both paternal and paternalistic. In each case the narrator legitimizes his own presence and authority by reading a young woman as alien or out of place. To borrow a formulation from Sara Ahmed, the body of the male narrator "comes to matter through the reduction of other bodies to matter out of place."[16] Labelling Phoebe's condition demonstrates the authority of the psychiatrist. His framing letter highlights the distinction between the institutionalized patient and the societal decision-makers. He takes for granted that he and his addressee share a cultural knowledge base, with phrases such as "I need hardly tell you" and an unfinished Latin quotation that he can expect his addressee to cap (*MIHK* 80). In "No One Goes Hungry," the narrator's efforts to analyze Lucie and her father give him the authority of an ethnographer and alleviate his loneliness. Initially isolated by his lack of fluency in English and estranged by small-town American life, he comes to see himself as Lucie's protector. As he gathers more information about Lucie, the narrator's tone becomes more confident, and he makes more and more judgments about the people before him. In both stories, the male narrators achieve their belonging through the power to judge the relative belonging of the women. Their efforts to make sense of the women bolster their authority and strip the women of authority to define themselves.

By contrast, Warner complicates the efforts of readers to make sense of the women through the ambiguities created by their metamorphoses. The bodily disappearances of the characters seemingly reflect the losses of self that result from subordination. Yet they ultimately challenge coherent readings. When Lucie vanishes at the end of "No One Goes Hungry," her absence could easily be read as a sign of subjugation, her body transformed into a commodity to feed her father's hunger. It might equally reflect her control over her movements, beyond the control her father tries to exert or the analytic authority the narrator seeks. The narrative perspective adds to this uncertainty. Neither the narrator nor readers ever have access to Lucie's thoughts. She may be helping her father out of force, fear, or loyalty – perhaps even a desire to inherit his software. Readers never learn her feelings or motives, just as they never learn what happens to her after her disappearance. The ambiguity in Warner's text mirrors the ambiguity of the source tale. Erysichthon, cursed with hunger, repeatedly sells his daughter into slavery, and each time she slips away by transforming herself. In Ovid's version, "she would easily escape: she'd take shape after shape: now she became a mare, a bird, a deer – and, through these changes, she saw to her avaricious father's needs, with food that he did not deserve."[17] Though Erysichthon objectifies his daughter, as she brings him food she ranges herself against the gods that have cursed him, undermining their power to reward and punish.

"The Belled Girl," too, invites readers to interpret its central metamorphosis through multiple lenses.[18] The loss of hands signifies a loss of agency, since hands play crucial roles in day-to-day competence. As I mentioned above, it also hints at sexual exploitation. The source tale, "The Maiden without Hands," is a variation on the fairy tale "Donkeyskin," where a bereaved king vows to marry his daughter. As Warner explains in her fairy tale study *From the Beast to the Blonde*, in early versions of "The Maiden without Hands," the maiden cuts off her hands to stop her father from forcing her to marry him (*BB* 347–8). "The Belled Girl" implies that Phoebe was previously subjugated by a controlling boyfriend (*MIHK* 85) and that she is willing to subjugate herself to male authorities. "I would do anything for you," she proclaims to the theatre producer. "Because I loved you when I first saw you last night on the telly. And you haven't tried the same with a girl   not yet   have you?" (*MIHK* 82; spaces in the original). She is referring to a performance he produced with a boy with disabilities, but the ambiguity of the question gives it a sexual resonance. However, if Phoebe's missing hands and her message to the producer connote willing subordination, the bells that replace them also signify agency. She is proud of their "rings of sound that go out and out for miles" (*MIHK* 87), even if a bell with its single note is a limited tool for communication. My argument here is not just that Phoebe's voice exceeds narrow interpretations of her vulnerability. The ontological status of her transformation is ambiguous. The story never clarifies whether readers should accept the doctor's account of Phoebe's illness or read this as a magic realist text and accept Phoebe's bells as real. As in "No One Goes Hungry," here the vanishing body stymies interpretive efforts.

These stories do not simply complicate characterizations based on subordination or agency. By invoking "the palpable unknown," to return to H. Porter Abbott's term, they produce spaces where, despite a desire for understanding, "the construction of knowledge stops."[19] Readers are caught between the desire to make sense of contradictions and the acceptance of a multiplicity that eludes cohesive interpretation.

The ambiguities of both stories invoke curiosity, particularly because much of the pleasure of reading involves solving mysteries or finding out "what really happened," but they never fulfill that curiosity. They disturb what Abbott refers to as the conventional "reading contract." Most fiction, Abbott contends, enables people to annex otherness through cognitive mastery. Literature depends on this process of annexation "as a condition that gives fiction its readability and appeal." However, "[u]nreadable characters intrude on this compact by removing the veil of readability and exposing the need for mastery that is generally hidden from us."[20] More important, they call on readers "to adopt a stance of humility and respect before the human unknowable."[21] Warner's unreadable characters call on readers to accept stories they cannot necessarily make sense of. This is inevitably an uncomfortable process, as it involves giving up claims to cognitive authority. Yet it may be a foundation for humility and respect toward other people, well beyond the moment of reading. Since both stories centre on vulnerable young women, they push readers to assess their ways of reading people in positions of vulnerability. By calling on readers to open themselves to that which exceeds their understanding, the stories suggest that responses to others in need can only be provisional and subject to change, and the responsibility they involve can never be fully discharged.

These stories do not just call on readers to interpret their *characters* differently. They ask who and what is excluded by the interpretive frameworks we apply to other people. To borrow Sara Ahmed's formulation, who do we define as "strange" in order "to secure [our] being – [our] place – [our] presence – in the world"?[22] Moreover, who is left out of the frameworks that secure our sympathy in the face of suffering? "No One Goes Hungry" tacitly poses the last question through the contrast between the sweeping title and the narrow cast of characters. The ironic title acknowledges the widespread problem of hunger in the United States, where the story takes place, in opposition to the narrator's reflection that in a country with this much food, no one should ever go hungry. Yet the one person who gains the narrator's sympathy is the vulnerable teenage girl: not her obese and aggressive (but starving) father, nor any of the other homeless and hungry people in the United States. This contrast prods readers to think about who lies outside their own witnessing gaze and what cultural and imaginative frameworks contribute to those exclusions. "The Belled Girl," for its part, provokes both sympathy and satisfaction as Phoebe's voice supplants the ones that discredit her. Yet since the story "gives voice" to Phoebe though fantastical means – the bells that may or may not be products of delusion – it hints that both sympathy and satisfaction thwart attention to people whose vulnerabilities cannot be redressed so easily.

These stories show that even nuanced efforts to understand a person's life can never grasp that life in full. Moreover, they call attention to the ways efforts to make sense of another person's life can act as forms of violence. Warner calls on readers to read differently. She invites them to respect experiences and identities that outstrip their understanding, and she asks them to consider what lives they fail to see when they respond with fascination or compassion to suffering subjects.

TRANSFORMING STORIES OF THE MIDDLE EAST

A number of Warner's short stories challenge the interpretive frameworks of readers in a more overtly political context. Since the new millennium she has written several stories responsive to violence in the Middle East, particularly the "war on terror" and the Israeli-Palestinian conflict. Warner's Middle East stories operate as metonyms for collective experiences at the same time as they show that one story, whether fiction or non-fiction, can never account for the experiences of an entire group. They challenge readers to move beyond compassion for their characters to recognize broader, more systematic injustices that risk falling outside individualized frameworks of sympathy.

Warner has been involved in Middle Eastern literary scholarship since the turn of the millennium. She is on the advisory board of New York University Press's Library of Arabic Literature. She became a Distinguished Visiting Professor at New York University Abu Dhabi in January 2012. In 2013, in collaboration with Clare Finburgh, she translated an excerpt from *Archaeology: Twelve Miniatures* by Moroccan writer Abdelfattah Kilito, a figure she speaks of often.[23] She has also become increasingly involved in activism regarding conflicts in the Middle East and the rights of refugees. She has signed open letters in response to Israeli government actions in the Israeli-Palestinian conflict.[24] As I mentioned in the Introduction, in 2015 she started a project to develop storytelling initiatives among refugee populations.

Warner's interest in representations of the Middle East stems from her childhood in Cairo and underpins her 2011 study *Stranger Magic: Charmed States and the Arabian Nights* as well as her novel-in-progress *Inventory of a Life Mislaid*. But it also stems from her abiding concern with social justice activism. In a 2015 interview with M. Lynx Qualey for New York University Press's Library of Arabic Literature, Warner asserted, "I think that the only thing someone like myself, who's a reader and a writer, can do in the present dangerous and very distressing situation of the world's conflicts, is to try and read across cultures, in order to understand a bit more."[25] Implicit here is not just an effort to learn about the conflicts in the Middle East, but a desire to move past the popular discourses that often shape public perceptions. Her short story "Cancellanda," first published in the journal *Raritan*, marks an effort to respond to the 2003 Iraq War. Over the following decade she wrote "At Night through a Gap" and "They Make a Desert and Call It Peace," both initially conceived for audio performance and inspired by the Arab-Israeli conflict, though the three stories also allude to other sites of violence, from the Vietnam War and the Siege of Sarajevo to Northern Ireland's Bloody Sunday. "At Night through a Gap" and "They Make a Desert and Call It Peace" were revised and republished in *Fly Away Home*, the former under the title "Breadcrumbs" and the latter under the title "Sing for Me."

In each case, Warner humanizes people whose voices are lost beneath Western political rhetoric and news media about the Middle East. Her stories oppose discourses that present the Arab world as "other" and Arab women as silent victims, which, as Warner observes, "happens far too glibly today."[26] They challenge "an imaginative geography of West versus East, us versus Muslims, cultures in which First Ladies give speeches [about human rights] versus others where women shuffle around silently in burkas."[27] Each story centres on a woman bearing witness to violence. To borrow a phrase that Warner uses about Victoria Brittain's *Shadow Lives*, a study of the families of men imprisoned in England as part of the "war on terror," her own Middle East stories take "a line of sight at an angle, and acknowledge the dignity and perseverance and survival skills of individuals under extreme pressure."[28] In this way the stories echo *The Lost Father*, *Indigo*, and *The Leto Bundle*. Their female protagonists, insisting on self-definition in the face of interlocking restrictions, are literary descendants of the Pittagora women, Sycorax and Ariel, and Leto and her daughter Phoebe. Warner's depictions of these complex responses to adversity are particularly important in light of the ways empathy both circulates and is denied to inhabitants of the Middle East. Empathy is available "in abundance for oppressed women in Islamic states," but is not granted as easily to men, who are regularly stereotyped as embodiments of Islamist oppression.[29] Moreover, the empathy accorded to oppressed women and children often attenuates in response to signs of agency or claims for justice. It dissipates even further when Middle Eastern citizens arrive as refugees at US or UK borders.[30]

However, these stories do not simply evoke empathetic or compassionate responses. A politics of compassion does not necessarily lead to a politics of human rights, which would recognize claims to justice by those who have suffered and would critique ongoing injustice on a broad scale. Too often, compassion situates "the powerful Western eye/I as the judging subject, never called upon to cast her gaze at her own reflection."[31] By contrast, I argue that Warner's Middle East stories suggest acts of witness call for exploration of "the wider public's complicity, including our own, in atrocities that continue to be committed in the here and now."[32]

On one level, "Cancellanda" tells a story of suffering and resistance. It provides an alternative to the dehumanization that characterizes so much Euro-American political rhetoric on the Middle East. The story offers a complex picture of an Iraqi woman at the onset of the US invasion of Iraq. It explores the human costs of the "war on terror," the many layers of day-to-day life and community destroyed by the war, and the capacity for courage and defiance within vulnerability. But it does more than that, pushing readers to ask what their responsibilities are as witnesses and what accountability they may hold for violence carried out in the Middle East.

A modernized version of the biblical story of Sodom, "Cancellanda" depicts the bombing of Sodom by soldiers from an unnamed country. Warner started writing the story after seeing news coverage of the march on Basra in 2003, though she has mentioned that she was also thinking about the 1972 napalm bomb at Trang Bang, Vietnam, fictionalized in *The Leto Bundle*, and the destruction at Sarajevo and Mostar during the Bosnian Genocide.[33] In an introduction to the story, Warner explains that she was galvanized by the interplay in the news between "two recurring pictures, the charred dead on the road, the burning city in the distance." The juxtaposition of distance and intimacy brought her "face to face with the reality that people live in these places under fire," forcing her to look directly at the personal cost of war. "Cancellanda" does the same to readers.[34]

The attack on Sodom is described in retrospect by the invading soldiers, their ally Lot, and his wife and daughters. Lot's wife Rahab offers a counterpoint to their abstractions, her narrative focused on the day-to-day details of her family's lives. In Warner's words, the story is written "as a kind of chorale for voices,"[35] giving the impression of a series of interviews or testimonies. At a plot level, though, the characters cannot be testifying *to* someone, for Rahab dies before she could ever do so. This means readers are interpellated as witnesses as the text allegorizes the losses of Iraqi civilians and imagines the effects of the war on a single family.

Rahab's memories challenge the reduction of Iraqi lives to the rhetoric of war, a challenge particularly important given that the stories of Iraqis killed in the "war on terror" have received low global circulation.[36] Rahab recalls "the crying of a baby next door through the wall, and the prostitute who lives in the next street and stands on the corner of ours, scratching her thighs … the sounds of our house in the night and the lumps in the mattress we've had since we were first married."[37] In a strategy reminiscent of *The Lost Father*, Warner conjures Rahab's past through sensory details: "Reality is the rhythm of the day, the fitfulness of sleep in older years, the ebbing of appetite too, the buttons you remember from the dress you wore when you were ten, it's the way your granny's hair smelled when you leant forward to kiss her goodnight."[38] These descriptions simultaneously evoke empathy and refuse to define Warner's characters through the lens of conflict. In Warner's 2015 Holberg Lecture, she quoted the Palestinian poet Mourid Barghouti musing, "The worst thing about wars is that they reduce the enemy to a single characteristic. The country ceases to be history, language, architecture, theatre, gardens, legends … The whole of history is now today, and today has become a reduction of every yesterday."[39] Rahab's narrative invites readers to view the Middle East in alternative ways, in which "histories might be recounted in their complexity, and accountability might be understood apart from the claims of vengeance."[40] Re-centring attention away from the battlefield, Warner undermines the authoritative power of Western media coverage and reveals the many ways in which war ruptures individual and communal lives.

The end of the story portrays both intimate suffering and courage. Rahab, fleeing the city with her family, turns back to look at the bombs, and her body is engulfed by fire. Rahab narrates her final moments: "Its heat takes me in its arms and wraps me close, so close … The fire is trying to eat me too, from my toes to the tips of my fingers and the ends of my hair."[41] Her vivid death contrasts with the portrayals of Iraqi deaths in British and North American news media, where "[o]ur own acts of violence do not receive graphic coverage … and so they remain acts that are justified in the name of self-defense, but by a noble cause, namely, the rooting out of terrorism."[42] Much like Warner's portraits of Sycorax in *Indigo*, horribly maimed when the British settlers burn her out of her tree, and Phoebe in *The Leto Bundle*, flayed by napalm, "Cancellanda" instantiates Rahab as a body in pain, forcing readers to look directly at the effects of a bomb on human flesh. At the same time, the story insists on her strength. When Rahab turns back she refuses to let others, whether her husband or the soldiers, dictate what she sees or how she sees it. As Daniela Corona argues, Rahab's "final parting look" at Sodom serves as "an act of cultural resistance and of self-affirmation as a woman."[43] The inspiration behind the character was sparked by a 1996 sculpture called "Lot's Wife" by artist Kiki Smith, a friend of Warner's. In Warner's words, Smith sculpted Lot's wife with "her flesh drooping and her limbs blasted, her legs ending in stumps," but the figure sparkles with a patina of salt, "heroic in her tragedy." Like the sculpture, Rahab "has presence ... [She] resists her annihilation. Her own *cancellation.*"[44]

However, Rahab's metamorphosis hints that she cannot be defined through either the suffering she endures or the resilience she demonstrates. Rahab transforms into "a living archive" as she contemplates the destruction of Sodom.[45] Her memories express both personal and collective identity. Moreover, whereas Lot's wife becomes a pillar of salt, a static object, Rahab is transformed into fire, an entity with the power to transform, purify, and destroy. Constantly changing shape, she becomes something that cannot be touched or held down. Just as Rahab takes a form that cannot be pinned down, "Cancellanda" prevents readers from pinning her down at an interpretive level, like so many characters in Warner's fiction. Warner shows that just as one story can never encompass a person's identity, it can never convey a community or culture in any complete way. The fragmentary nature of Rahab's memories illustrates this impossibility, reminding readers that no story can provide a complete account of a person, let alone a complex social and political context. In this way "Cancellanda" opposes a history of imperialist narratives whereby European writers assumed the ability to master the Middle East – a phenomenon that takes different but related form in the twenty-first century. The imperial fantasy of "the illicit penetration of the hidden and gendered spaces of 'the Islamic World'" is echoed by US State Department rhetoric about Islamist oppression of women and mass-marketed life writing about Middle Eastern women that promises to let readers into the secret world "behind the veil."[46] "Cancellanda" subverts that desire by offering readers only fragments of a life. Though the protagonist narrates her experiences, she is not fully conveying "the real"[47] – either making an entire life visible or providing a transparent view of the violence in her country.

As Rahab recalls the smell of her grandmother's hair, the cry of the neighbour's child, and the way her husband would call her name, the story leaves readers grappling with irresolvable questions. Should they accept the image of Rahab's body as a cenotaph, as Warner suggests in an introduction to the story,[48] or insist on the corporeality of that body, in pain as it burns? Does the story enjoin readers to witness the violation of Rahab's body or "[t]he violation of the body of the people," to borrow a phrase from Wendy Hesford and Wendy Kozol?[49] Warner has acknowledged that she strove to unsettle readers through the uncertainties of the text. She followed "the vagaries of Genesis, where the motives and the highly compressed succession of events inspire a queasy unease in the reader."[50] Drawn to the story of Sodom because of its gaps and unanswered questions, she reproduces those gaps in ways that bar readers from any position of analytic authority. To read an individual trauma as metaphor may be its own act of violence, co-opting that trauma into one's own interpretive system and abstracting away the pain involved. But Rahab is a fiction, and so reading her as an individual rather than a metaphor may do even greater violence, enabling readers to evade questions of ethics and responsibility and simply grieve for the dying woman within the text.

Warner's story calls attention to the ways in which our lives (all people's lives) are bound up in one another's. Selves are "invariably in community, impressed upon by others, impinging upon them as well."[51] As Rahab recalls her granny's face and smell, her husband's voice, and the young man who courted her daughter Belsaba, the story emphasizes the ways these people have shaped her. Repeated references to these networks of relations show that it is impossible to define an individual outside of that person's relationships to others. As Butler insists, "it is not just that this or that body is bound up in a network of relations, but that the body, despite its clear boundaries, or perhaps precisely by virtue of those very boundaries, is defined by the relations that make its own life and action possible."[52] The mingling voices in the text, as Rahab, her family, her neighbours, and even the US soldiers each deliver short monologues, emphasize this point. Moreover, Rahab's stories depict not only family members, but also people whose names she does not know, showing that the self is constituted by people well beyond the boundaries of family or community. Through Rahab's memories, "Cancellanda" intimates that, as Jill Stauffer argues, we must "think differently about how we come to be who we are, have what we have, and, accordingly, what we owe to the larger world."[53] The text suggests that bearing witness to the Iraq war requires that readers approach it as part of their history and their story, no matter where they are.

By directing readers away from the body at the centre of the story, Warner enjoins them to "look again" at the many Iraqis left out of Euro-American coverage of the war.[54] US and UK media outlets covering the "war on terror" emphasized military "shock and awe" tactics and conquering troops, with relatively few photos of casualties, damaged homes, or images from Iraqi perspectives.[55] When news media and human rights groups did represent Iraqis, it was often in decontextualized spectacles of suffering, without local community relationships or networks of support and solidarity.[56] Notably, even in the years since "Cancellanda" was first published, the human cost of the "war on terror" has been largely excluded from public view. The US–led multinational force in Iraq counted American deaths between 2003 and 2012, but did not keep a sustained record of Iraqi deaths. Among humanitarian organizations, debate rages about how to count casualties; methods based on passive investigation have yielded figures between 100,000 and 200,000, while active investigation methods estimate between 500,000 and one million deaths, possibly more.[57] In both the US and the UK, public willingness to investigate systematic rights violations has been low.[58] Even when official investigations of abuse have occurred, they have tended to focus on individual cases, allowing governments and a broader citizenry to avoid grappling with the scale of the accusations and attendant questions of responsibility. "Cancellanda" asks readers to consider the lives – and deaths – they do not see. Warner points out that all of the people affected by the war have a claim to human rights, even if – like the unnamed prostitute scratching her thighs on the corner – they are not easy to empathize with as emblems of suffering or dignity. Thus she invites readers to consider when empathy for individualized suffering distracts from stronger forms of mutual accountability. The social networks conjured by Rahab's memories gesture toward the potential for solidarity, cooperation, and interpersonal support that a simple politics of compassion and a focus on individualized trauma cannot account for.

By calling attention to "the instabilities inherent to boundary-making between self and other,"[59] Warner implicates herself and her readers in the violence of the Iraq war. In this way, she complicates the idea that the story invites reading across distance. "Cancellanda" suggests that, as Sara Ahmed contends, "there is a danger in assuming proximity *or* distance as the basis of an ethics. An ethics that assumes distance as its point of entry, fails to recognise the implication of the self in the encounter, and the responsibility the self has for the other to whom one is listening."[60] In the encounter with Warner's story, "'one' does not stay in place, or one does not stay safely at a distance (there is no space which is not implicated in the encounter)."[61] As in Derrida's formulation of hospitality, here the reader's place within existing social structures is unsettled.[62] Yet that unsettlement does not just result from a willingness to "give place" to another person. It comes from willingness to question the institutions and discourses that define one's social position and that present Iraqi lives as distant from Western readers.

Rahab disappears at the end of the story, her narrative lost among the countless losses in Sodom. The last word belongs to Lot: "We're on the threshold of a new time," he proclaims. "This is history in the making. It's a shame she isn't here to see it all happen. She would have seen how wrong she was."[63] Lot's oversimplification and Rahab's death call attention to the stories in Iraq that will never be told firsthand and that must somehow be commemorated. The title underscores this need. The word "cancellanda" refers to discarded manuscript pages or page proofs, stories that remain unfinished and unread.[64] Like *The Leto Bundle*, "Cancellanda" places the onus on readers to imagine refugee stories they have not encountered in the news or other mainstream media. It calls on them to look for the people absented by abstract descriptions and distant shots of burning cities. It insists that readers listen to the people in those spaces when they do tell their stories, while recognizing that those stories are always fragments of complex histories, mediated by the context of narration and the perceptions, goals, and desires of the speaker and listener.

"Breadcrumbs," written five years later, joins "Cancellanda" in encouraging readers to examine what lives and experiences might be excluded by their acts of witness. It raises the "question of how and when 'we' become emotionally attached to the bodies" of Middle Eastern women, a question Gillian Whitlock poses with reference to Afghan women. It asks, as Whitlock does, "When do these lives matter? When do life narratives give face and authority to these lives? How do 'we' become open to this haunting gaze? When do we look away (because of course we do)?"[65] Warner initially wrote the story under the title "At Night through a Gap" for a project called "1001 Nights Cast: A Durational Performance," created by performance artist Barbara Campbell. Every night from June 2005 to March 2008, Campbell gave an online reading of a story that a participant had written for the project during the day. The stories were inspired by excerpts that Campbell selected from news articles about the Middle East, and each one had a limit of 1001 words.[66] Campbell's project arose from the realization, during the Iraq War, that "what we knew of the Middle East was being relayed to us by reports from 'embedded' journalists acting as our proxy, but partisan, witnesses."[67] Warner's story echoes "Cancellanda" in telling a story of violence in the Middle East from the perspective of a woman confronted by an occupying force.

Much like "Cancellanda," on the surface "Breadcrumbs" can be read as a story of individual trauma and resilience. Desperate to find her children after being separated from them by an attack on her Gaza village, Maryam travels from one refugee camp to another. She cuts her ID photo into pieces and leaves a fragment at each one so that her children will recognize her from an eye, nose, or mouth. Her metaphorical fragmentation, much like Rahab's fragmentary narrative in "Cancellanda," literalizes the capacity of trauma to create "a violent rupture, or shattering break, that defies conventional narration."[68] At the same time, it illustrates Maryam's strength in the face of oppression. By dividing her picture into fragments, she insists on ownership over her body in opposition to the soldiers that drive her away from her home. She fights back against a double silencing, first by the violence against her community and then by the vulnerability of her status as a refugee. Telling her story becomes another way of asserting her voice. Like Rahab, Maryam recounts her story in her own words, once again challenging political discourses that present Middle Eastern women as either dangerous or mute. She speaks up when one colleague asks another how she came "here," to the unnamed city and hospital where "Breadcrumbs" takes place. Responding to a question not directed toward her, she tacitly proclaims that hers is a story she needs to tell and her colleagues need to hear. While her colleagues may fail to hear the weight of her story, she offers them – and readers – a provocation to think about the effects of the Israeli-Palestinian conflict and their own relationship to it.

Thus, the circumstances of the telling and the way Maryam tells her story are as important as its content. Maryam's tale is an active construction. She chooses when and how to tell it. "Breadcrumbs" provides a reminder that while acts of witnessing by people subjected to violence are often seen as unmediated forms of access to historical information,[69] they are always *acts*. To see Maryam's story as a transparent window onto her experience would be to deny her agency as a witness and speaker. Moreover, while Maryam's story gives the illusion of closure, with a happy ending and a reunited family, it ultimately leaves more questions than answers. As I pointed out in the introduction to this chapter, Warner undermines the desire for closure through Maryam's final words. The original, online version complicates the apparent closure of the story further. A nurse asks when the attack on Maryam's home took place, and Maryam points toward the ongoing nature of the Arab-Israeli conflict: "Look at me and you see how long it's been since the intifada started, and I've been here since …"[70] She trails off and never finishes the sentence. At the end, when a listener observes that Maryam has not answered the original question of how she came to this country, she does not respond; a colleague declares that a tale for another night. These responses undercut the sense that her narrative offers a complete account of her experience. Furthermore, they show that Maryam's story is not simply hers; it represents the experiences of a community.

Warner persistently hints at how much lies outside this one story. Maryam points out the impossibility of describing her children: "what do you say? My son is six, he has dark curly hair ... My daughter is eight, she's so pretty your heart melts, and she has a chip on her first front tooth from falling over as she was running one afternoon?" (*FAH* 195, ellipsis in the original). These fleeting, unconnected moments bear the weight of infinite unarticulated scenes. Like "Cancellanda," the tale is built on compression. A whole narrative of struggle, self-assertion, and courage is buried beneath Maryam's laconic statement that once her daughter recognized her photo, "[i]t took another five days but we were re-united" (*FAH* 195). The words on the page only hint at the pain of the separation. Maryam's story ends with reunion, but the psychic fragmentation often undergone by trauma survivors does not heal so easily.[71] The juxtaposition between the gaps in Maryam's story and the satisfaction of her listening colleagues offers a reminder that for stories of refugees to gain wide circulation, they often have to follow familiar conventions, such as journeys from danger to safety in the "West."[72] The original title, "At Night through a Gap," brings to mind the gap between the story Maryam's colleagues hear, with its happy ending, and the story Maryam tells. It underscores the effort readers must make to bridge that distance.

The original title, with its allusion to separation, also hints at the many dislocations caused by the conflict. This one story of separation and reunion stands in for widespread separations. Sherene Seikaly describes the Israeli-Palestinian conflict as a "condition of perpetual separation," a "relentless separation of Palestinians [from one another] ... through war, occupation, the separation wall."[73] The online version of the story places greater emphasis on the dislocations that lie outside Maryam's story. When she begins her narrative her voice changes, "becoming deeper and older," as if she is speaking of something beyond her own experience.[74] She becomes an embodiment of cultural memory, much like Rahab in "Cancellanda." Thus, while the quest narrative that structures the story may be a highly individualistic genre, the text directs readers toward broader structural conditions. "Breadcrumbs" may seem like a liberal individualist tale about one woman heroically overcoming tragedy through strength and perseverance – a familiar narrative frame that de-emphasizes collective responsibility and collective potential for transformation.[75] But Maryam's fleeting references to the larger context of the conflict hint at the incompletion of that story.

In alluding to other, untold stories, "Breadcrumbs" evokes Shahrazad, the celebrated storyteller of the sprawling Middle Eastern fantasy collection the *Arabian Nights*. The *Arabian Nights* is not just the inspiration behind Campbell's project; it is a text that Warner has analyzed at great length, most notably in *Stranger Magic*. In the well-known frame tale, the sultan Shahriyar learns that his wife has cheated on him. In revenge, he vows to marry a virgin every night and behead her in the morning. Shahrazad, daughter of the vizier charged with providing the virgins, insists on marrying the sultan. Every night she starts telling him a story, then breaks off in the middle so he has to keep her alive to assuage his curiosity. The Shahrazad motif in Warner's story points to the capacity of storytelling to connect people across political gulfs. Shahrazad's stories are not just clever ploys to save herself, but ethical and political lessons. They teach the sultan that women can be faithful and that people who have been hurt can find comfort by substituting kindness for vengeance. As Warner observed in a keynote lecture at the Edward Said Memorial Conference in 2013, Shahrazad's stories depict people learning to trust others whom they had defined as enemies.[76] Moreover, through Shahrazad's insistence on marrying the sultan, the *Arabian Nights* offers a portrait of mutual responsibility predicated both on the vulnerability of all human beings and on our capacity to respond to the needs of one another. Yet while this intertext reveals optimism about the power of stories in the face of conflict, the gaps in Maryam's story and the many things she does not say remind readers that stories of trauma "can never offer terminal solutions."[77] Stories that people tell about their own traumas may help them work through their experiences or make human rights claims, but do not necessarily provide catharsis or comfort. Fictions about trauma, like real-life testimonies, can serve as spurs for change. They can catalyze new relationships and promote efforts to increase justice. But they can only form part of the process of working toward repair.

The frame tale of "Breadcrumbs" offers a reminder that stories of violence can contribute to change or promote the status quo. A first-person narrator listens to Maryam's story from her hospital bed. The narrator's dreamlike prose, like the satisfied sighs of Maryam's colleagues, is at odds with Maryam's harrowing story. Though the text describes the narrator feeling "awkward" in a net of intravenous lines, her tone is meditative, almost trancelike. She describes how "the moon was soaring and she was carrying us," with "us" referring to the narrator and the rest of the hospital denizens, but extending to readers as well (*FAH* 192). Thus readers share the pleasure of eavesdropping with a narrator who seems to experience no discomfort, guilt, or anger in the face of Maryam's tale, and who has the power to turn away and stop listening at any time. When the story ends with the narrator falling asleep, Warner shows how easily people can be distracted or turn away from suffering. On the other hand, the narrator's position in a hospital bed demonstrates that she is not simply a distant witness; she is dependent on Maryam and her colleagues for her well-being. Thus the frame tale invites readers to question their own positions relative to Maryam and her story, and to ask what individual or collective responsibilities they might bear in response to conflict in the Middle East.

"Breadcrumbs" resists the illusion that the losses resulting from the Arab-Israeli conflict can be embodied in a single person or story. It joins "Cancellanda" in suggesting that witnessing involves uncertainty and vulnerability. Warner asks readers to hear not just the trauma of Maryam's tale but the ongoing reverberations that she does not articulate. She calls on readers to do more than "chuckle and sigh appreciatively" like Maryam's fictional listeners, and instead ask what they can do to help repair lifeworlds fractured by violence. Like "Cancellanda," "Breadcrumbs" enjoins readers to bear witness to events they may know little about, and to declare themselves accountable for distant suffering even if they know only the barest details of that suffering.

Warner returns to these themes in "Sing for Me." Like "Breadcrumbs," "Sing for Me" was written for performance, this time for BBC Radio 4's *From Fact to Fiction* program. Similar to Campbell's project, the Radio 4 series asks writers to respond to a piece of news, though the writers pick the news items themselves. Warner wrote the story in 2010 in response to two events. The first was an Israeli raid on a humanitarian aid flotilla that attempted to breach a naval blockade on Gaza. The second was the conclusion of the Saville Inquiry, established twelve years earlier to assess who was to blame for Bloody Sunday, when British troops killed thirteen unarmed protesters at a 1972 civil rights march in Northern Ireland.[78] Once again, what seems to be a relatively straightforward fiction about the importance of testimony and witnessing calls on readers to bear witness to what lies outside the bodies on the page.

Whereas "Cancellanda" and "Breadcrumbs" focus on a Middle Eastern woman testifying to the violence she has endured, "Sing for Me" focuses on the daughter and the wife of a perpetrator of violence, a military captain in an unnamed country. Like *Indigo*, which reflects Warner's struggle to come to terms with her status as a descendant of colonizers, "Sing for Me" explores the responsibilities and guilt that accrue to the families of perpetrators. It joins Warner's other Middle East stories in calling on readers to bear witness to violence in ways that may challenge their sense of who they are and the webs of relationships to which they belong.

The story centres on the daughter's effort to convince her father to testify about an atrocity variously referred to as "Operation May 12," "The Manoeuvres," "The Mistake," and "The Outrage." The climax occurs when the captain offers his daughter, Maia, anything she wants if she will sing for him on his birthday. In a variation on the biblical tale of Herod and Salome, Maia asks her father to testify before the coming inquiry, knowing that he will not be able to refuse after the promise he made her. Whereas Salome perpetuates violence, asking Herod for the head of John the Baptist because he criticized her mother's marriage, Maia strives to repair the violence carried out by her father.

On the surface, this story is an allegory about the importance of publicly condemning acts of violence. The original title, "They Make a Desert and Call It Peace," critiques justifications of violence. The line comes from the *Agricola*, a biography written by the first-century historian Tacitus to honor his father-in-law, a Roman general and governor of Britain. Tacitus depicts a Celtic general named Calgacus excoriating the Romans: "they plunder, they butcher, they ravish, and call it by the lying name of 'empire.' They make a desert and call it peace."[79] In Warner's story the captain does the same thing. He couches his resistance to transparency in speeches about protecting the nation, language familiar from oppressive regimes that range from the apartheid government in South Africa to the juntas in Argentina. He describes the military action in which he killed an innocent man as an effort at "making the peace" (*FAH* 184).

Yet the story intimates that naming atrocities – testifying and bearing witness to testimony – is only one step in the larger process of witnessing. Once again, the story has a seemingly happy ending. The captain agrees to testify before the government inquiry he had resisted. But Warner hints at the limits of official inquiries and truth commissions even while insisting on their importance.[80] She points toward the scope of suffering they invariably exclude. She invites readers to consider, as truth commissions often fail to do, "how widely the weight of responsibility for past [and present] injustice ought to be felt."[81] Central to the story are the transformations of the captain's wife and daughter due to their roles in the peace movement, but neither one is included in the government inquiry. Moreover, the courage to testify and the honesty the captain shows by keeping his promise fall outside the scope of a traditional war crimes tribunal. A tribunal cannot account for the ways the conflict has fractured his family or for what it means to live with a husband or father who has committed war crimes.

Nor can it accommodate the new relationships that emerge from Maia's request and the captain's compliance. The story alludes to these limits by continuing past the captain's appearance at the inquiry, a structural choice hinting that the changes the family undergoes are ongoing, and no single narrative can account for them all.

"Sing for Me" can be seen as a coming-of-age story for both Maia and her mother, and from this angle it gives the illusion of closure, much like "Breadcrumbs." As the mother struggles "to unpick what happened" to her daughter as part of the peace movement (*FAH* 186), Maia's activism gives her mother the strength to express her own fears and hopes. In the version published in *Fly Away Home*, the mother's newfound self-expression is reflected in her status as narrator. Maia herself comes to adulthood by persuading her father to testify and by transforming her mother, who reflects, "That a child should give breath to a parent, isn't that against nature?" (*FAH* 191). These transformations provide a satisfying ending, as does the resolution of the central conflict, Maia's fight to get her father to confess his actions. The tight focus on the three family members – the captain, his daughter, and his wife – contributes to this sense of closure. But this plotline raises many questions: Who are the unnamed victims of the massacre? What happened on that day – and the day before, and the day after, and the following weeks and months? What are the social and economic legacies of the conflict? Do the people subjugated on the day of the massacre face ongoing violence? The story hints at these questions through cryptic references to the broader context, "the ones whose homes have been ransacked and wrecked and demolished, the innocent who've been shot and killed," the victims to whom Warner refers only as "they" (*FAH* 188).

As in "Cancellanda" and "Breadcrumbs," the stories that exceed the inquiry point toward the complex responsibilities of readers. "Sing for Me" implies that as witnesses to the violence within Warner's stories, and to the real-world violence that inspired them, readers must oppose efforts to cover up injustice. They must commemorate lives cut short as well as lives fractured by the loss of loved ones and the loss of trust in state institutions. They must read beyond the frames of official news stories and legal inquiries and recognize day-to-day oppressions overlooked by journalists. Warner calls on readers to pay attention to the stories they hear in the news but also to the stories they do not hear. She asks readers to refuse the false comfort that they are not responsible for what they do not know. Like the mother in "Sing for Me," who expands her experiential horizons as witness to the actions of her husband and daughter, Warner asks readers to open themselves to new intersubjective roles as witnesses to real-world violence.

Maia and her unnamed mother become models for readers. For both women, bearing witness becomes a source of transformation. Looking back on the moment when Maia asks her father to testify, her mother recalls, "I felt a hollow under my ribs, and a bird caged there flew up and out" (*FAH* 190). This image recurs in the closing paragraph: "when my daughter speaks, it is as if she's inside me, voicing my trapped soul. I feel it flutter like a bird trying out its wings" (*FAH* 191). Maia and her mother become doubles for one another, each one both parent and child, as Maia gives new life to her mother. In addition, Maia becomes a double for Rahab from "Cancellanda," whose memories keep alive the generations before her. She too becomes an embodiment of collective memory. As her mother thinks, "I warm myself at her fire," Warner invokes the power of fire to protect and inspire. She points toward the strength necessary to keep communal histories from being forgotten, and she intimates that readers, too, should take inspiration from her protagonist. Yet the story does not evoke straightforward feelings of identification, whereby readers might imagine bravely standing up to a perpetrator to demand justice. Knowing that the story was inspired both by the Saville Inquiry into Bloody Sunday and by the deaths of activists trying to breach an Israeli blockade on Gaza places a different kind of accountability on readers. It pushes them to ask why the outcry about the flotilla deaths was not louder or longer. In the months after Warner wrote the story, the United Nations Secretary General and the United Nations High Commissioner for Refugees launched inquiries; in Israel the Attorney General called a halt to police investigations. The story invites readers to ask why the deaths caused by the Israeli-Palestinian conflict so often fall outside the frames of Euro-American public discourse.

The indeterminate location and time period, as well as the dual inspirations of Gaza and Northern Ireland, encourage readers to question why some injustices loom large in cultural consciousness where others do not. "Sing for Me" takes place sometime in the twentieth or twenty-first centuries, with computers and other contemporary technology, but it could be set anywhere, and the conflict it depicts is nonspecific. This ambiguity may contribute to empathy and fellow-feeling by universalizing the experiences of mother and daughter, a strategy bolstered by Warner's emphasis on the mother's efforts to understand her daughter's transformations. In this respect the story risks undermining its insistence on naming violence. One could argue that it enables readers to overlook the conflict in Gaza and simply to engage in what Megan Boler calls "passive empathy."[82] It is easy to identify with the privileged Maia in her righteous indignation or with her mother's bafflement about the changes in her daughter. These are relatively universal experiences. However, the abstractness of the story and the interwoven historical inspirations also defamiliarize ongoing violence by encouraging readers to apply political and ethical frameworks from one situation to another. At the time when Warner wrote the story, Bloody Sunday had been officially condemned as an atrocity after decades of official refusal to hold the British army responsible. By connecting Bloody Sunday to a scene of violence in Gaza that received comparatively little public attention, the story challenges the normalization of the conflict in Gaza. Moreover, while mainstream Western journalism tends not to allude to colonialism in the context of the Israeli-Palestinian crisis,[83] placing these two histories side by side offers a reminder that the conflict is not easily separable from colonial histories. The story's invitation to historical comparison is a political tool. It contributes to what Michael Rothberg calls "multidirectional memory," the idea that making connections between the collective memories of different groups can contribute to new alliances and claims for justice.[84]

CONCLUSION

The texts I have analyzed in this chapter are stories "of storytelling," to borrow a phrase from Adam Zachary Newton.[85] From Louie and Mélusine, who are constantly performing, to Maryam and Rahab, recounting familial traumas, Warner's characters tell stories about who they are and what they have witnessed. Their testimonies are ways of both expressing and constructing themselves. They illustrate that "the human being is a narrator, an irrepressible maker-up of stories, a gossip, a reporter, a dreamer, an anthologist, a recycler of old stories," as Warner said in her 2015 Holberg Lecture in a riff on Tzvetan Todorov's term *l'homme récit*.[86] But their testimonies are also means of making the self opaque. Warner's stories point toward the instability and multiplicity of selves and the inability of narrative to contain them. The fluidity of identity has become a touchstone of postmodern thought, yet in Warner's stories it has important ethical and political consequences. Warner's portrayal of the fluidity of identity challenges reductive representations of other people, particularly in conditions of precarity. Moreover, it calls on readers to read beyond the life of the individual, to consider broader structural conditions alongside the interpretive frameworks that make it easy to overlook these conditions. It provokes recognition that "[a]ll stories emerge in the midst of complex and uneven relationships of power,"[87] and bearing witness to stories of injustice involves calling those relations of power into question.

Along with *The Lost Father*, *Indigo*, and *The Leto Bundle*, as well as Warner's early biographical work and war journalism, these short stories ask readers to acknowledge the limits of their understanding. It is worth noting that such acknowledgment is not always an ethical response, as James Phelan warns in an analysis of Toni Morrison's *Beloved*, another text that highlights the impossibility of pinning down its characters. Phelan reflects, "A white reader like myself may try to escape the pain – and any responsibility – by confessing, as I just did, the limits of his understanding."[88] For him, Morrison's novel blocks that resistance by calling on readers to witness the pain of slavery. Readers do not live the experiences of Morrison's title character Beloved or her mother Sethe, but in reading the novel, they "have, in a sense, lived *with* Beloved," and turning their backs on the suffering they have witnessed would be an act of cowardice.[89] Warner's stories, too, call for acts of witnessing that implicate readers in what they have seen. They insist that, as Fuyuki Kurasawa proclaims, "[i]ntegral to testimonial performances is an appeal to audiences that must in turn respond to it," for both the speaker and the addressee "are constructed through mutual recognition of each by the other."[90] As in *Indigo* and *The Leto Bundle*, this call to witness makes readers vulnerable to the needs of others, undermining liberal humanist views of the self-sufficient, autonomous self. It invites readers to ask how to answer for themselves in the face of violence – particularly violence done in their name or accepted by governments that represent them. In Derrida's terms, it poses the question: "How be responsible *for* them [for the questions and needs that come from strangers]? How answer for oneself when faced with them?"[91] These stories invite anagnorisis in the way Warner describes in her 2009 essay "Mirror-Readings": they can "discover oneself to oneself" by calling on readers to recognize their responsibility in the face of suffering.[92]

With readers predominantly in the United Kingdom and North America, Warner's Middle East stories initiate transnational acts of witnessing. Like *Indigo* and *The Leto Bundle*, they invite the formation of global communities predicated on the recognition that identities are intersubjective. They illustrate that "responsibility for justice and recovery is, rather than a narrow legal concern, the very broadest of obligations."[93] This responsibility includes questioning the frameworks that shape acts of witness, and this means acts of witness can never be complete. They must be continual efforts that open the witness to change by calling into question the justice of their positioning within intersecting networks of power.

For this reason, the texts hint at how difficult it is to construct ethical communities through witnessing. Within the stories, acts of witnessing lay the groundwork for new ways of relating, but the texts stop short of depicting their development. There is no obvious change in the relationships between Maryam and her co-workers, the mother in "Sing for Me" and the rest of her society, or Louie and Phoebe and their listeners. The narratives that emerge within the diegeses simply hold out the potential for new relations between characters. By extension, they urge readers to envision new ways of relating without providing any assurances or models.

In the next chapter, I extend my analysis of the ways Warner calls attention to the limits of readers' understandings of other people, communities, and cultures. There, I turn from fiction about conflict zones to histories of myths and fairy tales. These may seem like unintuitive texts for exploring the ethics of representation, but they reveal provocative formal strategies for unsettling presumptions of knowledge about individuals and cultural groups. I argue that like *Indigo*, *The Leto Bundle*, and Warner's Middle East stories, her cultural histories disrupt the idea that they can recover the voices of people subjected to silencing. They insist that the people and cultures they pay tribute to cannot be accounted for by any single narrative. This insistence is particularly crucial now, two decades into the twenty-first century, as political discourses that homogenize social and cultural groups are regularly mobilized to justify exclusions and cruelty. The widespread detention of immigrants and refusals of refugee rights are only two recent examples.

5

Nervous Histories

Resistance to Scholarly Mastery in Warner's Studies of Myths and Fairy Tales

As I have shown throughout this book, Warner's work continually confronts the question of how to combat "othering" through narrative without claiming an authority denied to the people she writes about or purporting to account for the complexities of their lives. This problem takes on an added dimension in Warner's cultural histories, because scholarly writing about the lives or cultures of people that have been labelled "others" can present those people as objects of knowledge, figures to be known and theorized by academics rather than producers of knowledge themselves. The history of colonialism illustrates the harm that can be done by such presumptions of knowledge, since colonial powers used the interpretation and classification of colonized peoples to justify social, economic, and political violence. As I pointed out in chapter 4, political and journalistic discourses that claim the authority to speak for marginalized groups, such as the rhetoric used to justify the Iraq War, can promote further divisions and subordinate the people they purport to protect.

In this chapter I turn to three of Warner's best-known books, *From the Beast to the Blonde*, *No Go the Bogeyman*, and *Stranger Magic*, to explore this quandary. Examining how these books unsettle presumptions of understanding reveals striking continuities between Warner's early non-fiction and her contemporary scholarship. Moreover, it exposes some ways in which the formal attributes of literary and cultural histories can convey ethical commitments toward the people and cultures they depict. *From the Beast to the Blonde*, *No Go the Bogeyman*, and *Stranger Magic* are primarily studies of stories rather than studies of people, and they focus on fantastical stories rather than realistic ones. However, they are all centrally concerned with people and cultures that have been "othered," whether defined as alien, excluded from dominant discourses, or persecuted outright. Warner explains that wanderers, fugitives, and oppressed figures pervade myths and fairy tales. The two genres "tell of child slaves, buying and selling women, abduction, tyranny, poverty, hunger and family conflicts," situations that still arise with terrible frequency.[1] Tales of exile, such as Dido leaving Tyre and Leto desperately seeking a place to give birth, offer critically important "myths for our time."[2] *From the Beast to the Blonde* traces a lineage of female storytellers left out of fairy tale histories that, until the late twentieth century, centred on Charles Perrault and the Brothers Grimm. *No Go the Bogeyman*, a study of responses to fear, culminates in an investigation of jokes and songs about cultural otherness and the ways they were re-appropriated in genres such as Afro-Caribbean calypso music. *Stranger Magic* explores the global influences exerted by the *Arabian Nights* and the diverse Middle Eastern cultures that produced them. Warner uses this exploration to combat centuries of Orientalist rhetoric and contemporary anti-Arab prejudices that have homogenized and devalued the "Arab world." In all three studies, she faces the challenge of paying tribute to silenced or devalued voices without subsuming those voices to her analysis or, indeed, purporting to instantiate them on the page.

One common response to the risk of subsuming the voices of other people to that of the writer is to turn to polyphony. Experimental anthropologists embraced polyphony in the 1980s as a means of creating space for "othered" voices rather than simply writing about them. In his introduction to the path-breaking book *Writing Culture*, James Clifford argued that recognizing dialogue as central to the production of the ethnographic text called into question the singular authority of the anthropologist.[3] Ethnographers began to define "native informants" as "co-authors" and "admit to the plurality of the ethnographic document."[4] Yet the inclusion of multiple voices in any text is limited by the conditions of production and reception that shape what informants (or co-authors) say or write and which articulations are recorded. Moreover, the polyphony of a text cannot undo the power relations between a scholar and the people she studies, particularly when the motives behind their speech acts differ. The disciplinary expectations and formal conventions of academic writing underpin the ways embedded voices are framed and confer an authority on the voice of the academic that does not necessarily accrue to the voices she studies.[5] As Patricia Yaeger observes, "In trying to give the subject enough headroom the anthropologist compensates with ample quotation. But the danger here is in using quotation in a subordinate fashion as confirming testimony."[6] A writer cannot simply use her text to let other voices speak for themselves. Even to stage the process of sharing authority depends on and confirms the authority of the writer.

I suggest that Warner's studies of myths and fairy tales offer a different response to this representational dilemma. The anecdotal and eclectic style of her studies subverts the desire for conclusions and metanarratives and, in this way, refuses to reduce people or cultures to objects of knowledge for the historian. All three books leap from story to story, interweaving myth, history, and cultural studies with exuberance. This eclecticism is familiar from all of Warner's work, whether fiction, journalism, or museum exhibitions. Reviewers frequently comment on her ability to make surprising connections. Omar Berrada once mused that Warner's scholarly essays read "like fast-paced digressive detective novels."[7] Yet what reviewers and critics have not addressed are the implications of this eclecticism. Warner's studies privilege anecdote over argument. They operate in the non-linear and digressive manner of an oral storyteller instead of following a clear chronological or argumentative structure. In this way they invite readers to make their own connections and thus to play an active role in constructing the arguments of the texts. The oral storytelling style also suggests that Warner's studies could take many different forms. Like fairy tales, which often have countless variations, Warner implies that each of her studies offers just some of many possible lenses onto her material – much like the journalistic and biographical work I analyzed in chapter 1. With their non-linear approach and seductive digressions, these books resist the conventional authority of the scholar, even if they cannot simply give up that authority to the people they represent.

I draw on the work of Kathleen Stewart and Patricia Yaeger to argue that Warner's studies of myths and fairy tales carry out "nervous writing": writing that draws attention to what it cannot represent. Stewart developed the concept of nervous writing, adapted from Michael Taussig's 1992 collection of anthropological essays *The Nervous System*, to describe a strategy for doing ethnography in impoverished coal mining communities in the West Virginia Appalachians. In her 1996 ethnography *A Space on the Side of the Road*, she describes nervous writing as writing that resists totalizing interpretive systems and insists "there is always something more to be said."[8] Yaeger, too, turns to "nervous writing" to embrace uncertainty about the writer's task. She adopts Stewart's approach in the context of writing about violent deaths as she grapples with the implications of turning the voices and bodies of other people "into 'text.'" She asks how to prevent "usurping others' worlds with our words" or "seeming to read bodies, when we may really be reading, then reinscribing our own figurations."[9] Warner, too, explores ways to prevent "usurping others' worlds with our words," asserting authority over those worlds while framing them for the consumption of readers. Her studies of myth and fairy tale evince a similar "nervousness" to Yaeger and Stewart's work. These books do not pin down the people or cultures they depict. Instead they accrete information in ways that provoke but do not fulfill the curiosity of readers. As in her biographical work and war journalism, Warner tacitly suggests that the people and cultures at the centre of her books cannot be captured by any overarching interpretive frame.

This is not to proclaim that Warner deliberately structured her fairy tale studies based on concerns with the ethics of representing other people. The eclectic and exploratory style of these books is a hallmark of her work. Moreover, Warner's fairy tale studies are not self-reflexive like Stewart's text, which foregrounds her interpretive role and her variable positions within the communities she studies. However, Warner's fairy tale studies, with their non-linear structure and anecdotal style, subvert reason as an organizing principle. While reviewers rightly praise Warner for her academic mastery, particularly her command of vast swathes of historical and literary information,[10] these books resist cohesive portrayals of people or cultures. As they jump from one topic, place, and time to another, they both evoke and exhibit openness to wonder, uncertainty, and further discovery. I read these digressions as transgressions, borrowing from Jacques Derrida's play on the relationship between digression and transgression.[11] Warner's digressions transgress the academic conventions that might lead readers to expect a cohesive and conclusion-driven argument. The stylistic elements that disrupt that cohesion also disrupt the stability of a space from which to draw conclusions. They not only show the limits of recuperative projects but unsettle readers by inviting them to re-assess the standpoints from which they read the world. In this way Warner's digressive style offers readers a foundation for reconceptualizing their relationships with others – all other people and people "othered" by social and political hierarchies.

Warner does not present her subjects as inherently strange or beyond understanding. To claim that a person or group is fundamentally beyond understanding reifies us-versus-them boundaries.[12] Images of strangeness, exoticism, and incomprehensibility have been central to colonial and Orientalist rhetoric for centuries. In addition, to see people other than oneself as ineffably strange or "other" risks atomizing all people at the expense of potential connection or coalition.[13] By contrast, Warner's studies suggest that any overarching interpretation of the texts they address or the people that produced them would inevitably oversimplify people, cultures, and historical moments. She subverts the desire for conclusive knowledge that would reinscribe unjust hierarchies as she insists that neither she nor readers can define the people and cultures she writes about.

THE ENIGMATIC VOICES OF THE STORYTELLERS IN *FROM THE BEAST TO THE BLONDE*

Like *Indigo* and *The Leto Bundle*, Warner's fairy tale study *From the Beast to the Blonde* is often seen as a recovery project, an effort to give voice to silenced women. Donald Haase labels *From the Beast to the Blonde* "[t]he best-known and most comprehensive work of scholarship" devoted to "recovering the female fairy-tale tradition."[14] But while Warner traces the work of female fairy tale tellers, she does not recover their voices in any straightforward way. To the extent that she can locate and include the voices of those women, that inclusion neither enables the women to speak for themselves nor undoes the ways in which they were silenced in the past. To label *From the Beast to the Blonde* an act of retrieval removes the fairy tale tellers from their cultural circumstances and ignores the constraints they faced. At the same time, it oversimplifies the complex personae adopted by many, which disable any effort to identify authentic voices in their texts. Hence, much like *Indigo* and *The Leto Bundle*, *From the Beast to the Blonde* simultaneously insists on the importance of a historically marginalized group and resists the authority to recover their voices. The eclectic organization and anecdotal structure of the book leave the storytellers "hard to grasp," to borrow Stewart's formulation. The female storytellers who ostensibly form the core of the text are threaded in and around tales by Aesop, La Fontaine, and Charles Perrault, Renaissance woodcuts about gossiping women, and laws about female cursing. The digressive structure suggests that the book could expand indefinitely without ever encapsulating its subjects.

From the Beast to the Blonde analyzes the development and transmission of European fairy tales. In opposition to a history of fairy tale studies centred on Charles Perrault and the Grimm brothers, the most famous disseminators of European fairy tales, Warner shows that these men were preceded and outnumbered by female storytellers. She gives pride of place to the *conteuses*, the women in the court of Louis XIV who inaugurated the literary fairy tale in the 1690s. The first half of the book focuses on the changing iconography of storytellers, from the Sibyl of Greco-Roman myth to the Victorian Mother Goose. In the second half of the book, Warner turns to some of the best-known fairy tales, such as "Cinderella" and "Sleeping Beauty," and she reads them as sources of subversive power, boundless worlds where "anything can happen" (*BB* xvi). She aligns herself with Angela Carter's view of the fairy tale as "a territory of freedom to express ... rebellion" (*BB* 193). In this way she makes a case for the power of female storytellers to challenge gender-based constraints.

Thus *From the Beast to the Blonde*, like *Wonder Tales*, Warner's 1994 collection of stories by the *conteuses*, rebels against the silencing of female storytellers. Warner makes common cause with Carter, Michèle Roberts, Sara Maitland, and others who revive folk and fairy tales through heroines who "reclaim the night."[15] She joins feminist fairy tale scholars of the 1980s and 1990s who "reassert women's ownership of the genre."[16] Examples include figures such as Karen Rowe and Jeannine Blackwell in the United States, and Marcelle Welch and Gabrielle Verdier in France, who argue for the importance of female fairy tale tellers and present fairy tales as tools for questioning patriarchal mores.[17] For Warner, fairy tales critique social structures that tellers could not question outright, and the tellers are counterparts for fairy godmothers in their determination to challenge social and cultural constraints. But despite the praise Warner garnered for recovering the marginalized voices of female storytellers, *From the Beast to the Blonde* shows that fairy tales never pass down the voices of their tellers complete or unmediated, and neither can the contemporary scholar.

A good deal of feminist fairy tale scholarship casts female storytellers as emblems of voice, and by extension presents itself as a retrieval of silenced voices.[18] However, *From the Beast to the Blonde* undermines the idea that celebrating the voices of the storytellers can overcome past silencing. Warner shows that to cast fairy tale tellers as emblems of voice is to ignore their material and social vulnerabilities. Instead, Warner juxtaposes the ideological rebellions permitted by fairy tales with the material conditions that gave rise to them, showing that the agency involved in telling fairy tales was often partial and compromised. While Lewis Seifert proclaims that *From the Beast to the Blonde* "emphasize[s] especially the various manifestations of subversion" in fairy tales,[19] Warner also calls attention to the constraints on such subversion.

On one hand, *From the Beast to the Blonde* presents storytellers as figures of creative power capable of working outside the social order. In this respect Warner is in line with Rowe, who casts the *conteuses* as "transmitters of culture" passing on "secret lore,"[20] and Blackwell, who contends that "active feminine narrative voices" in stories told by the Grimms' female contemporaries restored part of "the ... utopian core of the oral tale."[21] She echoes Welch and Verdier in arguing that the *conteuses* laid claim to a narrative authority that enabled them to assert their agency as women.[22] At the same time, she points out that telling fairy tales did not necessarily empower women in their day-to-day lives. Many of the women who took on the roles of Mother Goose and Mother Stork – nurses, governesses, servants, and widows – remained in acutely vulnerable socio-economic circumstances (e.g. *BB* 227–31). Re-centring them in the history of fairy tales does not counteract the vulnerabilities they faced or the social structures that entrenched those vulnerabilities.

But *From the Beast to the Blonde* suggests that avoiding over-generalized portraits of the storyteller's voice is not simply a matter of accruing examples of oppression, just as the omission of female storytellers from historical accounts cannot be corrected just by gathering examples of their speech. While Warner mines the lives of female storytellers for signs of both subordination and resistance, the book hints at her inability to redeem their marginalizations by telling their stories. The past is "triply mediated," as Susan Stanford Friedman writes, in this case through any records the storytellers produced; "the fragmentary and partial survival" of those records, "dependent upon the politics of documentation and the luck, skill, and persistence of the historian-as-detective"; and Warner's interpretive decisions.[23]

Warner's style and organization reflect these limitations. This does not mean that Warner intentionally structured the book to hint at the limits of her historical project. Yet the digressive nature of *From the Beast to the Blonde* calls attention to the impossibility of telling "the stories" of "the storytellers." The book is divided into "Part I: The Tellers" and "Part II: The Tales," but individually named storytellers feature less prominently in Part I than Part II. Chapter titles do not designate specific periods, places, or people, but announce broad themes, such as "The Old Wives' Tale: Gossips I," "Word of Mouth: Gossips II," and "No Hideous Hum: Sibyls I." Thus, if *From the Beast to the Blonde* is a book "on fairy tales and their tellers," as the subtitle proclaims, it is both a way of replacing female storytellers at the centre of a history of fairy tales, and a story about the impossibility of pinning them down.

Warner's chatty and anecdotal style simultaneously aligns her with the *conteuses* and leaves the *conteuses* out of reach. *From the Beast to the Blonde* presents the mythical Sibyl, a quintessential female storyteller, as a guide for Warner's opus, and Warner adopts the Sibyl's tools. She seduces readers into a journey that abjures the chronology of a traditional history book and instead traverses vast landscapes in the spirit of the adventurers who seek the Sibyl's cave. She moves from one country and period to another as thematic linkages present themselves. Her anecdotal style and adoption of the Sibyl as model echo the rhetoric of the *conteuses*, who associated themselves with the Sibyls. When she describes the "intimate speech … apparently spontaneous explanations … [and] gossipy parentheses" of the storytellers, she could easily be referring to her own writing (*BB* 25). The closeness of her style to that of the storytellers she analyzes is not just a gesture of solidarity; it also suggests that her work is no more authoritative than theirs. Perhaps more important, while Warner's storytelling style pays homage to the *conteuses* as Warner's literary ancestors, it paradoxically leaves them out of reach.

Warner often mentions female storytellers in passing. For example: "Oscar Wilde's father … used to ask for stories as his fee from his poorer patients: his wife Speranza Wilde then collected them"; "At the end of the century, the omnivorous Scottish folklorist Andrew Lang relied on his wife Leonora Alleyne, as well as a team of women editors, transcribers and paraphrasers, to produce … the *Red, Yellow, Green, Blue, Rose Fairy Books*" (*BB* 20–1). Like *Indigo*, *The Leto Bundle*, and Warner's short stories of witnessing, *From the Beast to the Blonde* is haunted by stories that Warner gestures toward but does not tell. On the surface, women such as Speranza Wilde and Leonora Alleyne become emblems of voice, contributing to the publication of stories that circulate throughout the Anglo-American world. At the same time they function as symbols of silence, their names unknown beside those of their famous husbands. But they remain only symbols, their lives shadowy and their voices conspicuously absent from the text. *From the Beast to the Blonde* challenges the historiography that subordinates them to their husbands, but readers still learn little about them beyond their names. Warner provides extensive sociological detail about nannies, nurses, stepmothers, and mothers-in-law without individual names or stories, a reminder that many of the storytellers whose legacy she celebrates left no records at all. She shows that recognizing unacknowledged histories "does not have to be approached from the perspective of plugging the gaps, as if this could ever be finally achieved, or as if which gaps one prioritizes were in need of no further explanation."[24] Instead, the multiplicity of the past can be explored through hints, allusions, and suggestive moments, teasing glimpses that call for readers to imagine lives they know little about.

The only storytellers depicted in detail in *From the Beast to the Blonde* are the *conteuses*, the originating forces behind the literary fairy tale in Europe. Yet while the *conteuses* are central to Warner's analysis, they nevertheless remain fragmentary, enigmatic figures. Warner introduces the book with the frontispiece to a collection of fairy tales by

Marie-Catherine d'Aulnoy, who coined the term "fairy tales," or *contes de fées*, in 1699. She notes in the caption that d'Aulnoy was "one of the leading enthusiasts in the new literary fashion for telling fairy stories" in the court of Louis XIV (*BB* xi). Yet d'Aulnoy does not appear in the text itself until the next page, and then more than thirty pages after that. Introduced through the caption of an image, she is literally relegated to the margins of the page even as she frames Warner's history of the fairy tale. Details of her life remain sparse, located primarily in a chapter on "Beauty and the Beast" – a story she did not write (*BB* 284–91). These teasing references may not be deliberate metacommentaries on Warner's project, but they point toward the challenges of recovering the voices of the *conteuses.*

Warner simultaneously seeks out voices excluded from traditional accounts of the fairy tale and offers hospitality to figures that remain silent, such as the many storytellers inevitably excluded from her narrative. Even when she presents the voices of fairy tale tellers, they make only brief and fragmentary appearances, evoking Yaeger's efforts at writing that remains "nervous about its own certainties."[25] Her proliferating stories, comparisons, and digressions refuse the conventional authority of the historian at the same time as they reveal her immense range of knowledge. This "nervousness" is apt because, like the people whose lives she fictionalizes in *The Lost Father*, *Indigo*, and *The Leto Bundle*, the storytellers Warner addresses are too numerous to catalogue, and many left behind no retrievable evidence about their lives. Others produced copious writing, but much of that writing is fictional, and even the non-fictional texts such as letters and biographies deliberately invoke fictionalized personae.

The irretrievability of the storytellers' voices is not only a function of the constraints they faced and the limitations of the historian. It also results partially from their own masking strategies, the interwoven personae they used to represent themselves. These masking strategies simultaneously empowered the storytellers and reinforced their invisibility. They enabled storytellers to claim shifting sources of authority, increasing the public appetite for their work, but they also bolstered social systems that validated certain roles for women at the expense of others. For example, *conteuse* Marie-Jeanne l'Héritier adopted the nickname "Télésille" after the Greek poet who rallied a group of Argive women to join battle against the Spartans. With this alias, she presented herself taking up a traditionally male role, a "passage into an exalted sphere of action, normally marked out as a male preserve" (*BB* 176). In another claim to male voice, this time not classical but "noble, French, male and youthful" (*BB* 175), l'Héritier situated herself in the troubadour tradition. Both personae positioned her within a lineage of respected storytellers, but at the same time contributed to the valorization of male writers at the expense of female creativity.

The figure of Mother Goose also conferred both authority and marginality. Charles Perrault popularized the image of Mother Goose with his 1697 collection *Histoires ou contes du temps passé*, subtitled *Contes de ma Mère l'Oye* (*Histories or Stories of Times Past: Stories of Mother Goose*). Warner speculates that he may have gotten the idea from l'Héritier, who was his cousin and friend (BB 171). As Warner explains, taking on the voice of Mother Goose was a way for female storytellers to make common cause with less wealthy women and reject the scorn with which the *Dictionnaire de l'Académie* (*Dictionary of the Academy*) sneered at old wives' tales (BB 162). Moreover, it offered a means of seducing readers through the comforting voice of the nurse or governess, even if *conteuses* such as l'Héritier and d'Aulnoy "could never be read as the voice of the people" because their style marked them as nobles from the court of the Sun King (BB 174). But this stratagem marked "an acceptance of inferior status for their literary production [albeit] in an ironical manner" (BB 164). The lower-class Mother Goose and Mother Bunch personae "threatened to eclipse" the style and concerns of the *conteuses* (BB 166). For instance, later editions of d'Aulnoy's fairy tales modified their tone and contents to match the Mother Bunch persona, with the effect that "d'Aulnoy's bluff was called" and the subversiveness of her stories was minimized (BB 166).

Warner's attention to the "[c]ounterfeit and masquerade" (BB 176) of both the tales and their tellers shows that she cannot conjure the authentic voices of the *conteuses*. In this respect the book resonates with her stylized portrayal of the voices of slaves in *Indigo* and Leto in *The Leto Bundle*. She presents the *conteuses* almost exclusively through their writing, as if to let them speak for themselves, but she shows that enabling subjects to speak is far more complicated than simply amassing quotations. As Warner catalogues the tales, eulogies, and squibs of the *conteuses*, their writings emerge simultaneously as evidence of their self-expression and as screens that block access to their lives. The *conteuses* come across more as fairy tale heroines than as biographical subjects. Much like a teller of fairy tales, Warner provides fantastical details but seldom psychological interiority. She presents the *conteuses* as enigmatic figures with "mysterious" and "shadowy" histories (BB 285). As in her biography *The Dragon Empress*, she offers anecdotes only to call their veracity into question. For instance, Warner proclaims that the details of d'Aulnoy's youth are "difficult to verify, as a mixture of hearsay, false memory, self-justification, writerly inventiveness and hyperbole have stirred a rich brew" (*BB* 284). Her memoir was probably written by fellow *conteuse* Henriette-Julie de Murat (*BB* 285). She conspired with her lover to have her husband executed for treason (without success), and she jumped out a window to escape a warrant, "or so one version has it" (*BB* 285). In Warner's text, Mme de Murat (born Henriette-Julie de Castelnau) comes across even more like a fairy tale figure: ordered into exile for being *une femme déréglée* (a disorderly woman), accused of blasphemy, prone to wearing a red riding hood to church (*BB* 281). The fantastical quality of the lives Warner depicts emphasizes the distance between her descriptions and any authentic self, much like many of Warner's short stories do, and reminds readers that all selves are plural and subject to change. If this distance is a hazard of all efforts to tell a person's story, it is exacerbated by the masquerades that granted the *conteuses* their literary authority.

From the Beast to the Blonde joins fairy tale scholarship aimed at demonstrating the importance of female storytellers. Yet contrary to the reception of the book by critics and reviewers, it complicates the act of recovering marginalized voices. *From the Beast to the Blonde* suggests that to cast the work of the historian as a retrieval of voice ignores the conditions that limited the reception of storytellers' voices in their lifetimes, including their collusion in patriarchal constructions of authority. The text hints at the limits of Warner's ability to find and include the voices of storytellers because they were so numerous, because many left no records, and because those who left the most prolific records adopted varied literary personae. Through her anecdotal and digressive structure, her tantalizing allusions, and her depiction of the *conteuses* as if they were fairy tale heroines themselves, Warner resists any straightforward claim to retrieval. She shows that like so many of the people that inspire her fiction, the voices of the storytellers exceed the limits of her text.

THE PEOPLE BEHIND THE MONSTERS IN *NO GO THE BOGEYMAN*

Like *From the Beast to the Blonde*, *No Go the Bogeyman* uses the study of myths and fairy tales as a means to oppose silencing and marginalization. While *No Go the Bogeyman* centres on stories of monstrosity, from ogres to cannibals and child-stealers, it devotes considerable attention to the ways monster stories construct and police social boundaries. The book repeatedly comes back to the ways descriptions of monstrosity present people as freaks or outsiders, and it examines strategies for fighting back against stigmatizing labels. *No Go the Bogeyman* gives far less space than *From the Beast to the Blonde* to the material circumstances behind the myths, but people deemed "monstrous" haunt the text. However, *No Go the Bogeyman* does not give embodied or vocal presence to the people behind the myths, those labelled as witches or monsters. Much the opposite; the book shows how claims to "know" people as "strange" or "strangers" (or, indeed, monsters) serve as a technique of domination.[26] I argue that the text's refusal to embody the people behind the myths marks a variation on the "nervous writing" that characterizes *From the Beast to the Blonde*. Like *From the Beast to the Blonde*, as *No Go the Bogeyman* moves from one story and topic to another, the text resists claims to instantiate the people marginalized by monster stories.

No Go the Bogeyman originated as an effort to balance out the female focus of *From the Beast to the Blonde* through attention to the male figures in well-known stories. Warner soon decided that the most important males in myths and fairy tales were heroes and ogres, and ogres were far more interesting than heroes (NGB x). *No Go the Bogeyman* modulated into a study of coping mechanisms for fear, namely monster stories and their more soothing cousins, lullabies and jokes. "Othering" became central to the text because of Warner's attention to the ways monster stories remove misfits from the realm of the "human" and "civilized." As Warner explains in the opening chapter, "Monsters, ogres, and beasts … variously represent abominations against society, civilization and family, yet are vehicles for expressing ideas of proper behaviour and due order" (NGB 11). While images of monstrosity may respond to genuine dangers, they also contribute to collective self-definition by articulating social boundaries. Mythic female monsters such as Scylla become vehicles for fears about female independence, self-assertion, and sexuality. Tales of "New World" cannibalism feed the needs of European settlers to distinguish themselves from Indigenous peoples. Hence what seems like a playful book, a "startling and shocking and delightful … treasure trove of stories," as Michèle Roberts declares on the back cover of the Vintage edition, encodes concerns with marginalization familiar from all of Warner's work.[27] The stigmatizing capacity of monster stories takes central stage in the final section. Under the ostensibly jocular heading "making mock," Warner analyzes jokes "that attempt to deal with fear of the Other" (NGB 19). While silencing and the reclamation of voice occupy less space in *No Go the Bogeyman* than in *From the Beast to the Blonde*, the political and ethical import of the book crystallizes in these topics. And yet, far more than the storytellers of *From the Beast*, in *No Go the Bogeyman* the people "othered" by monster stories remain shadowy, fleeting images.

No Go the Bogeyman critiques the ways stories of monstrosity deny the corporeal experiences of people labelled "monstrous." Warner shows that monster stories that take real people as their subjects (from witch hunts to accusations of cannibalism) strip them of presence, abstracting them out of corporeal existence. Witch trials turned suspected witches into physical manifestations of stereotype, with "protracted, solemn *auto da fé*, during which they were paraded in the Inquisition's garb of shame – the tall cap and tabard inscribed with diabolical symbols" (NGB 40). The trials defined their victims through monstrous desires, such as butchering infants "to make the ointment they needed for flying to the Sabbath on their broomsticks" (NGB 40). These stories make their subjects simultaneously invisible and hypervisible. They transform people into horrifying bodies while ignoring their bodily suffering. They reduce the accused to bodies "out of place," in Sara Ahmed's phrase,[28] and turn them into the caricatured shapes of witches and ogres even while refusing reality to their pain and fear.

No Go the Bogeyman shows that colonial imagery of cannibalism does much the same thing, denying the corporeal realities of the people it claims to depict. Warner reproduces the seventeenth-century "New World" portraits of Albert Eckhout, a Dutch painter who travelled to Brazil and made one of "the first visual records of the native people of the Americas" (NGB 341). She points out that his images "are portraits only in a manner of speaking" (NGB 341). They are framed by the desire for exoticism and plenty – and evidence of monstrosity. A "portrait" of a Tarairiu woman features a severed foot sticking out of the basket on her shoulder and a severed hand in her hand (NGB 340–1). In Warner's analysis, Eckhout's sketches not only position the Tarairiu as the "Other" but refuse them individuality. Whereas paintings by Eckhout's contemporaries use physical features to express individual personalities, Eckhout strives to capture the behaviour and customs of a social group alongside the "curiosities" that make up their immediate environment (NGB 342). The paintings are artifacts of absence as much as presence. Models may have sat for some, but "the paintings themselves do not convince us that the models were Brazilians" (NGB 344). For all his focus on bodies, the people he depicts are "types," emblems of his vision of an Indigenous lifestyle.

Hence *No Go the Bogeyman* demonstrates the need for attention to the weight of bodies sidelined by stories of monstrosity. In this respect it echoes the attention to bodily suffering in *Indigo*, *The Leto Bundle*, and Warner's short stories about the Middle East. Yet Warner does not respond by looking directly at absent bodies. Instead, she sketches them with the barest outlines. This restraint forms a stark contrast to her vivid depictions of monsters, from woodcuts of the enormously fat *Kinderfresser* (Child-Guzzler) to Francisco de Goya's iconic painting "Saturn

Devouring His Child," which recurs like a musical refrain. Warner does not offer detailed histories of the lives or plight of accused witches; they haunt the text without ever emerging in concrete detail. Warner mentions towns that endured witch-hunts, such as the notorious persecutions in the Basque town of Logroño in the seventeenth century, but she does not tell the stories of individual victims. She does not replace Eckhout's "portraits" with thick descriptions of the Tarairiu to reclaim an authenticity of experience rendered invisible by monster stories. To the extent that Warner offers correctives to Eckhout's perspective, they are also artistic representations. She reproduces a nineteenth-century painting of a market vendor by a Mexican artist named José Agustín Arrieta to illustrate, *contra* Eckhout, that "the bounty of the rain forest can be scanty, its products puny, and husbandry not entirely effortless" (*NGB* 345–6). The painting emerges from two centuries' and half a continent's remove, emphasizing that in the absence of Indigenous paintings from Eckhout's lifetime, any effort to combat Eckhout's vision is itself shaped by a web of social constructions. Warner's bare sketches of accused "witches" and "cannibals" do not necessarily mark a deliberate silence; they may be necessitated by the absence of records. Nevertheless, they echo *Indigo*, *The Leto Bundle*, and *From the Beast to the Blonde* in showing that the bodies of the dead cannot be recuperated on the page, any more than their subjectivity can be represented in any complete or authentic way.

Warner's discussion of Josephine Baker, an African American dancer who performed in the music halls of Paris in the early twentieth century, exemplifies her recognition of the challenges to recovering overlooked subjectivities from behind popular stories and tropes. Baker appears in Warner's analysis of banana jokes and their resonance with colonial discourses. For European settlers in the Americas, the banana went from a symbol of the "New World" as a "tropical paradise" to a metonym for the Indigenous people who cultivated it. Banana jokes came to encode intertwined fears and desires about colonized people and later, immigrants, performing a social function akin to monster stories. Josephine Baker gave bodily form to this complex set of representations when, at the *Folies Bergères* in Paris in 1926, she performed a fantasy jungle scene wearing little more than a luau skirt made of sparkly bananas.

Warner's analysis of Baker's performance is among the book's most corporeal invocations of a person presented as "other" by popular iconography. As Warner explains, the jungle sketch turned Baker's body into a site of pleasure and projection for audience members. It domesticated the colonized "other" through an exoticism that could be contained and consumed within the stage. With one of the only full-body photographs in the text, Warner focuses on Baker's theatrical use of her body. The photograph reveals Baker on stage, in a costume that consists mainly of the banana skirt and several strings of pearls. She smiles at viewers with a sidelong glance. With this image, Warner seemingly insists on the need to restore attention to Baker's bodily experience and give space to a woman commodified by racist and colonial discourses.

But Warner does not combat this objectification through careful rendering of Baker's corporeal experience. Baker emerges not so much as an embodied subject, but rather, as a sign of the distance between bodily image, especially a staged body reproduced on the page, and subjectivity. As Warner shows, Baker's performance simultaneously provided and stripped her of agency, much like the personae adopted by the *conteuses* featured in *From the Beast to the Blonde*, and that performance constrains any search for an authentic voice concealed by the floodlights. Baker's show simultaneously subverted and perpetuated the racist trope of Blackness as a marker of nature and savagery. As Warner puts it, her show "constitutes one of the most precise historical moments when the Other becomes trapped in the definition [she] is mocking" (*NGB* 364). As Baker "bounce[s] her bananas" she is reduced to their symbolism: sexual, exotic, and consumable (*NGB* 364). However, even with this description of Baker simultaneously satirizing and colluding in racist imagery, Warner does not claim to show what the experience did to her sense of herself as a performer or individual.

Like the *conteuses* in *From the Beast to the Blonde*, Baker's subjective experience remains at a distance partly due to the time and space that separates her from readers, partly because of the ways her image was shaped by stereotype and audience desire, and partly because of her active construction of a stage persona. Readers see her solely in performance. Warner moves quickly from Baker to Carmen Miranda, a Brazilian stage performer, and back to the banana as signifier. The effect is to create what Stewart, in her own work, describes as a "nervous, overstuffed, insistent story."[29] This dense, multilayered narrative reminds readers that the material could be recounted in many different ways, and the text can offer only fragments of the lives and moments it presents. Warner rejects the traditional viewpoint of the historian or ethnographer, "a privileged eye, a voyeuristic eye, an all-powerful eye."[30] As in all of the texts I have analyzed in this book, her depiction calls upon readers to imagine more than the narrative proffered here.

No Go the Bogeyman suggests that no single act of imagination will suffice to combat past marginalizations. The structure of the book, much like that of *From the Beast to the Blonde*, emphasizes the need for a multiplicity of stories. The book may seem to offer a comprehensive history of the monster and the responses of fear and laughter. It binds together encyclopedic amounts of information with a storyteller's verve. But it joins *From the Beast to the Blonde* in accreting anecdotes and details that resist the closure of an overarching framework. To borrow a description that Stewart applies to her ethnographic work, in both texts Warner produces "not a smooth story that follows the lines of its own progress … as a master narrative would but a collection of fits and starts in the moves of master narrative itself."[31] *No Go the Bogeyman* calls attention to the ways monster stories and jokes separate "selves" from "others," but does not offer a master narrative about those "others" (or, for that matter, those "selves"). Warner responds to stigmatizing rhetoric with the density of multiplying representations, but resists implying that any of these, separately or together, can account for the people they portray.

"SPILL[ING] OUT FROM THE COVERS": JUXTAPOSITIONS, DISSONANCE, AND IRREPRESSIBLE ENERGY IN *STRANGER MAGIC*[32]

Like *From the Beast to the Blonde* and *No Go the Bogeyman*, *Stranger Magic* is an encyclopedic study of a corpus of stories and their transmission. And like them, *Stranger Magic* tells a story about stigmatized voices while showing that there are always more stories to tell. The book celebrates the diffusion and influence of the *Arabian Nights*. It ranges itself against centuries of Orientalist narratives that present Middle Eastern cultures as dangerous, irrational, and unable to speak for themselves. Much like Warner's short stories "Cancellanda" and "Breadcrumbs," *Stranger Magic* challenges the clichéd images and anti-Arab rhetoric that engulfed the UK and US after September 11, 2001. As Robert Irwin observes in the 2004 edition of his companion to the *Arabian Nights*, many people "in the West are familiar only with the grim Arab world of the headlines – Taliban, *fatwas*, suicide bombers, *Intifada*, disputes over water rights, OPEC meetings, demonstrations, arrests and executions."[33] With *Stranger Magic*, Warner seeks "to present another side of the culture cast as the enemy and an alternative history to vengeance and war" (SM 436). In an interview with Hermione Lee, she explains that the book arose from a question at the end of her 2006 study *Phantasmagoria: Spirit Visions, Metaphors, and Media into the Twenty-First Century*. Exploring the ways in which a shared imaginary can shape discourses about combat and conflict, she asked, "was there another possible story to tell about the Middle East?"[34] She started her research during the first Gulf War and finished the book during the Arab Spring, but it has its roots in her childhood in Cairo. During the first Iraq War, when she heard a radio address about a bombing in Basra, she realized she knew the name "Basra" from the *Arabian Nights*, one of her favourite childhood books. Thus when she decided to turn her academic focus to the Middle East, the *Arabian Nights* provided a natural starting point.[35]

In this respect *Stranger Magic*, like *From the Beast to the Blonde* and *No Go the Bogeyman*, may be seen as a project of recovery. The book offers "another possible story" about a region that Western countries have often labelled as an enemy. It strives to shed new light on countries whose cultural productions were devalued in the West. Yet *Stranger Magic* resists any straightforward claim to "recover" or "give voice" to a culture. As in her earlier fairy tale studies, Warner resists an overarching vision that would reduce people or cultures to cogs in her argument. She undermines interpretive frameworks such as Orient versus Occident, empire versus margins, even voice versus silence. *Stranger Magic* reflects her description of the *Arabian Nights*: with its multiplying stories, Warner's study "sing[s] out against [the] ultimate reduction to thingness" (*SM* 205) and refuses to reduce the *Arabian Nights* or the cultures that produced the text to a single interpretive lens. Like *From the Beast to the Blonde* and *No Go the Bogeyman*, *Stranger Magic* embodies the polyvocality of the stories it analyzes, weaving together multiple histories and traditions that cannot be contained within a singular scholarly vision.

Stranger Magic depicts the *Arabian Nights* as a text with irrepressible energy, a collection of voices that cannot be reduced to cohesion. In Warner's words, the stories within are "not confined by the texts they inhabit, or by the nights over which they are told … [but] spill out from the covers of the volumes … and escape from the limits of time that the narrative struggles to impose" (*SM* 7). With this depiction Warner insists on the power of the storytellers' voices, much as she does in *From the Beast to the Blonde* when she places the *conteuses* and other women who passed down fairy tales at the centre of a fairy tale history. In *Stranger Magic*, she re-centres a strand of Arab culture within a global literary history. To that end she traces the wide-ranging influence of the stories, which "flowed with the traffic across the frontier of Islam and Christendom, a frontier that was more porous, commercially and culturally, than military and ideological history will admit" (*SM* 12). Echoing Homi Bhabha's desire to construct communities shaped by "dissonant, even dissident histories and voices,"[36] she weaves a tale of cultural crossings, "a neglected story of reciprocity and exchange," to promote greater understanding between the "West" and the "Arab world" (*SM* 26).

However, *Stranger Magic* does not simply recover an Eastern literary history in the face of Western prejudices, or "write back to the centre" in the name of an East homogenized by Western discourses.[37] Warner insists that the histories and cultures of "West" and "East" overlap. In this respect she aligns herself with Irwin's portrait of the interconnectedness of "Eastern" and "Western" narratives in his companion to the *Arabian Nights*.[38] She shows that, as Saree Makdisi and Felicity Nussbaum write, "neither the West nor the East, neither Occident nor Orient, exists as such, in a way that can override distinctions among nations, languages, cultures, religions, sects, classes, and genders across extremely heterogeneous geographical zones."[39] Warner not only resists any simple relationship between "East" and "West," she resists the idea that she can "recover" or "give voice" to an Eastern culture "silenced" by the West.

Just as the histories of "East" and "West" cannot be reduced to a tale of imperial domination, Warner insists, neither can the history of the *Arabian Nights*. She complicates narratives of the *Arabian Nights* being appropriated and devalued by European readers. In *Sheherazade through the Looking Glass*, for instance, Eva Sallis describes Western readings of the *Arabian Nights* as "raids," acts of "capture and retreat to the security of a known identity." Sallis argues that the *Arabian Nights* was "enslaved to the service of a culture which wilfully misunderstood it."[40] By contrast, Warner provides a fluid, tangled history for the *Arabian Nights* and the cultures that produced, translated, and reinvented its stories. In this respect she draws inspiration from Edward Said's late work on "entanglement, reciprocity, and mutual interdependence."[41]

Warner met Said in the early 1990s at a BBC press reception for the Reith Lectures. He was scheduled to deliver the lectures the year before Warner. She thought immediately that "he was devastatingly seductive and charming," and she came to count him as a friend, ally, and valued source of support. Although Said was eleven years older than Warner, they had both grown up in Cairo, with Said's father's stationery shop around the corner from Warner's father's bookshop. Both shops were attacked in the Cairo Fire of January 1952, a series of anti-British protests catalyzed when British troops killed fifty Egyptian police officers.[42] Warner has been accused of misrepresenting Said in *Stranger Magic*, because Said's *Orientalism* centred on exposing the European construction and silencing of the "Orient."[43] Yet as she observes, Said's views changed profoundly after he published *Orientalism* in 1978. Said's oeuvre "develops ... an alternative story about intercultural exchange and influence,"[44] exemplified by his 1998 lecture "The Myth of 'The Clash of Civilizations'" and his work with Daniel Barenboim on the West-Eastern Divan Orchestra, which the two men founded in 1999 as a workshop for Israeli, Palestinian, and other Arab musicians.[45] In this vein Warner emphasizes the rich exchanges and dialogues between "East" and "West" in the history of the *Arabian Nights*. She echoes Said's insistence that no civilization is monolithic or homogenous, and that a historical narrative centred on conflict ignores the heterogeneity and fluidity of both "East" and "West." Sameer Rahim argues that with her focus on cultural exchange and cross-fertilization, Warner undervalues the Arab heritage of the *Arabian Nights*, abstracting the stories from their cultural context.[46] Yet Warner insists that the "Arab-ness" of the *Arabian Nights*, much like the relationships between its Arab and European audiences, cannot be easily defined.

Warner's resistance to "giving voice" to the cultures of the Middle East rejects the authority of scholars who have sought to "make sense" of the "Orient." Said famously describes Orientalism as "a kind of intellectual *authority* over the Orient within Western culture,"[47] a discourse that claims the power to judge what is worth knowing about the Orient and what is not. *Stranger Magic* refuses this authority. Much like the stories in the *Arabian Nights* "flout the generally accepted order of things" (*SM* 10), *Stranger Magic* moves from tale to tale, country to country, talisman to bazaar to tapestry, refusing to establish a straightforward "order of things." Like Warner's earlier studies of myths and fairy tales, in structure *Stranger Magic* echoes the stories it analyzes. As Dominique Jullien writes in a review of *Stranger Magic*, Warner's study is as sprawling as the *Nights* themselves. The book resembles a genie spilling out of a jar or "a flying carpet … transporting us over so many lands in the space of a few hundred pages."[48] In the manner of Shahrazad, the heroine-storyteller of the *Arabian Nights*, Warner weaves "an endless tapestry of stories" (*SM* 2), often incongruous in their linkages and impossible to order neatly. Her study often seems bound together by the same logic as Shahrazad's storytelling, where one tale is linked to the next by the promise to reveal ever more wondrous events. As Warner jumps from a folk tale motif to a Syrian legal treatise or a Persian manuscript illumination, her study reveals the same "energy of unpredictability" that powers Shahrazad's stories (*SM* 44). In a move familiar from her previous fairy tale studies, she rejects familiar disciplinary or chronological categories as organizing principles. Section titles interweave literary and historical motifs, from "Solomon the Wise King," "The Flying Carpet," and "The Word of the Talisman" to Sigmund Freud's couch and Lotte Reiniger's animated silhouettes. Interspersed between historical chapters are summaries of tales from the *Arabian Nights*. This structure, with its unpredictable organization and resistance to closure, declares an alliance with the text and the people who transmitted it and suggests that the *Arabian Nights* cannot be subsumed to any historical argument.

Like the *Arabian Nights*, *Stranger Magic* accretes voices. Warner weaves together texts from multiple places and periods. A chapter on King Solomon's magic describes the Solomon of the Bible and Koran, the story told by *The Testament of Solomon* (a Greek "phantasmagoria" from the third century CE), and the portrayal of Solomon in the *Divine Comedy*. In this respect *Stranger Magic* seems to take its cue from Warner's description of the *Nights*: "a tangle of styles and a polyphony of vocal registers: poetry and prose mingle; high-flown court lyrics from the Persian tradition will interrupt a comedy" (SM 9). Warner's changes in tone contribute to this "tangle of styles" as well. While her voice in *Stranger Magic* will be familiar to readers of her other work, with her richly descriptive and lyrical sentences, as she recounts stories from the *Nights* she takes on a more dramatic tone, her sentences shorter and quicker-paced. She refuses a singularity of vision. This does not mean that she gives up authority over the text and simply creates space for other voices. As I have noted, deciding how to frame other voices grants the writer an authority her sources do not share. But Warner tacitly insists that she cannot tell a cohesive, overarching story about the *Arabian Nights* or the cultures that produced them, nor can she embody those cultures on the page.

In some ways, the descriptions in *Stranger Magic* are highly material, as if to make the cultures and places that gave rise to the *Nights* palpable for readers. Warner offers vivid physical descriptions of objects. In the London Arcadian Library, she observes, one version of the *Nights* contains "30 octavo notebooks, written in a variety of hands, with a sprinkling of red-letter headings, [and] the boards have been softened by handling, the pages tattered and torn, in some places patched and edged" (SM 11). A discussion of flying carpets catalogues the uses to which carpets can be put, emphasizing their physicality. A carpet might be hung as "an arras, a curtain, and a coverlet," used to "cordon off a place of higher value," and "[c]arried into the countryside for picnics, and spread out beneath trees or beside springs and pools" (SM 66). Entire chapters are devoted to objects, from the flying carpet to "the thing-world of the Arabian Nights" (SM 195). Conspicuously, though, the book embodies objects far more than it does people. Even in its treatment of objects, it presents customs and practices that change continuously in meaning and form, emphasizing that Middle Eastern and European cultures are "living organism[s]" that cannot be captured by any text (SM 165).

Warner's account of amulets and talismans offers one of many examples of "nervous writing," to return to Kathleen Stewart's phrase, suggesting that the stories and cultures she depicts are too complex to grasp or pin down. Warner's accretion of details simultaneously evokes the richness of the cultures that shaped the *Arabian Nights* and pulls against a cohesive analysis. She introduces amulets and talismans in her discussion of the story "Abu Mohammed the Lazy," about a merchant who makes a fortune with the help of a monkey that is also a jinn. (Frequently translated as "genie," a jinn is a spirit with magic powers that often appears in human form.) The monkey steals the merchant's bride and the merchant embarks on a series of adventures to get her back. In the end the merchant seizes a secret talisman that enabled the monkey to control all the jinni in the city. As Warner observes, the situation that drives the story in the first place – a caliph's desire for an enormous jewel owned by the merchant – disappears from sight. The story ends up "so stuffed with riches of every kind" that the jewel "has become a trifle" (*SM* 214). The discussion that accompanies this story follows the same model, "stuffed with riches of every kind" until the story at its core becomes almost a trifle itself. Warner starts by explaining that "Abu Mohammed the Lazy" emerges from two traditions: it is a tale of instrumental magic and of trade and adventure (*SM* 215). She immediately retreats from both of these literary traditions to trace the histories of the terms "amulet" and "talisman." She describes how the "talisman" modulated from a receipt or promissory note to a magical object, an active force that was "sometimes baneful, sometimes benevolent" (*SM* 216). By the time she observes, "'[t]alisman' consequently entails something having been brought to fruition, completed, often a transaction or pact made for some sacred or religious purpose" (*SM* 217), her comment underscores the irony that little is completed in either the story of Abu Mohammed or her analysis. Any effort to pin down a driving force for the story is arbitrary. Warner notes that Abu Mohammed, idle and goalless, cannot be its motive force. Perhaps, she muses, his riches "are the true subject of the story," and the man who gives him the fortune-building monkey is its "ethical hero" (*SM* 215). But it is the talisman, not the riches or the man with the monkey, that drives her analysis. Far from clarifying the text, these multiplying readings indicate the impossibility of identifying a singular motive force behind it. By accreting analytical perspectives, linguistic insights, and historical facts, Warner offers readers an endless story, much like the *Arabian Nights* itself, which there is always yet another way of reading.

The effect of reading *Stranger Magic* is not intimate. Warner's insights into documents, places, and historical moments might seem to bring readers closer to the cultures that shaped and transmitted the *Nights*. Yet the accumulation of detail suggests the ever-receding boundaries of what there is to know, both for her and for readers. Warner does not make the "strange" or the "stranger" familiar. As she comes to rest only briefly in any given space or time period, readers are denied the sense of familiarity the title seems to hold out, with its invitation to explore the magic of "strangers." This refusal of familiarization is important because rendering the "strange" familiar can be a method of domination, subsuming a person or group to pre-existing interpretive lenses. Yet Warner does not replicate an Orientalist lens whereby the "East" is excessive, irrational, or resistant to comprehension. In her work, the European cultures that transmitted the *Arabian Nights* become equally hard to grasp. She does not present either Middle Eastern or European cultures as inherently foreign or "strange"; rather, she shows that she, like readers, has only limited access to cultures that extend over vast swathes of space and time.

Like *From the Beast to the Blonde* and *No Go the Bogeyman*, *Stranger Magic*, with its eclectic details and juxtapositions, opposes the reduction of a complex history to a single narrative. Warner creates a sense of infinite stories that echoes the *Arabian Nights*, whose alternative title *The Thousand and One Nights* has often been read as a metonym for infinite nights and tales.[49] She joins Shahrazad in resisting grand narratives. Shahrazad, the storyteller of the *Arabian Nights*, tells stories to save her life and the lives of the women around her. With her stories, as I explained in chapter 4, she challenges the anger toward women that drives her husband the sultan into a killing spree. She shows him that his story offers one way of looking at the world, but the world can be many ways, and no single story (nor even any finite collection of stories) can ever define it (SM 3–4). Warner makes this point as well. She shows that grand narratives about East and West are just some available stories, not to be replaced by a singular authoritative one but by countless alternative viewpoints. She shows that the cultures that originated the *Arabian Nights* cannot be understood through any single image or argument and cannot be brought to life on the page without oversimplifying their polyvocality. Despite her statements that she sought to "present another side" of Middle Eastern culture (SM 436), in style and structure *Stranger Magic* resists the idea that it can tell a cohesive story of a culture. Instead it offers an agglomeration of stories that resist coherence just as cultures and histories do.

CONCLUSION

From the Beast to the Blonde, *No Go the Bogeyman*, and *Stranger Magic* give space to voices, bodies, and cultures that have been stigmatized, but all three books hint that they cannot fully instantiate those voices or bodies on the page. Through Warner's anecdotal, wide-ranging style, which privileges analogy, parallel, and juxtaposition above chronological history, the texts gesture toward the impossibility of pinning down their subjects. They invite readers to fill in the gaps through acts of imagination, a process that can never be complete or authoritative but must be undertaken again and again, each time through new eyes. In this way they invite readers into an ongoing effort to understand the people and cultures behind the stories, just as *Indigo*, *The Leto Bundle*, and many of Warner's short stories do.

Like Warner's fiction, with its twin efforts to give space to marginalized voices and show how those voices overspill any narrative, all three studies create frameworks for new communities. These communities stand in opposition to the ones described in *No Go the Bogeyman*, where societies exclude people as part of "the drive to define and delimit 'home,' to name and circumscribe the abode … to which one belongs" (NGB 328). Along with *Indigo* and *The Leto Bundle*, the three studies invite entry into communities that challenge divisive histories. They produce unexpected linkages. *From the Beast to the Blonde*, despite its focus on European fairy tales, ranges across the globe, from Disney in the United States to the earliest written version of "Cinderella" in ninth-century China. It shows how porous political and geographical boundaries can be when faced with the transmission of stories. *No Go the Bogeyman* works against monster stories that circumscribe a space "where one feels safe" (NGB 328), where people can be named and categorized. Through the sheer accretion of myths and histories, it destabilizes any single vantage point for understanding those stories or using them to label others. *Stranger Magic* is most explicit in its bid for new forms of community, with its attention to the ways in which cultural encounters and moments of conflict have led to interminglings of ideas, practices, and people. With these portrayals, Warner offers a vision of community that takes shape in the spaces "in-between" cultures,[50] characterized, like the books themselves, by syncretism and surprising connections.

Coda

The Power and Limits of Narrative

"THE LANGUAGE OF THINGS": EXCAVATING STORIES FROM STUBBORN SOURCES

Warner's work reveals great optimism about the capacity of art and narrative to combat injustice alongside acute sensitivity to their limits. Her essays and lectures reflect with increasing frequency on those limits. In 2002, after judging the Jerwood Drawing Prize (the leading British award for contemporary drawing), Warner praised the submissions for inquiring into "the limits of drawing itself."[1] In an essay written for a 2016 museum exhibition by the artist Elizabeth Price, she comments that while museums strive to efface the distance between the present and the past, their success is always limited because "the present stubbornly resists disappearance."[2] Yet at the same time as she explores the limitations of her tools, Warner excavates stories from the most stubborn of sources. Since the turn of the millennium she has been increasingly fascinated by the capacity of objects to map memories and provide guideposts in the effort to retrace lives. Both "Cancellanda" and *The Lost Father*, written nearly two decades apart, depict domestic objects as metonyms for family histories. Relationships, customs, and identities are encoded in a mother's coffee set, a copper cauldron, and the buttons in an old sewing basket. *Stranger Magic*, too, conveys the magic of "things," tracing the social functions of talismans and enchanted lamps alongside the capacity of objects to illustrate economic networks and cultural influences.

The power of objects to convey life stories drives two of Warner's major projects from the new millennium, a 2006 web exhibition called "Memory Maps" and her novel-in-progress, provisionally titled

Inventory of a Life Mislaid. "Memory Maps" is Warner's first digital exhibition, though she has done curatorial work since the 1990s, when she produced a touring exhibition called "The Inner Eye: Art Beyond the Visible." She developed "Memory Maps" in collaboration with her then-department at the University of Essex and London's Victoria and Albert Museum. The project maps local histories through essays, poems, photos, paintings, and artifacts, and because of the founding role of the University of Essex, it takes the history of Essex as its starting point. Much like *Stranger Magic*, the exhibit tells a story of cultural syncretism, inviting viewers to define themselves as inheritors of a global history. In an echo of *Indigo*, *The Leto Bundle*, and *Stranger Magic*, "Memory Maps" presents the history of England as the history of its immigrants, colonized peoples, and cultural contacts. Discussing the project in a 2007 essay called "Imaginary Passages: The Metamorphoses of Europa," Warner explains that Essex and the east coast of England saw "some of the earliest colonial and mercantile traffic between England and the rest of the world," and she hopes for the exhibit to "stem the leaching of our common ground, our interwoven experience in time and space."[3] A section of the website titled "Objects Connected to Essex" tells a vivid story of cross-fertilization.[4] An East India Company coffee pot reflects how the docks at Tilbury received the first English imports of coffee, which "changed social encounters all over Europe."[5] A teapot from China displays a local couple's coat of arms, because many upper-class British families in the eighteenth century had their coats of arms enamelled on Chinese porcelain. Colonialism haunts the project alongside a celebration of cultural intermingling.

"Memory Maps" shows that telling one's story is always a process of telling the stories of others, unearthing pasts that might not initially seem to be part of a person's history. Those stories are endless. Hence "Memory Maps" accumulates recollections and images with no boundaries or conclusion, suggesting that its contents could keep accreting *ad infinitum*. Yet despite its inevitable incompletion, Warner contends that "Memory Maps" makes it possible "to listen in" to the ghosts of the past, and by doing so, to connect people across time and space. In a phrase she borrows from the writer Robert Macfarlane, the project strives to make viewers "more sensitive to the hidden histories" of the places it depicts.[6] It encapsulates Warner's hope that images and stories can subvert divisions and inspire solidarity.

The online exhibit disrupts the opposition between hosts and guests, or showing and receiving hospitality. These concepts have long been intertwined. In Greek, *xenos* refers to a stranger, guest, or host. The Latin *hospes*, which forms the root of "hospitality," does the same.[7] Warner's exhibit asks viewers to show hospitality – or, in the common-sense use of the term, welcome – to people who might seem like outsiders in Britain. It insists that "outsiders" have played a central role in shaping British history and identity. Yet it does not let viewers extend that hospitality from the position of insiders. In the language commonly used by museums, here viewers are the visitors. This is doubly true because the exhibit's focus on places interpellates viewers as guests in those places. In blurring the lines between host and guest, the exhibit strips viewers of the right to delineate their space and the power "of choosing, electing, filtering, selecting their invitees, visitors, or guests."[8] At the same time as it calls on viewers to reconsider their relationships to those they may see as foreign, it lets viewers see themselves as strangers. To use a Derridean turn of phrase, the exhibit puts readers in question. It challenges the liberal fiction of the autonomous individual by asking readers to think in new ways about who they are and what they might owe the world around them.

The location of this exhibit online is particularly valuable because there is so much hostility on the web, even more so now than in 2006 when Warner and her collaborators launched the project. "Memory Maps" resonates with Richard Kearney's 2018 exhortation, "If there's a lot of toxic violence going on in this anonymous, faceless, excarnate discourse online, get in there and change it. Go to the source of it and use anonymity for the good."[9] In the face of the internet's capacity to sow divisiveness, "Memory Maps" casts the internet as a site to bring people together by insisting on connections that are all too often overlooked. In stripping the viewer of the authority to decide whom to welcome or reject, Warner calls for hospitality not just to people whose influences or contributions one recognizes but to all who enter or might enter the space where one resides. In this sense the exhibit enacts something close to Derrida's ideal of unconditional hospitality, which involves opening one's home and oneself to any foreigner regardless of who they are and what they have done.[10] It calls into being a community not bounded by identity-based restrictions but instead characterized by "a fracturing openness": an openness that fractures or rejects feelings of cohesion based on sameness.[11] As I noted in the Introduction, the deconstructionist ideal of unconditional openness is not without its critics. Kearney argues that the ideal of absolute commitment to an ineffable other leads to ethical paralysis: it makes it impossible to distinguish between an "other" in need whom one should support and a murderous "other" whom one should oppose.[12] However, by inviting hospitality to all people who might enter one's space, the exhibit – and indeed, the deconstructionist ethics advanced by Derrida – does not ask viewers to give up critical thought about the acts of others. Instead, it asks viewers to accept all other people as members of a shared community in opposition to us-versus-them barriers. The "Objects Connected to Essex" page contributes to this end not just through the stories it tells but through histories that outstrip the information in the captions. These objects call on viewers to show hospitality to people and stories they may know almost nothing about – to undertake a continuous process of reassessing their relationships to those histories.

Warner's descriptions of her novel-in-progress once again invoke the limits and power of "the language of things" to help people imagine the lives of others.[13] In a 2011 talk at the twenty-first annual International Conference on Virginia Woolf, Warner declared that the novel "takes the form of lists," such as the objects her parents took with them when they moved from England to Cairo in 1947: "patum peperium, or Gentleman's Relish … Crumpets … Horlick's … Trumper's Bay Rum."[14] "I am trying to open into stories from the inventory," she explained.[15] In a 2017 essay called "Anglo-Egyptian Attitudes" in the *London Review of Books*, she describes the decanters and drinks cabinet her father shipped from London as "tribal stuff, to keep him moored to home ground."[16] "Those Brogues," published in the *London Review of Books* a year earlier, uses the handmade shoes her father bought her mother in 1945 as a symbol of her mother's entry into upper-class English society.[17] The artifacts of her parents' journeys function as memory maps, helping her retrace their experiences, though these objects give up their secrets grudgingly. They can only hint at the lives of her parents; opening from artifacts "into stories" requires imagination and guesswork.

Like *Indigo*, *The Leto Bundle*, and *Stranger Magic*, *Inventory of a Life Mislaid* strives to tell a story largely overlooked by Euro-American histories: that of mid-century Cairo, where Warner spent her childhood in a rooftop apartment on the island of Gezira overlooking the Nile.[18] In an article about the novel in the *Egypt Daily News*, Warner states, "I want to confront British colonial history. I want to see if I can dramatize it in ways that will speak to our time."[19] She labels Tahrir Square her starting point; the demonstration that helped launch the Arab Spring in 2011 took place right beside her childhood home.[20] For Warner, the story of her father's life in Cairo is intimately connected to contemporary developments in the Arab world and the need to counter stereotypes and homogenizations of Arab cultures. Thus the novel-in-progress joins her work of the past three decades in striving to cross the boundaries erected by mutual distrust and create the groundwork for new relationships.

Both "Memory Maps" and Warner's descriptions of *Inventory of a Life Mislaid* strive to harness the transformational power of narrative.

Much as Warner describes the *Arabian Nights*, both offer, in very different ways, a "story cycle that challenges current proclamations about a clash of civilisations."[21] They explore connections sidelined both by imperialist narratives that devalue Asian and African histories and by postcolonial narratives focused on intercultural conflict. Both projects insist on the capacity of stories to shape new relationships and on Seamus Heaney's hopeful vision that literature "can be strong enough to help."[22] And yet, like so much of her work, they call attention to gaps and silences, acknowledging that they can never be complete.

EMBRACING THE LIMITS OF NARRATIVE

If Warner's faith in the power of narrative is one hallmark of her work, so too are discomfort, tentativeness, and uncertainty. These features call attention to traumas that cannot be blithely healed through narrative and silences that cannot be redressed simply by transforming them into stories. They hint at the impossibility of instantiating their subjects on the page but hold readers accountable for imagining those subjects nonetheless.

Warner's Middle East stories may best encompass this tension between the power and limits of narrative. Rahab in "Cancellanda" becomes a repository of memory; the protagonists of "Breadcrumbs" and "Sing for Me" become symbols of voice. The Captain in "Sing for Me" testifies before a truth commission. But the most resonant images in these stories are portraits of loss. At the end of "Cancellanda," Rahab is engulfed in flames as her home is bombed. She does not even leave behind a pillar of salt, like her counterpart in the biblical source tale. Maryam in "Breadcrumbs" tears her ID photo into pieces to find her children, and though she succeeds, the web of connections that made her part of a community remains in fragments. "Sing for Me" does not show the hearings of the truth commission; in the end, readers cannot act as witnesses. These absences hint at how much more there is to know about the people and places that inspired the stories. Warner's novels do the same, through gaps and uncertainties that leave readers wondering instead of providing closure. So, too, does Warner's biography *The Dragon Empress*. In very different ways, similar resistance to closure is visible in *From the Beast to the Blonde*, *No Go the Bogeyman*, and *Stranger Magic*, where the eclecticism that reveals Warner's immense scholarly knowledge also rejects the authority to subsume individual stories or groups of people to single conclusions.

Gaps and silences in these texts can be read as gestures of solidarity.[23] They convey respect for people who remain silent about their losses to protect themselves, who remain silent because there is no space to articulate those losses, or who express loss through avenues other than speech – from Maryam in "Breadcrumbs," who does not talk about a spouse, friends, or home in Gaza, to Serafine in *Indigo*, who never speaks of the child she left behind when she came to England as a nanny. They acknowledge that, as Warner asserts in "Anglo-Egyptian Attitudes," unintelligibility can be powerful. Drawing inspiration from Abdelfattah Kilito, Warner observes that "since Malinche interpreted for Cortés and the Jesuits became proficient in local tongues," colonial powers have used linguistic expertise as a tool for domination. Yet "remaining unintelligible can also be a weapon," a way to evade prying eyes and retain control over one's story.[24]

Warner's silences acknowledge the stakes of telling other people's stories, stakes that multiply, Julie Salverson warns, when a writer or performer's choices about speech are privileged over the subject's silences.[25] Warner hints at those stakes in "Breadcrumbs" when Maryam's colleagues respond with pleasure to the end of her story but ignore the home Maryam lost, the people she left behind, and the struggles of reaching a new country. Warner's silences suggest that efforts to redress silencing must always fall short, that to some degree they are bound to fail.[26] To borrow a phrase from the late poet and literary scholar Joseph Duemer, perhaps failure is "*built in* to certain kinds of projects, as a feature [and] not a bug," especially those projects that strive to speak for others.[27] Salverson contends that witnessing stories of injustice in ways that make it possible to "live with … a courageous hope in a tragic world" is a task "rife with failure."[28] This may be especially true in fiction, where the witness is doubly removed: by the task of writing (or reading) about the lives of others and by the act of invention. And yet, as Kearney insists, it is natural for human beings to strive "to say the unsayable as if it were somehow sayable."[29] For him, this drive must be nurtured, for "if there are definite limits to what can be said, the resolve to try to say something is indispensable to both ethics and poetics."[30] Warner's writing embodies this resolve. To adapt a formulation that Salverson uses about theatrical performances of witnessing, Warner's works undertake "a dangerous witness, challenged with multiple responsibilities of integrity, imagination, inspiration and craft."[31] This danger is not merely the risk of "bad" writing, of stories that bore or fail to convince, but the perhaps inevitable failure to do justice to those who have suffered. The silences of Warner's stories embrace that inevitable failure. They embrace the task of telling stories that can never be enough and must be told nonetheless.

Warner's stories invite readers to reconceptualize personal and communal identity. They insist that, as Salverson puts it, "personal narratives of crisis are never merely personal."[32] Narratives of crisis delineate what kinds of community we form, what we permit to stand unchallenged, and what we consider to lie within the bounds of the humane, the permissible, and the just. They are collective enterprises. They require response to end the isolation caused by suffering.[33] Warner's books demonstrate this, albeit in very different ways. They insist that stories of violence – the colonization of St. Kitts, the treatment of immigrants and refugees, the war in Iraq – are our stories, the stories of all readers. At the same time as Warner's books call on readers to resist easy assumptions of empathy, she proclaims herself and her readers responsible for the people behind her stories. This is true not only for Warner's stories of violence but also for her stories of *stories*. Her studies of myths and fairy tales ask readers to accept responsibility for the people who told the stories and the conditions that gave rise to them. They ask readers to remain haunted by the people they depict and the questions they provoke. Warner persistently challenges herself and her readers to read other lives in ways that deconstruct boundaries between people, promote healing, and build new communities.

Warner shows that "[t]he exchange of stories may create a certain liberty of space to remake history, reinvent history, and open up new possibilities of history that have never been fulfilled in the past."[34] Kearney makes this claim about testimonies exchanged with so-called enemies, yet it applies to fiction as well. While neither testimony nor fiction can change past injustice, they can remake history by enabling people to think differently about the past and by changing the legacies of that past in the present and future. As Kearney argues, "Our inheritance is a set of promissory notes: not just what has happened, but what also has *not* happened, or *not yet* happened – but which could still exist."[35] Warner uses stories to create new possibilities for that which has not yet happened. She invites readers to imagine that things could have been different, but even more important, she invites readers to re-envision their relationships to other people and to the structural conditions that prop up unjust hierarchies and unequal living conditions. Her narratives "carry seeds of hope that the impossible can become possible," a capacity Kearney ascribes to all of the granular, local, intimate stories that challenge widely held metanarratives.[36] If this is a utopian goal, it is not a naïve one; it encapsulates the hope that literature can contribute to the repair of injustice by inspiring new ways of thinking about the world and one another. Warner reaches for "the impossible" in the sense in which Kevin Hart defines Derrida's "impossible": "not that which cannot happen [but] … the way in which we talk of how something genuinely inventive comes to be and thus extends the realm of the possible."[37] On the surface, these are very abstract goals, but Warner's oeuvre suggests that they are also concrete and immediate ones. They may not admit any norms or precepts but they call for active responses in specific places and times. Warner's own activist work illustrates the material stakes of these considerations.

TELLING OTHER STORIES

The challenges of telling other people's stories – and the importance of telling those stories – have become subjects of widespread public debate. In 2015, images of three-year-old Alan Kurdi, a Syrian refugee who drowned in the Mediterranean trying to get from Turkey to Greece, helped to spur public outcry about the conditions of refugees. But the image also revealed the thin line between publicizing and spectacularizing injustice. Alan Kurdi's photo, posted and reposted on Facebook, became a nexus for the circulation of images as a form of activism and spectacle, a reminder that sympathy for pain and outrage against violence are necessities in the face of injustice but can also mask inaction. In 2013, videos of police shootings of unarmed Black men in the United States galvanized the Black Lives Matter movement. But many have expressed anger that, in the words of Rutgers professor Brittney Cooper, "Black death has become a cultural spectacle." As Cooper observes, "We watched Eric Garner die on video. We watched Tamir Rice die on video." The videos did not save them or lead to convictions for their killers.[38] These cases emphasize the distance between bearing witness to violence and enacting justice.

Warner's oeuvre asks whether acts of witness can ever do justice to the lives – and deaths – of others. She approaches this question in multifaceted ways. From her early journalism onward, her work strives to combat silencing while negotiating the risk of silencing her subjects once more. She explores how to tell stories of violence in ways that push readers to assert responsibility for the suffering of others. She asks readers to reconsider what count as "our" stories and "our" history, to proclaim transnational identities premised on shared uncertainties. The language of invitation that pervades "Memory Maps" forms an undercurrent for her work: "[Y]ou can enrich and deepen connections"; "You … are invited to respond and contribute"; "[Y]ou take it from here."[39] Just as "Memory Maps" seeks to plant "common ground," her oeuvre seeks to establish common ground – even as it challenges readers to think beyond that common ground, to read the stories of others outside of familiar frameworks, and to acknowledge that there is always more to understand.

Warner offers varied and provocative interventions into the ethical and political challenges of representing silenced voices – challenges central not just to contemporary fiction, feminist studies, and postcolonial studies but to a range of artistic practices and academic disciplines, including visual art and photography, Holocaust and trauma studies, oral history, and ethnography. The concerns with representation that pervade her work reflect quandaries faced by all scholars who strive to represent the lives of others. Even more important, they are crucial to members of a broader public striving to formulate their own responses to silencing and erasure. Warner acknowledges that such responses are always insufficient, but they are necessary in a world filled with inequalities and structural violence. Her work invites readers to respond in ways that may only be partial and halting but that open us to unexpected possibilities and new ways of defining ourselves.

Notes

INTRODUCTION

1 Marina Warner, "Disembodied Eyes, or the Culture of Apocalypse," *openDemocracy: Free Thinking for the World*, 18 April 2005, https://www.opendemocracy.net/en/article_2431jsp/.
2 Warner, "Who's Sorry Now?" 467.
3 Ibid., 468–9.
4 Warner, "Between the Colonist and the Creole," 296.
5 Marina Warner, interview by the author, London, 4 August 2004.
6 Warner, "Between the Colonist and the Creole," 296.
7 Freed, *Haunting Encounters*, 16.
8 Jolly, *Cultured Violence*, 5.
9 See, for example, Warner's essays "The Silence of Sycorax" and "Castaway on the Ocean of Story."
10 Marina Warner, "A Right to Write," interview by Sateesh Maharaj, *Trinidad Express*, 5 May 2013.
11 For example, Todd, "The Retrieval of Unheard Voices"; Connor, *The English Novel in History*; Cakebread, "Sycorax Speaks"; Zabus, "What Next Miranda?"; Zabus, *Tempests after Shakespeare*.
12 Warner, "A Right to Write."
13 Warner, "Who's Sorry Now?" 459.
14 See, for example, Nussbaum, *Love's Knowledge*.
15 Keen, *Empathy and the Novel*, 4.
16 Ibid.
17 Ibid. For helpful additional discussion on this point, see Ahmed, *The Cultural Politics of Emotion*.

18 Marina Warner, "The Truth in Stories" (lecture for the "Truth to Be Told" series at the University College Dublin Humanities Institute, 7 December 2017), https://www.youtube.com/watch?v=oLUARrC9u6w.

19 Ibid.

20 Royal Society of Literature, "Marina Warner Is Elected First Female President of the RSL," 14 March 2017, https://rsliterature.org/2017/03/marina-warner-is-elected-first-female-president/.

21 Bal, "The Pain of Images," 101.

22 Jolly, *Cultured Violence*, 9.

23 Zabus, "Mingling and Metamorphing," 119.

24 Marina Warner, "Those Brogues," *London Review of Books*, 6 October 2016.

25 Nicholas Wroe, "Absolutely Fabulist," *Guardian* (Manchester), 21 January 2000, http://www.theguardian.com/books/2000/jan/22/history.

26 Warner, "Marina Warner: A European Woman's Heritage," 93.

27 Quoted in Wroe, "Absolutely Fabulist."

28 Marina Warner, "Oxford Now," *Vogue* (London), May 1967, 40, 53.

29 Wroe, "Absolutely Fabulist."

30 Marina Warner, "What I See in the Mirror," *Guardian* (Manchester), 2 November 2012, http://www.theguardian.com/fashion/2012/nov/02/marina-warner-critic-writer-interview.

31 Warner, interview by the author, 2004.

32 Warner, "Cunning and High Spirits," 429.

33 Quoted in Wroe, "Absolutely Fabulist."

34 Ibid.

35 Warner, interview by Gilles Menegaldo, 217.

36 Warner, "Bearer-Beings and Stories in Transit," 153.

37 Ibid., 150.

38 Marina Warner, Skype interview by the author, 31 July 2019.

39 For two brief examples, she is not included in the following lists: "The 50 Greatest British Writers since 1945," *Sunday Times* (London), 5 January 2008, https://www.thetimes.co.uk/article/the-50-greatest-british-writers-since-1945-ws3g69xrf90; "100 Greatest British Novels," *BBC*, 7 December 2015, http://www.bbc.com/culture/story/20151204-the-100-greatest-british-novels. These lists have their own biases. Both are disproportionately white and male. Still, Angela Carter, Jeanette Winterson, Monica Ali, and Zadie Smith all make appearances.

40 Warner, "Myth and Faerie," 446.

41 This definition of witnessing draws on Barbie Zelizer's characterization of "bearing witness" as an act whereby the witness takes responsibility for the violence they see, as well as E. Ann Kaplan's definition of witnessing as a response that transforms one's understanding of justice and injustice. See Zelizer, *Remembering to Forget*; Kaplan, *Trauma Culture*.

42 Warner, "Myth and Faerie," 446.
43 Ibid., 447.
44 Kaplan, *Trauma Culture*, 104.
45 Sanders, *Adaptation and Appropriation*, 26.
46 Ibid., 2.
47 One common alternative definition is that anyone from a dominant group using experiences or cultural materials from a less privileged group carries out cultural appropriation. James O. Young, for instance, uses this definition. Young thus employs "cultural appropriation" as a descriptive rather than evaluative term, with "wrongful cultural appropriation" for appropriations that subordinate the represented group. See Young, *Cultural Appropriation and the Arts*; Young and Brunk, eds., *The Ethics of Cultural Appropriation*. It is worth acknowledging that both Young's definition and the one I have offered risk essentializing notions of group identity. Yet while cultures and groups are never fixed, cultural groups can clearly be subjected to discrimination and subordination.
48 Kate Taylor, "Cultural Appropriation and the Privilege of Creative Assumption," *Globe and Mail* (Toronto), 12 May 2017, https://www.theglobeandmail.com/arts/cultural-appropriation-and-the-privilege-of-creative-assumption/article34969432/. A transcript of Lionel Shriver's speech is available in "Lionel Shriver's Full Speech: 'I Hope the Concept of Cultural Appropriation is a Passing Fad,'" *Guardian* (Manchester), 13 September 2016, https://www.theguardian.com/commentisfree/2016/sep/13/lionel-shrivers-full-speech-i-hope-the-concept-of-cultural-appropriation-is-a-passing-fad. Hal Niedzviecki's editorial, "Winning the Appropriation Prize," can be found in *Write Magazine*, May 2017, 8.
49 Spivak, "Can the Subaltern Speak?"; Chow, "Where Have All the Natives Gone?"
50 For example, Mohanty, "Under Western Eyes."
51 Clifford and Marcus, eds., *Writing Culture*; Frisch, *A Shared Authority*.
52 hooks, "Choosing the Margin," 151–2.
53 Sanders, *Adaptation and Appropriation*, 100–1.
54 Rich, "When We Dead Awaken," 18–19.
55 Sanders, *Adaptation and Appropriation*, 99.
56 Lanser, *Fictions of Authority*, 7.
57 See, for example, Warner's essay "Between the Colonist and the Creole."
58 Chow, "Gender and Representation," esp. 43–6.
59 Khanna, "Ethical Ambiguities and Specters of Colonialism," 101; Chow, "Gender and Representation," 46.
60 As in the title of Judith Roof and Robyn Wiegman's influential anthology, *Who Can Speak? Authority and Critical Identity*.
61 For example, see Jolly, *Cultured Violence*; Hesford, *Spectacular Rhetorics*; Kozol, *Distant Wars Visible*.

62 Arondekar, *For the Record*, 1.
63 Derrida and Dufourmantelle, *Of Hospitality*.
64 Kearney, *Strangers, Gods and Monsters*, 17–19.
65 This declaration echoes (though perhaps not deliberately) anthropologist James Scott's phrase "weapons of the weak," which refers to subtle day-to-day strategies of peasant resistance against oppression. See Scott, *The Weapons of the Weak*.
66 Benjamin, "Theses on the Philosophy of History," 257.
67 There is a large bibliography on this question. I have found the following particularly helpful: Boltanski, *Distant Suffering*; Sontag, *Regarding the Pain of Others*; LaCapra, *Writing History, Writing Trauma*.
68 Kozol, "Witnessing Genocide and the Challenges of Ethical Spectatorship," 211.
69 Caruth, *Unclaimed Experience*; Felman and Laub, *Testimony*.
70 See, for example, Craps and Buelens, eds., *Postcolonial Trauma Novels*.
71 Sontag, *Regarding the Pain of Others*, 71.
72 Ibid., 99–101.
73 Warner, interview by Gilles Menegaldo, 218.
74 Warner, "Come to Hecuba," 52.
75 For helpful discussions of this problem, see, for example, Sontag, *Regarding the Pain of Others*; Ahmed, *The Cultural Politics of Emotion*, ch. 1; Kozol, "Witnessing Genocide and the Challenges of Ethical Spectatorship."
76 Warner, "Disembodied Eyes."
77 Warner, "Angels and Engines," 33.
78 Ibid., 17.
79 Ibid., 33.
80 Marina Warner, "There's Method in Theatre's Blood and Gore," review of *Titus Andronicus* (directed by Lucy Bailey at Shakespeare's Globe, London), *Guardian* (Manchester), 12 May 2014, http://www.theguardian.com/commentisfree/2014/may/12/theatre-blood-gore-titus-andronicus.
81 Ibid.
82 Warner, "Who's Sorry Now?" 467–9.
83 Ahmed, *The Cultural Politics of Emotion*, 21.
84 Bal, "The Pain of Images," 94.
85 Oliver, *The Colonization of Psychic Space*, xiv.
86 Ibid., xii.
87 Warner, "Come to Hecuba," 51.
88 Marina Warner, conversation with the author, 9 June 2006.
89 Warner, "Angels and Engines," 41.
90 LaCapra, *Writing History, Writing Trauma*, 41.
91 Sontag, *Regarding the Pain of Others*, 102–3.
92 Kearney, "Writing Trauma," 135.

93 For two helpful accounts of this issue, see Said, *Orientalism*; Smith, *Decolonizing Methodologies*.
94 I am drawing this definition from Black, *Fiction across Borders*.
95 Ganteau and Onega, "Introduction: Performing the Void," 11.
96 Ahmed, *Strange Encounters*.
97 Derrida and Dufourmantelle, *Of Hospitality*, 58.

CHAPTER ONE

1 Black, *Fiction across Borders*, 19–20.
2 In contemporary writing, "Tz'u-hsi" is typically spelled "Cixi." I have retained Warner's conventions for spelling names and places.
3 I am drawing on Judith Butler's definition of precarity as the vulnerability faced by populations that are disproportionately exposed to violence and death because of socio-economic inequalities. See Butler, *Precarious Life* and *Frames of War*.
4 Marina Warner, editorial, in "Women," special issue, *Isis* (Oxford University student magazine), 19 October 1966.
5 Seagrave and Seagrave, *Dragon Lady*, 13.
6 Bland and Backhouse, *China under the Empress Dowager*, 478.
7 Ibid., 481.
8 Backhouse, *Décadence Mandchoue*.
9 Trevor-Roper, *Hermit of Peking*. Originally published in 1976 under the title *A Hidden Life: The Enigma of Sir Edmund Backhouse.*
10 Seagrave and Seagrave, *Dragon Lady*, 16.
11 Ibid.
12 Chang, *Empress Dowager Cixi*.
13 "The Concubine in the Well," *Beijing Tours*, http://www.beijing-tours.cn/forbidden-city/the-concubine-in-the-well.html. Accessed 30 May 2019.
14 Gluck and Patai, introduction to *Women's Words*.
15 McCooey, "The Limits of Life Writing," 277.
16 Rudnick, "The Male-Identified Woman and Other Anxieties," 118.
17 See, for example, Rowbotham, *Women, Resistance, and Revolution* and *Hidden from History*; Liddington and Norris, *One Hand Tied Behind Us*.
18 For a critique of this tradition, see Heilbrun, *Writing a Woman's Life*.
19 Marina Warner, "The Revolution of Rose Dugdale," *Sunday Times Magazine* (London), 18 August 1974, 8.
20 Lee, *Biography*, 2.
21 Seagrave and Seagrave, *Dragon Lady*, 18.
22 Alpern et al., introduction to *The Challenge of Feminist Biography*, 12.
23 Lee, *Virginia Woolf's Nose*, 5.
24 Backscheider, *Reflections on Biography*, 91.

25 In 2008, forensic science showed that the emperor died of acute arsenic poisoning. The story was widely reported in the popular press; see, for example, "Arsenic Killed Qing Emperor, Experts Find," *New York Times*, 4 October 2008, https://www.nytimes.com/2008/11/04/world/asia/04iht-emperor.1.17508162.html; Louisa Lim, "Who Murdered China's Emperor 100 Years Ago?" *NPR*, 14 November 2008, https://www.npr.org/templates/story/story.php?storyId=96993694. From a contemporary perspective, it seems the question is not whether the emperor was poisoned, but by whom.

26 Backscheider, *Reflections on Biography*, 10.

27 Woolf, "The New Biography," 98.

28 The reliability of the source for this quote has since been called into question; see *DE* xiv; Seagrave and Seagrave, *Dragon Lady*, 13. It is outside the scope of this volume to settle the question.

29 Warner, "Report to the Memoir Club," 62.

30 I am drawing inspiration from Sturken's discussion of the varied ways memories can act as screens in "The Wall, the Screen, and the Image."

31 Black, *Fiction across Borders*, 44.

32 Ibid., 44.

33 Warner, *Alone of All Her Sex*, xvi.

34 The bomb on the road to Trang Bang recurs in her novel *The Leto Bundle* and was one influence for her short story "Cancellanda."

35 Warner, "The Bitch Route 13," 12.

36 Ibid., 11.

37 Ibid., 12.

38 Warner, *Alone of All Her Sex*, xvi.

39 Kleinman and Kleinman, "The Appeal of Experience," 3.

40 Sontag, *Regarding the Pain of Others*, 37–8.

41 Bui, "Embodiments of Difference," 77. For one example among many, see Bernard Weinraub, "Footnotes on the Vietnam Dispatches; The Americans Ask, the Vietnamese Ask, 'Does Anybody Care?'" *New York Times*, 20 October 1968, https://www.nytimes.com/1968/10/20/archives/footnotes-on-the-vietnam-dispatches-the-americans-ask-the.html.

42 "Suddenly the World Woke Up … But This Has Been Going On for Years," *Guardian* (Manchester), 15 March 1968.

43 Photo caption, *Guardian*, 9 May 1972.

44 Kleinman and Kleinman, "The Appeal of Experience," 4.

45 Ahmed, *The Cultural Politics of Emotion*, 21.

46 Marina Warner, "Poor Little Bastards of Vietnam," *Spectator*, 12 August 1972, 262.

47 Warner, "The Crushed Butterflies of War," 15.

48 Bui, "Embodiments of Difference," 78–9.

49 Warner, "Poor Little Bastards of Vietnam," 262.

50 Warner, "The Crushed Butterflies of War," 16.
51 Warner, "Poor Little Bastards of Vietnam," 263.
52 Warner, "The Crushed Butterflies of War," 16–17.
53 Ibid., 17.
54 Ibid., 17.
55 Kozol, *Distant Wars Visible*, 11.
56 Salverson, "Performing Emergency," 184.
57 Warner, "The Crushed Butterflies of War," 17.
58 Salverson, "Performing Emergency," 184.
59 Kleinman and Kleinman, "The Appeal of Experience," 1.
60 Chouliaraki, *The Spectatorship of Suffering*, 4.
61 I am indebted to Pedwell, *Affective Relations*; Chouliaraki, *The Spectatorship of Suffering*; and Sontag, *Regarding the Pain of Others*, for their analyses of why feelings of proximity do not necessarily promote ethical relations.
62 Black, *Fiction across Borders*, 34.

CHAPTER TWO

1 As mentioned in the Introduction, there are many definitions of empathy. I am following the definition adopted by Keen (*Empathy and the Novel*, 4). It is worth noting that identification and empathy are closely related. As Keen points out, character identification (i.e. a reader identifying with a character) can contribute to empathy for that character. Many of the narrative strategies that narrative theorists associate with identification are also associated with empathy, such as point of view, roundness of characters, and emotional intensity.
2 For example, Nussbaum, *Poetic Justice*, 5–6.
3 Keen, *Empathy and the Novel*.
4 Chabot Davis, *Beyond the White Negro*, 12.
5 This argument has a long and complex history, from the work of organizations such as the Black Women's Action Committee, which grew out of Britain's Black Unity and Freedom Party in 1970, to scholars of intersectionality and critical race theory.
6 Oliver, *The Colonization of Psychic Space*, 33–6.
7 For a few valuable accounts of these problems, see Boler, "The Risks of Empathy"; Freed, "The Ethics of Identification"; Delgado, "Rodrigo's Eleventh Chronicle"; Pedwell, *Affective Relations*.
8 deGravelles, "You Be Othello," 153. DeGravelles is drawing on Boler, "The Risks of Empathy"; Britzman, "If the Story Cannot End"; Eppert, "Entertaining History."
9 Freud, "Group Psychology and the Analysis of the Ego," 105. For a helpful discussion of Freud's view, see also Chabot Davis, "Oprah's Book Club."

10 Harlow, "Sites of Struggle."
11 Chabot Davis, "Oprah's Book Club." She expands on this argument in *Beyond the White Negro*.
12 Pedwell, *Affective Relations*, 47–8.
13 Ahmed, *Strange Encounters*, 180.
14 Keen, "A Theory of Narrative Empathy," 213, and *Empathy and the Novel*, 96–9, though Keen emphasizes that reader identification and empathy for literary characters are hard to predict.
15 With this portrait of the varied motives that shape responses to the visions, the novel echoes Warner's journalistic work on the 1879 visions of the Virgin Mary in Knock, Ireland. Warner wrote about Knock as early as 1976, in *Alone of All Her Sex,* and three years later she published an essay titled "What the Virgin of Knock Means to Women" (*Magill: Ireland's Current Affairs Monthly Magazine*, September 1979). In both cases she analyzed how conflicting agendas shaped competing narratives of the apparition.
16 Coupe, *Marina Warner*, 19.
17 In thinking about the relationships between idealization and identification, I am indebted to Scott, "Fantasy Echo," and Eppert, "Entertaining History."
18 Scott, "Fantasy Echo," 289.
19 Ibid., 293.
20 Lugones and Spelman, "Have We Got a Theory for You," 574.
21 Benjamin, *Like Subjects, Love Objects*, 7–8.
22 Warner, interview by Elaine Williams, 264.
23 Wyatt, *Risking Difference*, 6–7.
24 Keen, *Empathy and the Novel*, 94. Keen notes that there is debate about whether or not increased pacing promotes identification, but I am inclined toward the argument that quick reading leads to immersion, which promotes a strong feeling of involvement in a character's situation.
25 Spivak, "Can the Subaltern Speak?" 296.
26 Mohanty, "Under Western Eyes," 337.
27 Ibid., 337.
28 Warner, "Marina Warner in Conversation," 36.
29 Boler, "The Risks of Empathy," 255.
30 hooks, "Eating the Other," 31.
31 Ibid., 32.
32 Oliver, *Witnessing*.
33 Scott, "Fantasy Echo," 285.
34 Lanser, "Toward (a Queerer and) More (Feminist) Narratology."
35 Ibid., 27.
36 Warner, "Angela Carter: Bottle Blonde, Double Drag."
37 Butler, "Contingent Foundations," 14–15.
38 Kilian, "Visitations from the Past," 57.

39 Warner, "Marina Warner in Conversation," 36.
40 Warner, "Spinning a Yarn with Marina Warner," 520.
41 Warner, "Making It Big in the New World," 47.
42 The 1980s were a watershed decade for historiographic metafiction. A short list of influential examples includes Rushdie, *Midnight's Children*; Swift, *Waterland*; Carter, *Nights at the Circus*; Barnes, *Flaubert's Parrot* and *A History of the World in 10½ Chapters*; Morrison, *Beloved*; Winterson, *The Passion*; and Lively, *Moon Tiger*.
43 Warner, "Myth and Faerie," 446.
44 Warner, "Who's Sorry Now?" 467.
45 Giunta, afterword to *Umbertina*, 427.
46 Warner, "Marina Warner in Conversation," 36.
47 Barolini, interview by Dorothée von Huene Greenberg, 92.
48 Abu-Lughod, "The Romance of Resistance," 47.
49 Jenkins, "Authorizing Female Voice and Experience," 62.
50 Spivak, "Can the Subaltern Speak?"; Chow, "Gender and Representation," 47.
51 Milosz, "My Faithful Mother Tongue."
52 Pedwell, *Affective Relations*, 147.
53 Chabot Davis, *Beyond the White Negro*, 110.
54 Freed, "The Ethics of Identification."

CHAPTER THREE

1 Warner, "Who's Sorry Now?" 467.
2 Keats, *The Letters of John Keats*, 72.
3 Ibid., 227–8.
4 Warner, "Who's Sorry Now?" 467.
5 For two influential expressions of this view, see Caruth, *Unclaimed Experience*, and Scarry, *The Body in Pain*.
6 I have found Craps and Buelens, eds., *Postcolonial Trauma Novels*, particularly helpful in this regard.
7 Warner, "Who's Sorry Now?" 467.
8 Ibid., 467.
9 Tuck and Yang, "Decolonization Is Not a Metaphor."
10 Warner, "Who's Sorry Now?" 468–9.
11 Ibid., 467.
12 Freed, *Haunting Encounters*, 5.
13 Connor, *The English Novel in History*; Cakebread, "Sycorax Speaks"; Zabus, *Tempests After Shakespeare*, "What Next Miranda?" "Mingling and Metamorphing."
14 Connor, *The English Novel in History*, 184, 97.
15 Weaver-Hightower, "Revising the Vanquished," 88–9.

16 Ibid., 98–9.
17 Harris, "Imagine. Investigate. Intervene?" 172–3.
18 Todd, "The Retrieval of Unheard Voices"; Williams-Wanquet, "Marina Warner's *Indigo*"; Franková, "Marina Warner's Sibyls and Their Tales."
19 Newton, *Narrative Ethics*, 19.
20 See, for example, Phillips, *Cambridge*; Coetzee, *Foe*.
21 Newton, *Narrative Ethics*, 16.
22 Warner, "Marina Warner in Conversation," 36.
23 Warner, "Between the Colonist and the Creole," 302.
24 Marina Warner, "Those Brogues," *London Review of Books*, 6 October 2016, 29–32.
25 Marina Warner, "My Grandfather, Plum," *Guardian* (Manchester), 10 June 2004, http://www.theguardian.com/books/2004/jun/11/sportandleisure.cricket.
26 Warner, "The Silence of Sycorax," 264–5.
27 Warner, interview by David Dabydeen, 122.
28 Warner, "Between the Colonist and the Creole," 301.
29 Warner, "Marina Warner with Robert Fraser," 367–8.
30 Darío, "The Triumph of Caliban"; Rodó, *Ariel*.
31 Lee, *A Life of William Shakespeare*. I have drawn the phrase "the Americanization of *The Tempest*" from Vaughan and Vaughan, introduction to *The Tempest*, 100.
32 Stoll, "Certain Fallacies and Irrelevancies in the Literary Scholarship of the Day," 487.
33 For more detailed discussion, see Kermode's introduction to *The Tempest* in *The Arden Edition of the Works of William Shakespeare*, xxvi–xxx.
34 Shakespeare, *The Tempest*, 1.2.229.
35 For a detailed account of this linguistic transformation, see ch. 1 of Hulme, *Colonial Encounters*.
36 Robinson, "Caribbean Caliban," 431–2.
37 Warner, "Shakespeare's Caliban," 262.
38 Warner, "Between the Colonist and the Creole," 302.
39 Ibid., 297.
40 Warner, "The Silence of Sycorax," 266–7.
41 E.g. Warner, "Its Own Dark Styx," 269, and "Zombie," 342.
42 Brathwaite, *Contradictory Omens*, 38.
43 Warner, "The Silence of Sycorax," 264.
44 O'Callaghan, "'Jumping into the Big Ups' Quarrels'"; deCaires Narain, "Caribbean Creole"; Savory, "Jean Rhys, Race and Caribbean/English Criticism."
45 Zabus, "What Next Miranda?" 81.
46 Lamming, *Water with Berries*, 57.

47 Thieme, *Postcolonial Con-Texts*, 7.
48 Brathwaite, "A Post-Cautionary Tale of the Helen of Our Wars," 77; O'Callaghan, *Woman Version*, 4.
49 Other emblems of the grandmother tradition include Ma Chess in Jamaica Kincaid's *Annie John*; Ma in Merle Hodge's *Crick, Crack, Monkey*; and Mma Alli in Michelle Cliff's *Abeng*.
50 Cliff, *Abeng*, 21.
51 Warner, "The Silence of Sycorax," 268.
52 Warner, "Siren/Hyphen," 309–12.
53 Ibid., 311.
54 Hulme, *Colonial Encounters*, 155.
55 Ibid., 156.
56 Ibid., 3.
57 Boehmer, *Colonial and Postcolonial Literature*, 15.
58 Cakebread, "Sycorax Speaks," 228.
59 Warner, "Between the Colonist and the Creole," 302.
60 Connor, *The English Novel in History*, 192.
61 Warner, "Between the Colonist and the Creole," 302.
62 Brecht, "A Short Organum for the Theatre," 195–6.
63 Newton, *Narrative Ethics*, 13.
64 Warner, *Managing Monsters*, 66.
65 Chivite de León, *Echoes of History*, 117.
66 Hulme, *Colonial Encounters*, 8. Warner echoes this point in "Pavane for Her Wildwoman Symmetries."
67 Warner, "Rough Magic and Sweet Lullaby," 242.
68 Zabus, *Tempests after Shakespeare*, 141.
69 de la Concha, "Crossing the Lines, Crossing the Squares," 90.
70 Warner, "Myth and Faerie," 445.
71 Connor, *The English Novel in History*, 190.
72 Marina Warner, interview by Lisa Hopkins, *Sheffield Thursday*, Autumn 1994, 91.
73 Said, *Culture and Imperialism*, 19.
74 Zabus, *Tempests after Shakespeare*, 145.
75 López, "Historiographic Metafiction and Resistance Postmodernism," 220.
76 Opie and Opie, *The Classic Fairy Tales*, 11–12.
77 Bronwyn Rivers, "Eclectic, Academic Writing with a Spiritual Dimension," *Courier Mail* (Queensland), 18 January 2003.
78 Marina Warner, interview by the author, London, 4 August 2004.
79 Ibid.
80 Ibid.
81 Warner, "Castaway on the Ocean of Story," 290.
82 Warner, interview by the author, 2004.

83 Warner, "Castaway on the Ocean of Story," 281.
84 See Warner, *Fantastic Metamorphoses*, ch. 2, for more information about variations on the story.
85 Ibid., 76.
86 Rushdie, "In Good Faith," 394; Levi, *The Periodic Table*, 34; Warner, *Managing Monsters*.
87 Fetterley, *The Resisting Reader*.
88 For an analysis of this kind of desacralization process, see Anderson, *Imagined Communities*, 181–2.
89 Sontag, *Regarding the Pain of Others*, 87.
90 Nora, "Between Memory and History," 19.
91 Warner, *Fantastic Metamorphoses*, 99.
92 Yaeger, "Consuming Trauma," 33–4.
93 Warner, "Castaway on the Ocean of Story," 290.
94 Aeschylus, *Prometheus Bound*, 38.
95 Hennecke, *New Testament Apocrypha*, 375.
96 Spivak, "Ethics and Politics," 22.
97 Attridge, "Ethical Modernism," 664.
98 Warner, "Those Brogues."
99 Warner, "Donkey Business, Donkey Work," 395.
100 Warner, "Castaway on the Ocean of Story," 289–90.
101 Marais, "J.M. Coetzee's *Disgrace*," 88–9.
102 Marais, "Little Enough," 164.
103 Scarry, *The Body in Pain*, 4.
104 Bennett, *Empathic Vision*, 10.
105 Sontag, *Regarding the Pain of Others*, 102, 117.
106 Yaeger, "Consuming Trauma," 29.
107 Marais, "Literature and the Labour of Negation"; Monson, "An Infinite Question."
108 Monson, "An Infinite Question," 100.
109 Hartman, "Tele-Suffering and Testimony in the Dot Com Era," 118.
110 Attridge, "Ethical Modernism," 660.
111 Bakhtin, *Problems of Dostoevsky's Poetics*, 123.
112 Bhabha, *The Location of Culture*, 1–2.
113 Derrida, *Politics of Friendship*, 14.
114 Butler, "Sex Rights," 59.
115 Levinas, *Otherwise than Being, or, Beyond Essence*, 12.
116 Derrida and Dufourmantelle, *Of Hospitality*.
117 See, for example, Spivak, "In Response: Looking Back, Looking Forward."
118 Marina Warner, "Burning Intellect," *Financial Times* (London), 17 July 2004.

CHAPTER FOUR

1 Smith and Schaffer, *Human Rights and Narrated Lives*, 5.
2 Stauffer, *Ethical Loneliness*.
3 Marina Warner, interview by the author, London, 4 August 2004.
4 Whitlock, *Soft Weapons*.
5 Berlant, "Poor Eliza," 641.
6 Oliver, *Witnessing*; Esmeir, "On Making Dehumanization Possible"; Hesford, *Spectacular Rhetorics*, 48–52.
7 Oliver, *Witnessing*.
8 Ibid., 2.
9 Stauffer, *Ethical Loneliness*, 70.
10 Said, *Orientalism*.
11 Oliver, *Witnessing*, 106.
12 Kearney, *Strangers, Gods and Monsters*, 9.
13 Abbott, *Real Mysteries*, 3.
14 For a helpful analysis of this phenomenon, see Hesford and Kozol, *Haunting Violations*.
15 Oliver, *Witnessing*, 106.
16 Ahmed, *Strange Encounters*, 52.
17 Ovid, *The Metamorphoses of Ovid*, 283.
18 I have analyzed the shifting connotations of Phoebe's metamorphosis in "Bloody Chambers and Labyrinths of Desire," 137–9.
19 Abbott, *Real Mysteries*, 17.
20 Ibid., 142.
21 Ibid., 146.
22 Ahmed, *Strange Encounters*, 54.
23 Warner, *Stranger Magic*, 144; Marina Warner, interview by Elizabeth Dearnley, *The White Review*, July 2013, http://www.thewhitereview.org/feature/interview-with-marina-warner/; Marina Warner, "Story-Bearers," review of *Je parle toutes les langues, mais en arabe*, by Abdelfattah Kilito, *London Review of Books*, 17 April 2014.
24 For example, Warner was a signatory on a 2013 open letter in the *Guardian* opposing the Prawer-Begin Plan, which would displace Palestinian Bedouins in the Negev region: "UK Must Protest at Bedouin Expulsion," *Guardian* (Manchester), 29 November 2013, https://www.theguardian.com/world/2013/nov/29/uk-protest-bedouin-expulsion.
25 Marina Warner, "Dissolving the Barriers of Literature: A Conversation withMarina Warner about Cultural Diplomacy, Remapping Literature, and Her Upcoming Conference on LAL [Library of Arabic Literature] at Oxford," interview by M. Lynx Qualey, *Library of Arabic Literature*, 17 April 2015, http://www.libraryofarabicliterature.org/2015/dissolving-the-barriers-

of-literature-a-conversation-with-marina-warner-about-cultural-diplomacy-remapping-literature-and-her-upcoming-conference-on-lal-at-oxford/.

26 Warner, foreword to *Memoirs of an Early Arab Feminist*, ix.
27 Abu-Lughod, "Do Muslim Women Really Need Saving?" 784.
28 Warner, afterword to *Shadow Lives*, 165.
29 Whitlock, *Soft Weapons*, 112.
30 Ibid., 79–80.
31 Boler, "The Risks of Empathy," 259.
32 Chaudhuri, *Cinema of the Dark Side*, 51.
33 Warner, introduction to "Cancellanda."
34 Ibid., 189–90.
35 Ibid., 190.
36 Butler, *Precarious Life*, 34; Griffin, "Picturing America's 'War on Terrorism'"; Schwalbe, Silcock, and Keith, "Visual Framing of the Early Weeks of the U.S.-Led Invasion of Iraq."
37 Warner, "Cancellanda," 208.
38 Ibid., 208.
39 Marina Warner, "Losing Home, Finding Words: Transformations of Story" (Holberg Lecture, University of Bergen, 9 June 2015), https://www.youtube.com/watch?v=AaLrl9qFHRA.
40 Butler, *Precarious Life*, 3.
41 Warner, "Cancellanda," 209.
42 Butler, *Precarious Life*, 6.
43 Corona, "Risky Memory," 307.
44 Warner, introduction to "Cancellanda," 190.
45 Warner, "Cancellanda," 207.
46 Whitlock, *Soft Weapons*, 58. For an example of US State Department rhetoric, see the 2001 State Department "Report on the Taliban's War Against Women," https://2001-2009.state.gov/g/drl/rls/6185.htm.
47 I am drawing this term from Hesford and Kozol, *Haunting Violations*.
48 Warner, introduction to "Cancellanda," 192.
49 Hesford and Kozol, *Haunting Violations*, x.
50 Warner, introduction to "Cancellanda," 191.
51 Butler, *Precarious Life*, 27.
52 Butler, *Notes toward a Performative Theory of Assembly*, 130.
53 Stauffer, *Ethical Loneliness*, 3.
54 The phrase is from Warner's afterword to Brittain's *Shadow Lives*.
55 Griffin, "Picturing America's 'War on Terrorism,'" 397.
56 Ibid., 397. Kozol makes the same point about images of Afghan women that circulated in the US during the "war on terror" (*Distant Wars Visible*, 57).
57 Hagiopian et al., "Mortality in Iraq Associated with the 2003–2011 War and Occupation: Findings from a National Cluster Sample Survey by

the University Collaborative Iraq Mortality Study"; Physicians for Social Responsibility, *Body Count: Casualty Figures after 10 Years of the 'War on Terror.'* "Passive investigation" refers to compiling reported deaths from sources such as hospitals, morgues, and news outlets, a method shown to under-report casualties. The deceased may never reach a hospital or morgue; hospitals and morgues are sometimes prohibited from reporting figures; news reports of deaths are often concentrated in urban centres; etc. "Active investigation" refers to methods such as on-site polls that extrapolate from available data. According to Physicians for Social Responsibility, "active investigation" is more likely to yield accurate figures.

58 Andrew Williams, "Hear No Evil See No Evil: The UK and the Iraq Allegations," *Lacuna Magazine*, 27 September 2016, https://lacuna.org.uk/justice/hear-no-evil-see-no-evil-uk-iraq-allegations/.
59 Kozol, *Distant Wars Visible*, 12.
60 Ahmed, *Strange Encounters*, 157.
61 Ibid., 157.
62 Derrida and Dufourmantelle, *Of Hospitality*.
63 Warner, "Cancellanda," 209.
64 Warner, introduction to "Cancellanda," 190.
65 Whitlock, *Soft Weapons*, 72.
66 Barbara Campbell, "1001 Nights Cast: A Durational Performance by Barbara Campbell," 2005–08, http://1001.net.au.
67 Barbara Campbell, "Artist Statement."
68 Kozol, *Distant Wars Visible*, 52.
69 Chow makes this point in a discussion of third world women in "Gender and Representation." Hesford and Kozol make a similar argument in *Haunting Violations*.
70 Marina Warner, "At Night through a Gap," in "1001 Nights Cast: A Durational Performance by Barbara Campbell," 2006, https://1001.net.au/story/206/1001-nights-cast-story-206.pdf.
71 See, for example, Stauffer, *Ethical Loneliness*; Phelps, *Shattered Voices*.
72 Chaudhury, *Cinema of the Dark Side*, 118.
73 Seikaly, "Return to the Present," 237.
74 Warner, "At Night through a Gap."
75 Brophy and Hladki, "Visual Autobiography in the Frame," 4.
76 Marina Warner, "Burning the Many-Coloured Fish: Re-readings in the 1001 Nights" (keynote lecture, Edward Said Memorial Conference, Centre for the Humanities, Utrecht University, Utrecht, Netherlands, 22 October 2013), https://www.youtube.com/watch?v=7NT9juBl2eY.
77 Kearney, "Writing Trauma," 141.
78 Marina Warner, "Marina Warner Hits the High Notes," interview by Mark Reynolds, *Bookanista* 2016, http://bookanista.com/marina-warner/.

79 Tacitus, *Agricola*, section 30.

80 Numerous scholars have analyzed the limits of official truth recovery processes such as truth commissions. I have found the following particularly helpful: Jolly, "Spectral Presences"; Ross, "Speech and Silence"; Chakravarti, *Sing the Rage*.

81 Stauffer, *Ethical Loneliness*, 48. One historical example is the South African Truth and Reconciliation Commission. While the commission made important efforts to acknowledge the whole system of apartheid as a crime against humanity, neither the hearings nor the final report could fully address the structural injustices of the apartheid regime. See the introduction to the Truth and Reconciliation Commission of South Africa, *Truth and Reconciliation Commission of South Africa Report*; Mamdani, "Amnesty or Impunity."

82 Boler, "The Risks of Empathy."

83 Chaudhuri, *Cinema of the Dark Side*, 147.

84 Rothberg, *Multidirectional Memory*.

85 Newton, *Narrative Ethics*, 3.

86 Warner, "Losing Home, Finding Words."

87 Smith and Schaffer, *Human Rights and Narrated Lives*, 5.

88 Phelan, *Narrative as Rhetoric*, 186.

89 Ibid., 186–7, italics mine.

90 Kurasawa, "A Message in a Bottle," 97.

91 Derrida and Dufourmantelle, *Of Hospitality*, 131.

92 Warner, "Mirror-Readings," 231.

93 Stauffer, *Ethical Loneliness*, 4.

CHAPTER FIVE

1 Marina Warner, "Richard Dawkins Is Wrong to Dismiss the Power of Fairytales," *Guardian* (Manchester), 7 June 2014, http://www.theguardian.com/books/2014/jun/08/richard-dawkins-fairytales-pernicious-wrong.

2 Marina Warner, "On Myth," *The Liberal: Poetry-Politics-Culture*, no. 11 (Autumn 2007).

3 Clifford, "Introduction: Partial Truths," 15.

4 Ahmed, *Strange Encounters*, 62.

5 Ibid., 63–4.

6 Yaeger, "Consuming Trauma," 43.

7 Marina Warner, interview by Omar Berrada, *Bidoun Magazine*, Spring 2013, http://bidoun.org/articles/marina-warner.

8 Stewart, *A Space on the Side of the Road*, 7.

9 Yaeger, "Consuming Trauma," 30.

10 See, for example, Christina Hardyment, "Feasts Cooked in Magic Cauldrons," review of *From the Beast to the Blonde*, *Independent* (London), 12 November

1994; Michèle Roberts, "Women Who Tell Tales," review of *From the Beast to the Blonde*, *Independent* (London), 30 October 1994.

11 Derrida and Dufourmantelle, *Of Hospitality*, 89–90.

12 Ahmed, *Strange Encounters*.

13 Kearney, *Strangers, Gods and Monsters*, 229.

14 Haase, "Feminist Fairy-Tale Scholarship," 17. For additional praise of *From the Beast to the Blonde* as a feminist recovery project, see Zipes, preface to the 1999 edition of *When Dreams Came True*, ix.

15 Warner, introduction to *The Bloody Chamber and Other Stories*, x.

16 Haase, "Feminist Fairy-Tale Scholarship," 14–15.

17 For example, Rowe, "To Spin a Yarn"; Blackwell, "Fractured Fairy Tales"; Welch, "La femme, le mariage et l'amour"; Verdier, "Figures de la conteuse dans les contes de fées feminins."

18 Examples include Zipes, preface to *Don't Bet on the Prince*; Blackwell, "Fractured Fairy Tales."

19 Seifert, "On Fairy Tales, Subversion, and Ambiguity," 56.

20 Rowe, "To Spin a Yarn," 63–4.

21 Blackwell, "Fractured Fairy Tales," 163.

22 Welch, "La femme, le mariage et l'amour"; Verdier, "Figures de la conteuse dans les contes de fées feminins."

23 Friedman, *Mappings*, 201.

24 Hemmings, *Why Stories Matter*, 16.

25 Yaeger, "Consuming Trauma," 45.

26 My thinking here is indebted to Ahmed's analysis, in *Strange Encounters*, of the effects of labelling people "strange" or "strangers."

27 Michèle Roberts, "Tricks and Treats from the Boy Zone of Fear," review of *No Go the Bogeyman*, *Independent* (London), 31 October 1998.

28 Ahmed uses the phrase frequently in *Strange Encounters*, e.g. 39.

29 Stewart, *A Space on the Side of the Road*, 7.

30 Behar, *The Vulnerable Observer*, 21.

31 Stewart, *A Space on the Side of the Road*, 7.

32 The quote is from Warner, *Stranger Magic*, 7.

33 Irwin, *The Arabian Nights: A Companion*, viii.

34 Warner, "Phantasmagoria," 44.

35 Warner, "Marina Warner … Talks about Life as an Independent Scholar," 37.

36 Bhabha, *The Location of Culture*, 6.

37 As in the phrase popularized by Salman Rushdie with his article "The Empire Writes Back with a Vengeance," *Times* (London), 3 July 1982.

38 Irwin, *The Arabian Nights: A Companion*.

39 Makdisi and Nussbaum, eds., *The Arabian Nights in Historical Context*, 7.

40 Sallis, *Sheherazade through the Looking Glass*, 7, 11.

41 Warner, interview by Omar Berrada.

42 Ibid.

43 Ibid.
44 Marina Warner, "Through the Looking Glass," *New Statesman*, 5 June 2006, http://www.newstatesman.com/node/164498.
45 Edward Said, "The Myth of 'The Clash of Civilizations'" (lecture, University of Massachusetts-Amherst, 1998), https://www.youtube.com/watch?v=aPS-pONiEG8; a revised version of this argument was published as "The Clash of Ignorance," *The Nation*, 22 October 2001, https://www.thenation.com/article/clash-ignorance/.
46 Sameer Rahim, review of *Stranger Magic*, *Telegraph* (London), 4 January 2012, http://www.telegraph.co.uk/culture/books/bookreviews/8981193/Stranger-Magic-by-Marina-Warner-review.html.
47 Said, *Orientalism*, 19, italics his.
48 Jullien, review of *Stranger Magic*, 206.
49 One example is Borges's article "The Thousand and One Nights," 566–7.
50 I am drawing this phrase from Homi Bhabha's description of the task of the writer as an effort to identify "the living relationship" between cultures, "'in-between' colony and metropole, 'in-between' the powerful and the powerless" ("Afterword: A Personal Response," 198).

CODA

1 Marina Warner, catalogue note to *Jerwood Drawing Prize 2002*. London: Jerwood Foundation, 2002.
2 Marina Warner, "A Restoration," Ashmolean Museum of Art and Archaeology, 2016, http://www.ashmolean.org/exhibitions/arestoration/essay/.
3 Warner, "Imaginary Passages," 497–8.
4 Marina Warner, "Objects Connected to Essex," in "Memory Maps," Victoria and Albert Museum, 2006, http://www.vam.ac.uk/content/articles/m/memory-maps-objects-connected-to-essex/.
5 Marina Warner, "About the Project," in "Memory Maps," Victoria and Albert Museum, 2006, http://www.vam.ac.uk/content/articles/m/memory-maps-about-the-project/.
6 Ibid.
7 My thinking here is indebted to the ways Derrida and Kearney play on this slippage in their theorizations of hospitality. See Derrida and Dufourmantelle, *Of Hospitality*; Kearney, "Intercultural Encounters as Hospitality," 28; Kearney, "Narrative and Recognition in the Flesh," 786.
8 Derrida and Dufourmantelle, *Of Hospitality*, 55.
9 Kearney, "Intercultural Encounters as Hospitality," 38.
10 Derrida and Dufourmantelle, *Of Hospitality*.
11 Derrida, "Avowing – The Impossible," 21.
12 Kearney, *Strangers, Gods and Monsters*.
13 *Inventory of a Life Mislaid* is tentatively due to be published by HarperCollins

in Spring 2021. Warner uses the phrase "the language of things" in *Stranger Magic*, 178; the introduction to Kennedy and Warner, eds., *Scheherazade's Children*, 2; and Warner's article "The Writing of Stones," *Cabinet Magazine*, Spring 2008, http://www.cabinetmagazine.org/issues/29/warner.php. As Warner acknowledges in *Stranger Magic*, she draws the phrase from the introduction to Lorraine Daston's *Things that Talk*, 15.

14 Warner, "Report to the Memoir Club," 63–4.

15 Ibid., 62.

16 Marina Warner, "Anglo-Egyptian Attitudes," *London Review of Books*, 5 January 2017.

17 Marina Warner, "Those Brogues," *London Review of Books*, 6 October 2016.

18 Warner, "Anglo-Egyptian Attitudes."

19 Marina Warner, "A Life in Flames," *Daily News* (Cairo), 29 January 2009, http://www.dailynewsegypt.com/2009/01/29/a-life-in-flames/.

20 Marina Warner, interview by Omar Berrada, *Bidoun Magazine*, Spring 2013, http://bidoun.org/articles/marina-warner.

21 Warner, "Imaginary Passages," 487.

22 Quoted in ibid., 487.

23 For the idea that silence can function as a sign of solidarity, I am indebted to Sarah Kastner's article "Only Words Can Bury Us, Not Silence."

24 Warner, "Anglo-Egyptian Attitudes."

25 Salverson, "Performing Emergency," 182–3.

26 I am grateful to the fellow organizers and participants in the 2016 Impossible Projects Mini-Conference at Clarkson University for helping me think through the necessity of failure, especially Joseph Duemer, Julie Salverson, and Jenn Cole.

27 Joseph Duemer, e-mail correspondence, 1 October 2016.

28 Salverson, "Taking Liberties," 245.

29 Kearney, *Strangers, Gods and Monsters*, 230–1.

30 Ibid., 231.

31 Salverson, "Taking Liberties," 245.

32 Salverson, "Performing Emergency," 182.

33 Stauffer, *Ethical Loneliness*.

34 Kearney, "Intercultural Encounters as Hospitality," 29.

35 Ibid., 29.

36 Ibid., 37.

37 Hart, "Four or Five Words in Derrida," 178.

38 Brittney Cooper, "Black Death Has Become a Cultural Spectacle: Why the Walter Scott Tragedy Won't Change White America's Mind," *Salon*, 9 April 2015, https://www.salon.com/2015/04/08/black_death_has_become_a_cultural_spectacle_why_the_walter_scott_tragedy_wont_change_white_americas_mind/.

39 Warner, "About the Project."

Works Cited

For a comprehensive bibliography of Warner's work, see https://webspace.clarkson.edu/~lpropst/marina-warner-bibliography.pdf.

Abbott, H. Porter. *Real Mysteries: Narrative and the Unknowable*. Columbus: Ohio State University Press, 2013.

Abu-Lughod, Lila. "Do Muslim Women Really Need Saving? Anthropological Reflections on Cultural Relativism and Its Others." *American Anthropologist* 104, no. 3 (2002): 783–90.

– "The Romance of Resistance: Tracing Transformations of Power through Bedouin Women." *American Ethnologist* 17, no. 1 (February 1990): 41–50.

Aeschylus. *Prometheus Bound*. In *"Prometheus Bound"; "The Suppliants"; "Seven Against Thebes"; "The Persians."* Translated by Philip Vellacott. London: Penguin, 1961.

Ahmed, Sara. *The Cultural Politics of Emotion*. Edinburgh: Edinburgh University Press, 2004.

– *Strange Encounters: Embodied Others in Post-Coloniality*. London and New York: Routledge, 2000.

Alpern, Sara, Joyce Antler, Elisabeth Israels Perry, and Ingrid Winther Scobie. "Introduction." In *The Challenge of Feminist Biography: Writing the Lives of Modern American Women*, edited by Sara Alpern, Joyce Antler, Elisabeth Israels Perry, and Ingrid Winther Scobie, 1–15. Urbana: University of Illinois Press, 1992.

Anderson, Benedict. *Imagined Communities: Reflections on the Origin and Spread of Nationalism*. 2nd ed. [1983.] London: Verso, 1991.

Arondekar, Anjali. *For the Record: On Sexuality and the Colonial Archive in India*. Durham, NC: Duke University Press, 2009.

Attridge, Derek. "Ethical Modernism: Servants as Others in J.M. Coetzee's Early Fiction." *Poetics Today* 25, no. 4 (Winter 2004): 653–71.
Backhouse, Edmund. *Décadence Mandchoue: The China Memoirs of Sir Edmund Trelawny Backhouse*. Edited by Derek Sandhaus. Hong Kong: Earnshaw Books, 2011.
Backscheider, Paula R. *Reflections on Biography*. Oxford, UK: Oxford University Press, 1999.
Bakhtin, Mikhail. *Problems of Dostoevsky's Poetics*. Translated by Caryl Emerson. Manchester, UK: Manchester University Press, 1984.
Bal, Mieke. "The Pain of Images." In *Beautiful Suffering: Photography and the Traffic in Pain*, edited by Mark Reinhardt, Holly Edwards, and Erina Duganne, 93–115. Chicago, IL: Williams College Museum of Art in association with University of Chicago Press, 2007.
Barnes, Julian. *Flaubert's Parrot*. London: Jonathan Cape, 1984.
– *A History of the World in 10½ Chapters*. London: Jonathan Cape, 1989.
Barolini, Helen. Interview by Dorothée von Huene Greenberg. In "Varieties of Ethnic Criticism," special issue, *MELUS* 18, no. 2 (Summer 1993): 91–108.
– *Umbertina, A Novel*. [1979.] New York: Feminist Press at the City University of New York, 1999.
Behar, Ruth. *The Vulnerable Observer: Anthropology that Breaks Your Heart*. Boston, MA: Beacon, 1996.
Benjamin, Jessica. *Like Subjects, Love Objects: Essays on Recognition and Sexual Difference*. New Haven, CT: Yale University Press, 1995.
Benjamin, Walter. "Theses on the Philosophy of History." Translated by Harry Zohn. In *Illuminations: Essays and Reflections*, edited by Hannah Arendt, 253–64. New York: Schocken, 1968.
Bennett, Jill. *Empathic Vision: Affect, Trauma, and Contemporary Art*. Stanford, CA: Stanford University Press, 2005.
Berlant, Lauren. "Poor Eliza." In "No More Separate Spheres!" special issue, *American Literature* 70, no. 3 (September 1998): 635–68.
Bhabha, Homi. "Afterword: A Personal Response." In *Rethinking Literary History: A Dialogue on Theory*, edited by Linda Hutcheon and Mario J. Valdes, 194–204. Oxford, UK: Oxford University Press, 2002.
– *The Location of Culture*. London: Routledge, 1994.
Black, Shameem. *Fiction across Borders: Imagining the Lives of Others in Late-Twentieth-Century Novels*. New York: Columbia University Press, 2010.
Blackwell, Jeannine. "Fractured Fairy Tales: German Women Authors and the Grimm Tradition." *Germanic Review* 62, no. 4 (Fall 1987): 162–74.
Bland, J.O.P., and Edmund Backhouse. *China under the Empress Dowager: The History of the Life and Times of Tzu Hsi*. [1910.] Hong Kong: Earnshaw, 2010.
Boehmer, Elleke. *Colonial and Postcolonial Literature: Migrant Metaphors*. Oxford, UK: Oxford University Press, 1995.

Boler, Megan. "The Risks of Empathy: Interrogating Multiculturalism's Gaze." *Cultural Studies* 11, no. 2 (1997): 253–73.
Boltanski, Luc. *Distant Suffering: Morality, Media and Politics*. Translated by Graham D. Burchell. Cambridge: Cambridge University Press, 1999.
Borges, Jorge Luis. "The Thousand and One Nights." Translated by Eliot Weinberger. *Georgia Review* 38, no. 3 (Fall 1984): 564–74.
Brathwaite, Kamau. *Contradictory Omens: Cultural Diversity and Migration in the Caribbean*. Monograph. Mona, Jamaica: Savacou, 1974.
– "A Post-Cautionary Tale of the Helen of Our Wars." *Wasafiri*, no. 22 (1995): 69–81.
Brecht, Bertolt. "A Short Organum for the Theatre." In *Brecht on Theatre: The Development of an Aesthetic*, edited and translated by John Willett, 179–205. [1948.] New York: Hill and Wang, 1984.
Brittain, Victoria. *Shadow Lives: The Forgotten Women of the War on Terror*. Foreword by John Berger; afterword by Marina Warner. London: Pluto, 2013.
Britzman, Deborah P. "If the Story Cannot End: Deferred Action, Ambivalence, and Difficult Knowledge." In *Between Hope and Despair: Pedagogy and the Remembrance of Historical Trauma*, edited by Roger I. Simon, Sharon Rosenberg, and Claudia Eppert, 27–57. Lanham, MD: Rowman and Littlefield, 2000.
Brophy, Sarah, and Janice Hladki. "Visual Autobiography in the Frame: Critical Embodiment and Cultural Pedagogy." In *Embodied Politics in Visual Autobiography*, edited by Sarah Brophy and Janice Hladki, 3–29. Toronto: University of Toronto Press, 2014.
Bui, Diem-My Thi. "Embodiments of Difference: Representations of Vietnamese Women in the U.S. Cultural Imaginary." Ph.D. diss. Urbana-Champaign: University of Illinois at Urbana-Champaign, 2008.
Butler, Judith. "Contingent Foundations: Feminism and the Question of 'Postmodernism.'" In *Feminists Theorize the Political*, edited by Joan W. Scott and Judith Butler, 3–21. London: Routledge, 1992.
– *Frames of War: When Is Life Grievable?* [2009.] London: Verso, 2016.
– *Notes toward a Performative Theory of Assembly*. The Mary Flexner Lectures of Bryn Mawr College. Cambridge, MA: Harvard University Press, 2015.
– "On Being Beside Oneself: On the Limits of Sexual Autonomy." In *Sex Rights: The Oxford Amnesty Lectures 2002*, edited by Nicholas Bamforth, 48–78. Oxford, UK: Oxford University Press, 2005.
– *Precarious Life: The Powers of Mourning and Violence*. London: Verso, 2004.
Cakebread, Caroline. "Sycorax Speaks: Marina Warner's *Indigo* and *The Tempest*." In *Transforming Shakespeare: Contemporary Women's Re-Visions in Literature and Performance*, edited by Marianne Novy, 217–35. New York: Palgrave, 2000.

Campbell, Barbara. "Artist Statement." *Media-N: Journal of the New Media Caucus* (2007). http://median.newmediacaucus.org/archives_in_progress/pre_2009_issues/2007_fall/statements/campbell_barbara/campbell_barbara.html (accessed 27 February 2020).

Carpentier, Alejo. *The Kingdom of This World*. 1957. Originally published as *El reino de este mundo* [1949]. Translated by Harriet de Onís. Harmondsworth, UK: Penguin Modern Classics, 1980.

Carter, Angela. *Nights at the Circus*. London: Chatto and Windus, 1984.

Caruth, Cathy. *Unclaimed Experience: Trauma, Narrative and History*. Baltimore, MD: Johns Hopkins University Press, 1996.

Césaire, Aimé. *Une Tempête: d'après «la Tempête» de Shakespeare – Adaptation pour une théâtre nègre*. Paris: Éditions de Seuil, 1969.

Chabot Davis, Kimberly. *Beyond the White Negro: Empathy and Anti-Racist Reading*. Urbana: University of Illinois Press, 2014.

– "Oprah's Book Club and the Politics of Cross-Racial Empathy." *International Journal of Cultural Studies* 7, no. 4 (2004): 399–419.

Chakravarti, Sonali. *Sing the Rage: Listening to Anger after Mass Violence*. Chicago, IL: University of Chicago Press, 2014.

Chang, Jung. *Empress Dowager Cixi: The Concubine who Launched Modern China*. New York: Knopf, 2013.

Chaudhuri, Shohini. *Cinema of the Dark Side: Atrocity and the Ethics of Film Spectatorship*. Edinburgh: Edinburgh University Press, 2014.

Chivite de León, María José. *Echoes of History, Shadowed Identities: Rewriting Alterity in J.M. Coetzee's Foe and Marina Warner's Indigo*. Bern, Switzerland: Peter Lang, 2010.

Chouliaraki, Lilie. *The Spectatorship of Suffering*. London: SAGE, 2006.

Chow, Rey. "Gender and Representation." In *Feminist Consequences: Theory for the New Century*, edited by Elisabeth Bronfen and Misha Kavka, 38–57. New York: Columbia University Press, 2001.

– "Where Have All the Natives Gone?" In *Writing Diaspora: Tactics of Intervention in Contemporary Cultural Studies*, 27–54. Bloomington, IN: Indiana University Press, 1993.

Cliff, Michelle. *Abeng*. [1984.] New York: Plume, 1995.

Clifford, James. "Introduction: Partial Truths." In *Writing Culture: The Poetics and Politics of Ethnography*, edited by James Clifford and George E. Marcus, 1–26. Berkeley, CA: University of California Press, 1986.

Clifford, James, and George Marcus, eds. *Writing Culture: The Poetics and Politics of Ethnography*. Berkeley, CA: University of California Press, 1986.

Coetzee, J.M. *Disgrace*. London: Secker and Warburg, 1999.

– *Foe*. New York: Viking, 1986.

Connor, Steven. *The English Novel in History 1950–1995*. London: Routledge, 1996.

Corona, Daniela. "Risky Memory: Preventive Strategies and Emancipatory Resistance in *Cancellanda* by Marina Warner." *Textus* 22, no. 2 (May 2009): 305–21.

Coupe, Laurence. *Marina Warner*. Horndon, UK: Northcote House, 2006.

Craps, Stef, and Gert Buelens, eds. "Postcolonial Trauma Novels." Special issue, *Studies in the Novel* 40, no. 1–2 (Spring–Summer 2008).

Darío, Rubén. "The Triumph of Caliban." [1898.] Translated by Andrew Hurley, Greg Simon, and Steven F. White. In *Selected Writings*, edited by Ilan Stavans, 507–12. New York: Penguin, 2005.

Daston, Lorraine. "Introduction: Speechless." In *Things that Talk: Object Lessons from Art and Science*, edited by Lorraine Daston, 9–24. Brooklyn, NY: Zone, 2004.

de la Concha, Ángeles. "'Crossing the Lines, Crossing the Squares': Marina Warner's New Cartography of *The Tempest*." In *Beyond Borders: Re-defining Generic and Ontological Boundaries*, edited by Ramón Plo-Alastrué and María Jesús Martínez-Alfaro, 81–93. Heidelberg, Germany: Universitätsverlag C. Winter, 2001.

deCaires Narain, Denise. "Caribbean Creole: The Real Thing? Writing and Reading the Creole in a Selection of Caribbean Women's Texts." In *Reading the "New" Literatures in a Postcolonial Era*, edited by Susheila Nasta, 105–27. Cambridge: D.S. Brewer, 2000.

deGravelles, Karin H. "You Be Othello: Interrogating Identification in the Classroom." *Pedagogy* 11, no. 1 (Winter 2011): 153–75.

Delgado, Richard. "Rodrigo's Eleventh Chronicle: Empathy and False Empathy." *California Law Review* 84, no. 1 (January 1996): 61–100.

Derrida, Jacques. "Avowing – The Impossible: 'Returns,' Repentance, and Reconciliation." In *Living Together: Jacques Derrida's Communities of Violence and Peace*, edited by Elisabeth Weber, 18–41. New York: Fordham University Press, 2013.

– *Politics of Friendship*. Translated by George Collins. London: Verso, 1997.

Derrida, Jacques, and Anne Dufourmantelle. *Of Hospitality: Anne Dufourmantelle Invites Jacques Derrida to Respond*. Translated by Rachel Bowlby. Stanford, CA: Stanford University Press, 2000.

Eppert, Claudia. "Entertaining History: (Un)heroic Identifications, Apt Pupils, and an Ethical Imagination." *New German Critique* 86 (Spring–Summer 2002): 71–101.

Esmeir, Samera. "On Making Dehumanization Possible." *PMLA* 121, no. 4 (October 2006): 1544–51.

Felman, Shoshana, and Dori Laub. *Testimony: Crises of Witnessing in Literature, Psychoanalysis, and History*. New York: Routledge, 1992.

Fetterley, Judith. *The Resisting Reader: A Feminist Approach to American Fiction*. Bloomington, IN: Indiana University Press, 1981.

Franková, Milada. "Marina Warner's Sibyls and Their Tales." *Brno Studies in English*, no. 29 (2003): 117–21.

Freed, Joanne Lipson. "The Ethics of Identification: The Global Circulation of Traumatic Narrative in Silko's *Ceremony* and Roy's *The God of Small Things*." *Comparative Literature Studies* 48, no. 2 (2011): 219–40.

– *Haunting Encounters: The Ethics of Reading across Boundaries of Difference*. Ithaca, NY: Cornell University Press, 2017.

Freud, Sigmund. "Group Psychology and the Analysis of the Ego." In *Beyond the Pleasure Principle, Group Psychology and Other Works*, edited by James Strachey, 65–144. [1921.] London: Hogarth and the Institute of Psychoanalysis, 1955.

Friedman, Susan Stanford. *Mappings: Feminism and the Cultural Geographies of Encounter*. Princeton, NJ: Princeton University Press, 1998.

Frisch, Michael. *A Shared Authority: Essays on the Craft and Meaning of Oral and Public History*. Albany: State University of New York Press, 1990.

Ganteau, Jean-Michel, and Susana Onega. "Introduction: Performing the Void: Liminality and the Ethics of Form in Contemporary Trauma Narratives." In *Contemporary Trauma Narratives: Liminality and the Ethics of Form*, edited by Jean-Michel Ganteau and Susana Onega, 1–18. New York: Routledge, 2014.

Giunta, Edvige. "Afterword." In *Umbertina, A Novel*, by Helen Barolini, 425–53. New York: Feminist Press at the City University of New York, 1999.

Gluck, Sherna Berger, and Daphne Patai. "Introduction." In *Women's Words: The Feminist Practice of Oral History*, edited by Sherna Berger Gluck and Daphne Patai, 1–5. Abingdon, UK: Routledge, 1991.

Griffin, Michael. "Picturing America's 'War on Terrorism' in Afghanistan and Iraq: Photographic Motifs as News Frames." *Journalism* 5, no. 4 (2004): 381–402.

Haase, Donald. "Feminist Fairy-Tale Scholarship." In *Fairy Tales and Feminism: New Approaches*, edited by Donald Haase, 1–36. Detroit, MI: Wayne State University Press, 2004.

Hagiopian, Amy, et al. "Mortality in Iraq Associated with the 2003–2011 War and Occupation: Findings from a National Cluster Sample Survey by the University Collaborative Iraq Mortality Study." *PLOS Medicine* (15 October 2013). https://journals.plos.org/plosmedicine/article?id=10.1371/journal.pmed.1001533.

Harlow, Barbara. "Sites of Struggle: Immigration, Deportation, Prison, and Exile." In *Criticism in the Borderlands: Studies in Chicano Literature, Culture, and Ideology*, edited by Héctor Calderón and José David Saldívar, 149–63. Durham, NC: Duke University Press, 1991.

Harris, Siân. "Imagine. Investigate. Intervene?: A Consideration of Feminist Intent and Metafictive Invention in the Historical Fictions of A.S. Byatt and Marina Warner." In *The Female Figure in Contemporary Historical Fiction*, edited by Katherine Cooper and Emma Short, 171–88. London: Palgrave Macmillan, 2012.

Hart, Kevin. "Four or Five Words in Derrida." In *Living Together: Jacques Derrida's Communities of Violence and Peace*, edited by Elisabeth Weber, 168–87. New York: Fordham University Press, 2013.

Hartman, Geoffrey. "Tele-Suffering and Testimony in the Dot Com Era." In *Visual Culture and the Holocaust*, edited by Barbie Zelizer, 111–24. New Brunswick, NJ: Rutgers University Press, 2001.

Heilbrun, Carolyn G. *Writing a Woman's Life*. [1988.] New York: Norton, 2008.

Heller-Roazen, Daniel, ed. *Arabian Nights*. Translated by Husain Haddawy based on the text edited by Muhsin Mahdi. New York: Norton, 2009.

Hemmings, Clare. *Why Stories Matter: The Political Grammar of Feminist Theory*. Durham, NC: Duke University Press, 2011.

Hennecke, Edgar. *New Testament Apocrypha*, vol. 1. Translated by R.McL. Wilson, A.J.B. Higgins, George Ogg, and Richard E. Taylor. Edited by Wilhelm Schneemelcher. Philadelphia, PA: Westminster, 1963.

Herd, David, and Anna Pincus, eds. *Refugee Tales*. 3 vols. Manchester, UK: Comma Press, 2016–2019.

Hesford, Wendy. *Spectacular Rhetorics: Human Rights Visions, Recognitions, Feminisms*. Durham, NC: Duke University Press, 2011.

Hesford, Wendy, and Wendy Kozol. *Haunting Violations: Feminist Criticism and the Crisis of the "Real."* Urbana: University of Illinois Press, 2001.

Hodge, Merle. *Crick, Crack, Monkey*. London: Heinemann, 1970.

Homer. *The Odyssey of Homer*. Translated by Richmond Lattimore. New York: Harper Perennial, 2007.

hooks, bell. "Choosing the Margin as a Space of Radical Openness." In *Yearning: Race, Gender, and Cultural Politics*, 145–53. [1990.] London: Turnaround, 1991.

– "Eating the Other." In *Black Looks: Race and Representation*, 21–39. Boston, MA: South End Press, 1992.

Hulme, Peter. *Colonial Encounters: Europe and the Native Caribbean 1492–1797*. London: Methuen, 1986.

Irwin, Robert. *The Arabian Nights: A Companion*. [1994.] London: Taurus Parke, 2004.

James, C.L.R. *Beyond a Boundary*. London: Stanley Paul, 1963.

Jenkins, Ruth Y. "Authorizing Female Voice and Experience: Ghosts and Spirits in Kingston's *The Woman Warrior* and Allende's *House of the Spirits*." In "Intertextualities," special issue, *MELUS* 19, no. 3 (Autumn 1994): 61–73.

Jolly, Rosemary. *Cultured Violence: Narrative, Social Suffering, and Engendering Human Rights in Contemporary South Africa*. [2010.] Liverpool, UK: Liverpool University Press, 2013.

– "Spectral Presences: Narrating Women in the Context of South Africa's Truth and Reconciliation Commission." *Canadian Journal of African Studies / Revue canadienne des études africaines* 38, no. 3 (2004): 622–37.
Jullien, Dominique. "Review of *Stranger Magic*, by Marina Warner." *Marvels and Tales: Journal of Fairy Tale Studies* 28, no. 1 (2014): 203–6.
Kaplan, E. Ann. *Trauma Culture: The Politics of Terror and Loss in Media and Literature*. New Brunswick, NJ: Rutgers University Press, 2005.
Kastner, Sarah. "'Only Words Can Bury Us, Not Silence': Reading Yvonne Vera's Difficult Silences." *Safundi: The Journal of South African and American Studies* 17, no. 2 (April 2016): 213–30.
Kearney, Richard. "Intercultural Encounters as Hospitality." Interview by Breffni O'Rourke. *Journal of Virtual Exchange*, no. 1 (2018): 25–39.
– "Narrative and Recognition in the Flesh." Interview by Gonçalo Marcelo. *Philosophy and Social Criticism* 43, no. 8 (2017): 777–92.
– *Strangers, Gods and Monsters: Interpreting Otherness*. London: Routledge, 2003.
– "Writing Trauma: Narrative Catharsis in Homer, Shakespeare, and Joyce." In *Making Sense: Beauty, Creativity, and Healing*, edited by Bandy Lee, Nancy Olson, and Thomas P. Duffy, 131–43. New York: Peter Lang, 2014.
Keats, John. *The Letters of John Keats*. Edited by Maurice Buxton Forman. London: Geoffrey Cumberlege–Oxford University Press, 1954.
Keen, Suzanne. *Empathy and the Novel*. Oxford, UK: Oxford University Press, 2007.
– "A Theory of Narrative Empathy." *Narrative* 14, no. 3 (October 2006): 207–36.
Keeshig-Tobias, Lenore. "Stop Stealing Native Stories." In *Borrowed Power: Essays on Cultural Appropriation*, edited by Bruce Ziff and Pratima V. Rao, 71–3. [1990.] New Brunswick, NJ: Rutgers University Press, 1997.
Kennedy, Philip F., and Marina Warner, eds. *Scheherazade's Children: Global Encounters with the Arabian Nights*. New York: New York University Press, 2013.
Kermode, Frank, ed. *The Arden Edition of the Works of William Shakespeare*. Cambridge, MA: Harvard University Press, 1958.
Khanna, Ranjana. "Ethical Ambiguities and Specters of Colonialism: Futures of Transnational Feminism." In *Feminist Consequences: Theory for the New Century*, edited by Elisabeth Bronfen and Misha Kavka, 101–25. New York: Columbia University Press, 2001.
Kilian, Eveline. "Visitations from the Past: The Fiction of Marina Warner." *Anglistik und Englischunterricht* 60 (1997): 55–69.
Kincaid, Jamaica. *Annie John*. New York: Farrar, Straus and Giroux, 1985.
Kleinman, Arthur, and Joan Kleinman. "The Appeal of Experience: The Dismay of Images: Cultural Appropriations of Suffering in Our Times." *Daedalus* 125, no. 1 (Winter 1996): 1–23.

Kozol, Wendy. *Distant Wars Visible: The Ambivalence of Witnessing.* Minneapolis: University of Minnesota Press, 2014.

– "Witnessing Genocide and the Challenges of Ethical Spectatorship." In *Embodied Politics in Visual Autobiography*, edited by Sarah Brophy and Janice Hladki, 209–24. Toronto: Toronto University Press, 2014.

Kurasawa, Fuyuki. "A Message in a Bottle: Bearing Witness as a Mode of Transnational Practice." *Theory, Culture and Society* 26, no. 1 (2009): 92–111.

LaCapra, Dominick. *Writing History, Writing Trauma*. Baltimore, MD: Johns Hopkins University Press, 2001.

Lamming, George. "A Monster, a Child, a Slave." In *The Pleasures of Exile*, 95–117. London: Michael Joseph, 1960.

– *Water with Berries*. [1971.] New York: Holt, Reinhart and Winston, 1972.

Lanser, Susan Snaider. *Fictions of Authority: Women Writers and Narrative Voice*. Ithaca, NY: Cornell University Press, 1992.

– "Toward (a Queerer and) More (Feminist) Narratology." In *Narrative Theory Unbound: Queen and Feminist Interventions*, edited by Robyn Warhol and Susan S. Lanser, 23–42. Columbus: Ohio State University Press, 2015.

Lee, Hermione. *Biography: A Very Short Introduction*. Oxford, UK: Oxford University Press, 2009.

– *Virginia Woolf's Nose: Essays on Biography*. Princeton, NJ: Princeton University Press, 2005.

Lee, Sidney. *A Life of William Shakespeare*. 4th ed. [1898.] London: Smith, Elder, 1899.

Levi, Primo. *The Periodic Table*. Translated by Raymond Rosenthal. London: Abacus, 1986.

Levinas, Emmanuel. *Otherwise than Being, or, Beyond Essence*. Translated by Alphonso Lingis. Dordrecht, Netherlands: Kluwer Academic Publishers, 1997.

Liddington, Jill, and Jill Norris. *One Hand Tied Behind Us: The Rise of the Women's Suffrage Movement*. London: Rivers Oram, 1978.

Lively, Penelope. *Moon Tiger*. London: André Deutsch, 1987.

López, Marta Sofía. "Historiographic Metafiction and Resistance Postmodernism." In *Theme Parks, Rainforests and Sprouting Wastelands: European Essays on Theory and Performance in Contemporary British Fiction*, edited by Richard Todd and Luisa Flora, 215–26. Amsterdam: Rodopi, 2000.

Lugones, María, and Elizabeth V. Spelman. "Have We Got a Theory for You! Feminist Theory, Cultural Imperialism and the Demand for 'The Woman's Voice.'" *Women's Studies International Forum* 6, no. 6 (1983): 573–81.

Makdisi, Saree, and Felicity Nussbaum, eds. *The Arabian Nights in Historical Context: Between East and West*. Oxford, UK: Oxford University Press, 2008.

Mamdani, Mahmood. "Amnesty or Impunity? A Preliminary Critique of the Report of the Truth and Reconciliation Commission of South Africa (TRC)." *Diacritics: A Review of Contemporary Criticism* 32, no. 3–4 (Fall–Winter 2002): 33–59.

Mannoni, Octave. *Psychologie de la colonisation. Collections Esprit "Frontière ouverte."* Paris: Éditions du Seuil, 1950.

Marais, Mike. "J.M. Coetzee's *Disgrace* and the Task of the Imagination." *Journal of Modern Literature* 29, no. 2 (Winter 2006): 75–93.

– "Literature and the Labour of Negation: J.M. Coetzee's *Life and Times of Michael K*." *Journal of Commonwealth Literature* 36, no. 1 (2001): 107–25.

– "'Little Enough, Less than Little: Nothing': Ethics, Engagement, and Change in the Fiction of J.M. Coetzee." *Modern Fiction Studies* 46, no. 1 (Spring 2000): 159–82.

McCooey, David. "The Limits of Life Writing." *Life Writing* 14, no. 3 (2017): 277–80.

Milosz, Czeslaw. "My Faithful Mother Tongue." In *Selected Poems 1931–2004*, 90. [1968.] New York: Harper Collins, 2006.

Mohanty, Chandra Talpade. "Under Western Eyes: Feminist Scholarship and Colonial Discourses." *Feminist Review* 30 (Autumn 1988): 61–88.

Monson, Tamlyn. "An Infinite Question: The Paradox of Representation in *Life and Times of Michael K*." *Journal of Commonwealth Literature* 38, no. 3 (July 2003): 87–106.

Morrison, Toni. *Beloved*. New York: Vintage, 1987.

Newton, Adam Zachary. *Narrative Ethics*. Cambridge, MA: Harvard University Press, 1995.

Nora, Pierre. "Between Memory and History: *Les Lieux de Mémoire*." *Representations*, no. 26 (Spring 1989): 7–14.

Nussbaum, Martha C. *Love's Knowledge: Essays on Philosophy and Literature*. Oxford, UK: Oxford University Press, 1990.

– *Poetic Justice: The Literary Imagination and Public Life*. Boston, MA: Beacon, 1995.

O'Callaghan, Evelyn. "'Jumping into the Big Ups' Quarrels': The Hulme/Brathwaite Exchange." *Wasafiri*, no. 28 (1998): 34–6.

– *Woman Version: Theoretical Approaches to West Indian Fiction by Women*. London: Macmillan Caribbean, 1993.

Oliver, Kelly. *The Colonization of Psychic Space: A Psychoanalytic Social Theory of Oppression*. Minneapolis: University of Minnesota Press, 2004.

– *Witnessing: Beyond Recognition*. Minneapolis: University of Minnesota Press, 2001.

Opie, Iona, and Peter Opie. *The Classic Fairy Tales*. Oxford, UK: Oxford University Press, 1974.

Ovid. *The Metamorphoses of Ovid*. Translated by Allen Mandelbaum. San Diego, CA: Harvest, 1993.

Pedwell, Carolyn. *Affective Relations: The Transnational Politics of Empathy*. Basingstoke, UK: Palgrave Macmillan, 2014.

Phelan, James. *Narrative as Rhetoric: Technique, Audiences, Ethics, Ideology*. Columbus: Ohio State University Press, 1996.

Phelps, Teresa Godwin. *Shattered Voices: Language, Violence, and the Work of Truth Commissions*. Philadelphia, PA: University of Pennsylvania Press, 2004.

Phillips, Caryl. *Cambridge*. London: Bloomsbury, 1991.

Physicians for Social Responsibility. *Body Count: Casualty Figures after 10 Years of the 'War on Terror.'* March 2015. https://www.psr.org/wp-content/uploads/2018/05/body-count.pdf (accessed 27 February 2020).

Propst, Lisa. "Bloody Chambers and Labyrinths of Desire: Sexual Violence in Marina Warner's Fairy Tales and Myths." *Marvels and Tales: Journal of Fairy Tale Studies* 22, no. 1 (2008): 125–42.

Rhys, Jean. *Wide Sargasso Sea*. London: André Deutsch, 1966.

Rich, Adrienne. "When We Dead Awaken: Writing as Re-Vision." *College English* 34, no. 1 (October 1972): 18–30.

Robinson, James E. "Caribbean Caliban: Shifting the 'I' of the Storm." *Comparative Drama* 33, no. 4 (Winter 1999–2000): 431–53.

Rodó, José Enrique. *Ariel*. Translated by F.J. Stimson. [1900.] Boston, MA: Houghton Mifflin, 1922.

Roof, Judith, and Robyn Wiegman, eds. *Who Can Speak? Authority and Critical Identity*. Urbana: University of Illinois Press, 1995.

Ross, Fiona. "Speech and Silence: Women's Testimony in the First Five Weeks of Public Hearings of the South African Truth and Reconciliation Commission." In *Remaking a World: Violence, Social Suffering, and Recovery*, edited by Veena Das, Arthur Kleinman, Margaret Lock, Mamphela Ramphele, and Pamela Reynolds, 250–80. Berkeley, CA: University of California Press, 2001.

Rothberg, Michael. *Multidirectional Memory: Remembering the Holocaust in the Age of Decolonization*. Stanford, CA: Stanford University Press, 2009.

Rowbotham, Sheila. *Hidden from History: 300 Years of Women's Oppression and the Fight against It*. London: Pluto, 1973.

– *Women, Resistance, and Revolution: A History of Women and Revolution in the Modern World*. New York: Pantheon, 1972.

Rowe, Karen. "To Spin a Yarn: The Female Voice in Folklore and Fairy Tale." In *Fairy Tales and Society: Illusion, Allusion, and Paradigm*, edited by Ruth B. Bottigheimer, 53–74. Philadelphia, PA: University of Pennsylvania Press, 1986.

Rudnick, Lois. "The Male-Identified Woman and Other Anxieties: The Life of Mabel Dodge Luhan." In *The Challenge of Feminist Biography: Writing the Lives of American Women*, edited by Sara Alpern, Joyce Antler, Elisabeth Israels Perry, and Ingrid Winther Scobie, 116–38. Urbana: University of Illinois Press, 1992.

Rushdie, Salman. "In Good Faith." In *Imaginary Homelands: Essays and Criticism 1981–91*, 393–414. [1990.] London: Granta, 1992.
– *Midnight's Children*. London: Jonathan Cape, 1981.
Said, Edward. *Culture and Imperialism*. London: Chatto and Windus, 1993.
– *Orientalism*. [1978.] New York: Vintage, 1994.
Sallis, Eva. *Sheherazade through the Looking Glass: The Metamorphosis of the Thousand and One Nights*. [1999.] London: Routledge, 2010.
Salverson, Julie. "Performing Emergency: Witnessing, Popular Theatre, and the Lie of the Literal." *Theatre Topics* 6, no. 2 (September 1996): 181–91.
– "Taking Liberties: A Theatre Class of Foolish Witnesses." *Research in Drama Education* 13, no. 2 (June 2008): 245–55.
Sanders, Julie. *Adaptation and Appropriation*. London: Routledge, 2006.
Savory, Elaine. "Jean Rhys, Race and Caribbean/English Criticism." *Wasafiri*, no. 28 (1998): 33–4.
Scarry, Elaine. *The Body in Pain: The Making and Unmaking of the World*. New York: Oxford University Press, 1985.
Schwalbe, Carol B., B. William Silcock, and Susan Keith. "Visual Framing of the Early Weeks of the U.S.-Led Invasion of Iraq: Applying the Master War Narrative to Electronic and Print Images." *Journal of Broadcasting and Electronic Media* 52, no. 3 (Sept. 2008): 448–65.
Scott, James. *The Weapons of the Weak*. New Haven, CT: Yale University Press, 1985.
Scott, Joan W. "Fantasy Echo: History and the Construction of Identity." *Critical Inquiry* 27, no. 2 (Winter 2001): 284–304.
Seagrave, Sterling, and Peggy Seagrave. *Dragon Lady: The Life and Legend of the Last Empress of China*. New York: Vintage, 1992.
Seifert, Lewis C. "On Fairy Tales, Subversion, and Ambiguity: Feminist Approaches to Seventeenth-Century *Contes de fées*." In *Fairy Tales and Feminism: New Approaches*, edited by Donald Haase, 53–72. Detroit, MI: Wayne State University Press, 2004.
Seikaly, Sherene. "Return to the Present." In *Living Together: Jacques Derrida's Communities of Violence and Peace*, edited by Elisabeth Weber, 227–41. New York: Fordham University Press, 2013.
Shakespeare, William. *The Tempest*. Edited by Virginia Mason Vaughan and Alden T. Vaughan. The Arden Shakespeare, 3rd ser. Surrey, UK: Thomas Nelson and Sons, 1999.
Smith, Linda Tuhiwai. *Decolonizing Methodologies: Research and Indigenous Peoples*. 2nd ed. [1999.] London: Zed Books, 2012.
Smith, Sidonie, and Kay Schaffer. *Human Rights and Narrated Lives: The Ethics of Recognition*. New York: Palgrave Macmillan, 2004.
Sontag, Susan. *Regarding the Pain of Others*. New York: Farrar, Straus and Giroux, 2003.

Spivak, Gayatri Chakravorty. "Can the Subaltern Speak?" In *Marxism and the Interpretation of Culture*, edited by Cary Nelson and Lawrence Grossberg, 271–314. Urbana: University of Illinois Press, 1988.

– "Ethics and Politics in Tagore, Coetzee, and Certain Scenes of Teaching." *Diacritics* 32, no. 3–4 (Fall–Winter 2002): 17–31.

– "In Response: Looking Back, Looking Forward." In *Can the Subaltern Speak: Reflections on the History of an Idea*, edited by Rosalind Morris, 227–36. New York: Columbia University Press, 2010.

Stauffer, Jill. *Ethical Loneliness: The Injustice of Not Being Heard*. New York: Columbia University Press, 2015.

Stewart, Kathleen. *A Space on the Side of the Road: Cultural Poetics in an "Other" America*. Princeton, NJ: Princeton University Press, 1996.

Stoll, Elmer Edgar. "Certain Fallacies and Irrelevancies in the Literary Scholarship of the Day." *Studies in Philology* 24, no. 4 (1927): 485–508.

Sturken, Marita. "The Wall, the Screen, and the Image: The Vietnam Veterans Memorial." In "Monumental Histories," special issue, *Representations*, no. 35 (Summer 1991): 118–42.

Swift, Graham. *Waterland*. London: Heinemann, 1983.

Tacitus, Cornelius. *Agricola*. Translated by A.R. Birley. In *"Agricola" and "Germany."* Oxford, UK: Oxford University Press, 1999.

Thieme, John. *Postcolonial Con-Texts: Writing Back to the Canon*. London: Continuum, 2002.

Todd, Richard. "The Retrieval of Unheard Voices in British Postmodern Fiction: A.S. Byatt and Marina Warner." In *Liminal Postmodernisms: The Postmodern, the (Post-) Colonial, and the (Post-) Feminist*, edited by Theo D'haen and Hans Bertens, 99–114. Amsterdam: Rodopi, 1994.

Trevor-Roper, Hugh. *Hermit of Peking: The Secret Life of Sir Edmund Backhouse*. [1976.] New York: Knopf, 1977.

Truth and Reconciliation Commission of South Africa. *Truth and Reconciliation Commission of South Africa Report*. 1998–2003. https://www.justice.gov.za/trc/report/ (accessed 27 February 2020).

Tuck, Eve, and K. Wayne Yang. "Decolonization Is Not a Metaphor." *Decolonization: Indigeneity, Education, and Society* 1, no. 1 (2012): 1–40.

Vaughan, Virginia Mason, and Alden T. Vaughan. "Introduction." In *The Tempest*, by William Shakespeare, edited by Virginia Mason Vaughan and Alden T. Vaughan, 1–138. London: The Arden Shakespeare, 1999.

Verdier, Gabrielle. "Figures de la conteuse dans les contes de fées feminins." *Dix-septième siècle*, no. 180 (July–September 1993): 481–99.

Walcott, Derek. *Omeros*. New York: Farrar, Straus and Giroux, 1990.

Warner, Marina. Interview by Elaine Williams. In *Beyond the Glass Ceiling: Forty Women whose Ideas Shape the Modern World*, edited by Sian Griffiths, 259–63. Manchester, UK: Manchester University Press, 1996.

– Interview by David Dabydeen. *Kunapipi: Journal of Postcolonial Writing* 14, no. 2 (1992): 115–23.
– Interview by Gilles Menegaldo. In *Jeux d'écriture: Le roman britannique contemporain*, edited by Marie-Françoise Cachin and Ann Grieve, 217–35. Paris: *Publications de l'Université Paris VII – Denis Diderot*, 1995.
– "Afterword." In *Shadow Lives: The Forgotten Women of the War on Terror*, by Victoria Brittain, 165–8. London: Pluto, 2013.
– *Alone of All Her Sex: The Myth and Cult of the Virgin Mary*. [1976.] Oxford, UK: Oxford University Press, 2013.
– "Angela Carter: Bottle Blonde, Double Drag." In *Flesh and the Mirror: Essays on the Art of Angela Carter*, edited by Lorna Sage, 243–56. London: Virago, 1994.
– "Angels and Engines: The Culture of Apocalypse." *Raritan* 25, no. 2 (Fall 2005): 12–41.
– "Bearer-Beings and Stories in Transit / *Storie in Transito*." *Marvels and Tales: Journal of Fairy Tale Studies* 31, no. 1 (2017): 149–61.
– "Between the Colonist and the Creole." Originally published as "Between the Colonist and the Creole: Family Bonds, Family Boundaries," in *Unbecoming Daughters of the Empire*, edited by Shirley Chew and Anna Rutherford (Sydney, Australia: Dangaroo Press, 1993). In *Signs and Wonders*, 295–302.
– "The Bitch Route 13." Originally published in *Spectator*, 1972. In *Signs and Wonders*, 9–13.
– "Cancellanda." In *Myth and Violence in the Contemporary Female Text: New Cassandras*, edited by Sanja Bahun-Radunović and V.G. Julie Rajan, 195–209. With an introduction to the story by Warner (189–93). Farnham, UK: Ashgate, 2011.
– "Castaway on the Ocean of Story." Revised from paper presented at *Shakespeare Deutsche Gesellschaft* Conference, Weimar, Germany, 2002. Earlier version published in *Jahrbuch*, 2003. In *Signs and Wonders*, 274–91.
– "'Come to Hecuba': Theatrical Empathy and Memories of Troy." In *Placing Michael Neill: Issues of Place in Shakespeare and Early Modern Culture*, edited by Jonathan Gil Harris, 61–87. London: Ashgate, 2011.
– "The Crushed Butterflies of War." Originally published in *Guardian Extra*, 1972. In *Signs and Wonders*, 13–18.
– "Cunning and High Spirits." Introduction to *The Second Virago Book of Fairy Tales*, edited by Angela Carter (London: Virago, 1992). In *Signs and Wonders*, 428–35.
– "Donkey Business, Donkey Work: In the House of Crossed Desires." Revised from W.D. Thomas Memorial Lecture, University of Wales Swansea, 1996. In *Signs and Wonders*, 393–405.
– *The Dragon Empress: Life and Times of Tz'u-hsi 1835–1908: Empress Dowager of China*. [1972.] London: Vintage, 1993.

– *Fantastic Metamorphoses, Other Worlds: Ways of Telling the Self: The Clarendon Lectures in English 2001*. [2002.] Oxford, UK: Oxford University Press, 2004.
– *Fly Away Home: Stories*. Cromer, UK: Salt, 2015.
– "Foreword." In *Memoirs of an Early Arab Feminist: The Life and Activism of Anbara Salam Khalidi*, by Anbara Salam Khalidi, translated by Tarif Khalidi, viii–xii. London: Pluto, 2013.
– *From the Beast to the Blonde: On Fairy Tales and Their Tellers*. [1994.] London: Vintage, 1995.
– "Imaginary Passages: The Metamorphoses of Europa." *Third Text* 21, no. 5 (September 2007): 487–98.
– *In a Dark Wood*. [1977.] London: Penguin, 1980.
– *Indigo, or, Mapping the Waters*. [1992.] London: Vintage, 1993.
– "Introduction." In *The Bloody Chamber and Other Stories*, by Angela Carter, ix–xvi. London: Folio Society, 2012.
– "Its Own Dark Styx: Caryl Phillips." Review of *The Nature of Blood* by Caryl Phillips. Originally published in *London Review of Books*, 1997. In *Signs and Wonders*, 269–74.
– *Joan of Arc: The Image of Female Heroism*. [1981.] Oxford, UK: Oxford University Press, 2013.
– *The Leto Bundle*. [2001.] London: Vintage, 2002.
– *The Lost Father*. [1988.] London: Vintage, 1998.
– "Making It Big in the New World." Originally published in *Listener*, 1986. In *Signs and Wonders*, 45–8.
– *Managing Monsters: Six Myths of Our Time: The 1994 Reith Lectures*. London: Vintage, 1994.
– "Marina Warner: A European Woman's Heritage." Interview by Richard Kearney. In *States of Mind: Dialogues with Contemporary Thinkers on the European Mind*, 93–100. Manchester, UK: Manchester University Press, 1995.
– "Marina Warner in Conversation." Interview by Nicolas Tredell. *PN Review* 18, no. 6 (July–August 1992): 31–9.
– "Marina Warner … Talks about Life as an Independent Scholar, and Why Fairy Tales Matter So Much to Us." Interview by British Academy Review. *British Academy Review*, no. 28 (Summer 2016): 34–9.
– "Marina Warner with Robert Fraser." Interview by Robert Fraser. In *Writing Across Worlds: Contemporary Writers Talk*, edited by Susheila Nasta, 364–75. London: Routledge, 2004.
– "Mirror-Readings: An Afterword." In *Recognition: The Poetics of Narrative: Interdisciplinary Studies on Anagnorisis*, edited by Philip F. Kennedy and Marilyn Lawrence, 227–34. New York: Peter Lang, 2008.
– *Murderers I Have Known, and Other Stories*. London: Chatto and Windus, 2002.
– "Myth and Faerie: Rewritings and Recoveries." Paper given in French at the colloquium "*Où est-on avec la théorie littéraire*" ("Literary Theory: Where

Is It At?"), University of Paris VII, 1999, and subsequently published in *Textuel* 37 (2000). In *Signs and Wonders*, 444–57.
– *No Go the Bogeyman: Scaring, Lulling, and Making Mock*. [1998.] London: Vintage, 2000.
– "Pavane for Her Wildwoman Symmetries." In *Francesco Clemente: The Book of the Sea*, edited by Mark Francis, n.p. London: Gagosian Gallery, 2002.
– "Phantasmagoria: Professor Marina Warner FBA in Conversation with Professor Hermione Lee FBA." *British Academy Review*, no. 18 (Summer 2011): 41–4.
– *Phantasmagoria: Spirit Visions, Metaphors, and Media into the Twenty-First Century*. Oxford, UK: Oxford University Press, 2006.
– "Report to the Memoir Club: Scenes from a Colonial Childhood." In *Contradictory Woolf: Selected Papers from the Twenty-First Annual International Conference on Virginia Woolf*, edited by Derek Ryan and Stella Bolaki, 57–65. Clemson, SC: Clemson University Digital Press, 2012.
– "Rough Magic and Sweet Lullaby." BBC Radio 3 lecture, 2000. In *Signs and Wonders*, 237–50.
– "Shakespeare's Caliban." Review of *Shakespeare's Caliban: A Cultural History*, by Alden T. Vaughan and Virginia Mason Vaughan. Originally published in *Times Literary Supplement*, 1992. In *Signs and Wonders*, 260–3.
– *Signs and Wonders: Essays on Literature and Culture*. London: Chatto and Windus, 2003.
– "The Silence of Sycorax." Revised version of paper presented at the Free University of Berlin, 1996. In *Signs and Wonders*, 263–8.
– "Siren/Hyphen; or 'The Maid Beguiled.'" Originally published in *New Left Review*, 1997, and reprinted in *Caribbean Portraits: Essays on Gender Ideologies and Identities*, edited by Christine Barrow (Kingston, Jamaica: Ian Randle, 1998). In *Signs and Wonders*, 309–22.
– *The Skating Party*. [1982.] London: Vintage, 1992.
– "Spinning a Yarn with Marina Warner." Interview by Chantal Zabus. In "Post-Colonial Women's Writing," special issue, *Kunapipi: Journal of Postcolonial Writing and Culture* 16, no. 1 (1994): 519–29.
– *Stranger Magic: Charmed States and the Arabian Nights*. Cambridge, MA: Harvard University Press, Belknap, 2013.
– "Who's Sorry Now? Personal Stories, Public Apologies." Amnesty Lecture in Human Rights, Oxford, 14 February 2002; early version published at http://www.opendemocracy.net in 2002. In *Signs and Wonders*, 459–80.
– "Zombie: The Devil Inside." Originally published in *Guardian* (Manchester), 2001. In *Signs and Wonders*, 341–4.
– ed. *Wonder Tales: Six French Stories of Enchantment*. London: Chatto and Windus, 1994.

Weaver-Hightower, Rebecca. "Revising the Vanquished: Indigenous Perspectives on Colonial Encounters." *Journal for Early Modern Cultural Studies* 6, no. 2 (Fall/Winter 2006): 84–102.

Welch, Marcelle Maistre. "La femme, le mariage et l'amour dans les contes de fées mondains du XVIIe siècle français." *Papers on French Seventeenth Century Literature* 18 (1983): 47–58.

Whitlock, Gillian. *Soft Weapons: Autobiography in Transit.* Chicago, IL: University of Chicago Press, 2007.

Williams-Wanquet, Eileen. "Marina Warner's *Indigo* as Ethical Deconstruction and Reconstruction." *Critique: Studies in Contemporary Fiction* 46, no. 3 (Spring 2005): 267–82.

Winterson, Jeanette. *The Passion.* London: Bloomsbury, 1987.

Woolf, Virginia. "Mr Bennett and Mrs Brown." London: Hogarth, 1924.

– "The New Biography." In *Selected Essays*, edited by David Bradshaw, 95–100. [1927.] Oxford, UK: Oxford University Press, 2008.

– *Orlando.* London: Hogarth, 1928.

Wyatt, Jean. *Risking Difference: Identification, Race, and Community in Contemporary Fiction and Feminism.* Albany: State University of New York Press, 2004.

Yaeger, Patricia. "Consuming Trauma; or, The Pleasures of Merely Circulating." In *Extremities: Trauma, Testimony, and Community*, edited by Nancy K. Miller and Jason Tougaw, 25–51. Urbana: University of Illinois Press, 2002.

Young, James O. *Cultural Appropriation and the Arts.* London: Blackwell, 2008.

Young, James O., and Conrad G. Brunk, eds. *The Ethics of Cultural Appropriation.* London: Blackwell, 2009.

Zabus, Chantal. "Mingling and Metamorphing: Articulations of Feminism and Postcoloniality in Marina Warner's Fiction." In *The Contemporary British Novel*, edited by James Acheson and Sarah Ross, 118–28. Edinburgh: Edinburgh University Press, 2005.

– *Tempests After Shakespeare.* New York: Palgrave, 2002.

– "What Next Miranda? Marina Warner's *Indigo*." *Kunapipi: Journal of Postcolonial Writing* 16, no. 3 (1994): 81–92.

Zelizer, Barbie. *Remembering to Forget: Holocaust Memory through the Camera's Eye.* Chicago, IL: University of Chicago Press, 1998.

Zipes, Jack. "Preface." In *Don't Bet on the Prince: Contemporary Feminist Fairy Tales in North America and England*, xi–xiv. New York: Routledge, 1986.

– "Preface to the 1999 Edition." In *When Dreams Came True: Classical Fairy Tales and Their Tradition*, ix–x. New York: Routledge, 2007.

Index

The abbreviation MW refers to Marina Warner.